THE
PSYCHOLOGY
OF POWER

Also by Ronald V. *Sampson*

PROGRESS IN THE AGE OF REASON:
The Seventeenth Century to the Present Day

THE
PSYCHOLOGY
OF POWER

Ronald V. Sampson

PANTHEON BOOKS
A DIVISION OF RANDOM HOUSE
NEW YORK

FIRST PUBLISHED IN THE UNITED STATES, *1966*

© *Copyright, 1965, by R. V. Sampson*

All rights reserved under International and Pan-American
Copyright Conventions. Published in New York by Pantheon
Books, a division of Random House, Inc., and in London,
England by Heinemann Educational Books Ltd.

MANUFACTURED IN THE UNITED STATES OF AMERICA

Library of Congress catalog card number: 66-10771

24689753

Contents

⊏ Introduction

IT WILL be the central argument and purpose of this book to deny that there is more than one plane of reality in which the moral judgement functions; so that it is possible to argue that what appears to be right on one plane or from one standpoint somehow becomes wrong or less right from another and equally valid plane or standpoint. In other words, what is morally right cannot be pragmatically wrong or politically wrong or invalidated on grounds of apparent futility. The variety of the scales of moral value accepted in the world, the number of people at any given time who are blind to the truth of the moral law, is irrelevant to the existence of that universal and unchanging moral law which binds and governs all men, whether they obey it or not. That there is a plurality of 'true' values, that moral truth is no more than the expression of a subjective appraisal relative to and valid only within the culture in question, this it is my concern to deny. The nature of this moral law is, moreover, understood to some degree by all rational men; it is the only sure source of their welfare in this world; it can be spelt out and be clearly understood by all, and will be found to hold good at whatever point of human experience we may seek to test it. I shall in the following pages seek to test its relevance on a number of different planes of human experience: those of psychology, politics, history, and creative art. It is necessary, first, to give dimension to the abstraction of 'moral law', the knowledge of which derives from our many-sided experience, and the love of which derives from within ourselves. The moral law rests on the fact that it is possible for every human being to develop in greater or lesser degree in one direction or another. He may seek to order his life and his relations with others on the basis of love or on the basis of power. The two forces are antithetical, but are directly related to each other, in so far as it is impossible to develop in both directions at the same time. To the extent that we develop our capacity for power we weaken our capacity for love; and conversely, to the extent that we grow in our ability to love we disqualify ourselves for success in the competition for power. To the extent that the forces of love in men triumph over the forces of power, equality among men prevails. And conversely, to the extent that the forces of power prevail over the forces of love, domination and subjection characterize human relations. The former is good and leads to human well-being; the latter is bad and leads to human suffering and strife. The struggle between these dialectical forces is always the same. No one may contract out of it, however much he may wish to do so. For of necessity, everyone at all times and in all positions stands on a relation with other men which will be predominantly of one category or the other. In this sense, what happens in the world, what happens in history, inevitably reflects the contribution, active or passive, of everybody who participates in the vast web of human inter-relations. There are not diverse planes of reality to be judged by different standards. There are no separate, insulated planes of the cloister and the Chancellory Office. Jesus Christ and Adolf Hitler belong together to the common plane of our single human experience. It is merely that they represent extreme polarized positions within our common moral spectrum. I cite them only as rough examples, or rather symbols, to demarcate the limits of the scale on which the rest of us must also find a place. At the one extreme is to be found the strength of a courageous and selfless non-violence. At the other end of the scale is to be found the extreme of violence to which the logic of power, when pushed far enough, can degenerate.

At the level of popular discussion, the commonest way of avoiding any close examination of the contradiction lurking beneath the surface of accepted moral usage in politics is an imprecise terminology. The example I take is from yesterday's newspaper. The name of the paper, of the commentator or of his subjects, these are equally unimportant. The significance of the passage lies in its being so commonplace.

> Within the Cabinet, there is no more fascinating conjunction: these two men have so much and so little in common. Both of them Eton scholars, very clever and very ambitious; . . . both Christians,

regular churchgoers, and strict believers in personal morality; . . .
it was clear to everybody that X could not stand Y.

This observation, made casually and without irony, conceals
an obvious contradiction. But it is a contradiction which
apparently, at any rate on the surface, millions of newspaper
readers experience no difficulty in assimilating and accepting
as the basis of their evaluation of what is reasonable. The
passage is *not* noteworthy because it is closely attuned to the
universally felt realities of social and political experience; and
most people are generally most anxious to remain harmoniously
related to the realities of their immediate environment. On one
plane of experience, it might appear odd that ambition, rivalry,
animus should be considered perfectly compatible with Christianity, strict morality, eminence and public service. One reply
might be that no such contradiction is very evident or felt to be
particularly relevant by the masses of ordinary people whose
attitudes and behaviour make reality what it is. If pressed, a con-
cession might be made to the effect that 'it depends from which
standpoint you consider it'. There are, in fact, a number of
expressions in current usage for dealing with embarrassments of
this kind. 'Perhaps there is something in what you say from a
moral standpoint, but I am a practical man,' or, 'Yes, but the
world just isn't like that,' or quite simply, 'Morality has nothing
to do with business of State or with the affairs of this Court'
as the case may be. If pressed still further (in the absence of
symptoms of suppressed irritation), answers of a more metaphysical character might be elicited. 'After all, the world is many-
sided,' 'Reality is complex' or 'We must be careful not to over-
simplify things' or even simply 'Truth is relative'. In other
words, what might appear to be contradictory to a rather literal-
minded and simple individual, applying the strict canons of
logic, can really be made to appear quite free from difficulty
when seen in its proper light. And any lingering doubt can
be finally disposed of by the reminder that the supposed contradiction is undoubtedly considered perfectly normal and respectable by millions of perfectly normal and respectable men.

In the same issue of the newspaper quoted above is an extract
from Hannah Arendt's book, *Eichmann in Jerusalem*, in which
she discusses the question as to why the Jewish leaders for the

most part themselves co-operated with the Nazis in the administrative tasks of organizing the destruction of their own people. Why was there comparatively little active resistance even in the face of certain death? Exceptions there were – she cites the case of the German sergeant, Anton Schmidt, executed for his courageous and disinterested help to Jewish partisans. But why, she asks, are there comparatively so few such instances? Why so terribly few Anton Schmidts in the presence of organized savagery on so vast a scale? Why indeed so little attempt at protest of any kind? The answer is, of course, terror. But this still leaves the question of how people lived with the guilt of their acquiescence in the doing of evil so immeasurable. Miss Arendt quotes from the memoirs of a German army physician, recounting his experience on the Russian front. Peter Bamm (*Die Unsichtbare Flagge*, 1952) describes how the Jews were rounded up and killed by the S.S. in Sevastopol, and is then candid enough to admit that they, the ordinary troops, knew what was happening and did nothing about it. The 'justification' then follows.

> Anyone who had seriously protested or done anything against the killing unit would have been arrested within twenty-four hours and would have disappeared. It belongs among the refinements of totalitarian governments in our century that they don't permit their opponents to die a great, dramatic martyr's death for their convictions. A good many of us might have accepted such a death. The totalitarian state lets its opponents disappear in silent anonymity. It is certain that anyone who had dared to suffer death rather than silently tolerate the crime would have sacrificed his life in vain. This is not to say that such a sacrifice would have been morally meaningless. It would only have been practically useless. None of us had a conviction so deeply rooted that we could have taken upon ourselves a practically useless sacrifice for the sake of a higher moral meaning.

Here it is the promptings of moral unease or guilt in a horrifying situation which lead to the familiar assertion of the dichotomy of morality and political realism. Moral or right behaviour, even if the courage had been available, would have been pointless. Or rather the only point would have been on a plane of meaning without practical relevance. It is not clear how the mind can conceive of something being at one and the same time significant and futile. Miss Arendt quite rightly draws attention to the falsity of this alleged dichotomy of different planes of reality. She points out that the Nazi attempt to establish 'holes of oblivion into which all deeds, good and evil, would disappear' was an impossible attempt and failed as all such attempts must fail. 'The holes of oblivion do not exist. . . . One man will always be left alive to tell the story. Hence, nothing can ever be "practically useless," at least, not in the long run.' We suffer today, and the German people in particular suffer, not because of all the goodness that has been effaced in oblivion, but because of the rarity of instances of the highest example.

This fundamental moral issue is essentially about the nature of the conditions which govern man's life and welfare. Closely related to and arising out of this problem is the question of the status of man himself, confronted by these conditions. Who is man? How well or otherwise is he qualified to meet these conditions? What are his chances of governing his life in accordance with the law of his being? What do we mean when we speak of our common human nature? Of what is it capable, and what are its limits? No debate has been more fundamental than the argument whether or not it is possible for man to work out his own salvation. The schism between St Augustine and Pelagius, for example, on this issue is one which divides men with equal consistency in morals and politics as well. What activities are appropriate to men? What is the meaning of man's earthly life? Is there a meaning to be found? Or is the question itself meaningless? What confidence can be placed in answers to questions so vexed and perennial? The questions concealed within the original proposition crowd upon us, and have elicited widely divergent answers. Is it that men observe differently? Or do they react with different emotions to what they observe? Man is so richly endowed and complex that perhaps disinterested observers might arrive at differing conclusions as to his nature. The voice of Philinte in Molière's *Le Misanthrope* expresses the authentic voice of conservatism in every generation.

> I take men as they are, quite calmly,
> I school my heart to suffer what they do;
> Yes, those faults against which your heart murmurs I see

As vices inseparable from human nature;
And finally my mind is not more offended
At seeing a rogue, an unjust, a covetous man,
Than in seeing vultures famished for carrion,
Treacherous monkeys, and ravening wolves.[1]

The outlook of Philinte is so far removed from that of Alceste that Molière seems to suggest that a collision of this order goes altogether too deep for rational argument. It is an instinctual, intuitive conflict grounded in root differences of temperament. Philinte acknowledges that error, vice and ugliness exist in man; but retorts that no man need choose to repine at this condition of affairs. We need only observe that marks of imperfection are uniform throughout nature, and accustom our hearts to respond in a befitting manner. If Alceste for his part finds this impossible, this is his misfortune.

We see here one of the classical conservative arguments in turning the attack of what is sometimes referred to as 'the emotional Left': the appeal to Nature. The world of Nature no less than the world of man conforms, it is said, to my practice rather than to your aspiration. So cease repining. The next step in the argument has sometimes been to assimilate man himself to the level of the beasts, at any rate in his need to be set under powerful controlling agencies. The offence of the Left, according to Henry St John, Earl of Bolingbroke, has been to threaten 'to take at least one curb out of the mouth of that wild beast man, when it would be well if he was checked by half a score of others'. More usually, however, the attack on human nature and the crude appeal to power are softened. The commoner argument appeals to the inequality in nature, as the proper model for an ordered and harmonious society. This argument has the double advantage of justifying the privilege of those who are set on high, and of giving due meed to those who occupy a necessary but humbler place in the hierarchical order, which they must not be encouraged to disturb. Conservatives are fond of quoting at least one passage from the book of Ecclesiasticus:

---

[1] Alceste replies not with argument, but by expressing his sense of outrage at Philinte's attitude.

'I will see myself betrayed, broken, robbed,
Rather than I should be . . . Heavens! I will not speak,
So full of insolence is this reasoning.'

The wisdom of a learned man cometh by opportunity of leisure: and he that hath little business shall become wise. How can he get wisdom that holdeth the plough, and that glorieth in the goad, that driveth oxen, and is occupied in their labours, and whose talk is of bullocks? . . . Without these cannot a city be inhabited: . . . they shall not be sought for in publick counsel, nor sit high in the congregation: . . . But they will maintain the state of the world.

The leisured and powerful are justified by their function, while the poor and humble who by their labours maintain them have the consolation of knowing that they 'maintain the state of the world'. To each his providentially appointed condition and estate! And if the people should murmur in their hearts, cavil at their lot, question the providential nature of the arrangement, and seek to shake the foundations of authority itself? Then the conservative can appeal direct to his own power and his opponent's weakness and ignorance.

In Ibsen's dialogue between the Provost and Brand, it is the mocking castigation of their own inferiority by the Provost that is effective in undermining the people's will to take up the challenge in the face of their fears.

> What can you achieve,
> Humble people born in a humble village?
> Were you created to shake the world,
> To right wrongs, liberate the oppressed?

The taunt strikes at each man's own sense of personal impotence ever to alter the conditions under which he suffers. It shrivels his weakly developed sense of self-respect; it reminds him of his customary status with its attendant feelings of deference to those set in authority over him. It reminds him that he is the subject and that others are the rulers; and it suggests that this dichotomy is eternal as Nature herself. But is it? The debate turns on the issue as to what is human nature. It is precisely the issue as to who we are that is the most fiercely disputed. Can man by his own understanding and endeavours work out his own salvation? Or is he irredeemably a fallen creature, seeing the better but following the worse? suffering by virtue of his own folly and then wallowing in his own self-pity?

You grind away God's image, live like beasts,
Then join the grovelling queue to beg for grace.

Often it would seem that both pessimist and perfectibilist
agree as to the facts, differing only in their attitudes towards the
facts. The conservative has no difficulty in convincing himself
that human nature is what it is. On the contrary, it is his
main stock-in-trade. The progressive radical contemplates the
spectacle with anguish, but would often seem to concede that the
facts are as Ibsen's Provost and Brand too in the end would have
us believe. When Edmund Burke attacked the radicals struggling
to achieve an extension of the suffrage, he was quick to fasten
on an allusion by Dr Price to the existing voters as a few thousands
of 'the dregs of the people'. 'You will smile here,' Burke comments, 'at the consistency of those democratists, who, when they
are not on their guard, treat the humbler part of the community
with the greatest contempt, whilst, at the same time, they
pretend to make them the depositories of all power.' None
struggled more devotedly to enlighten mankind than Denis
Diderot in the face of crushing blows by his enemies. But even
Diderot, in a mood of despondency as he considered in retrospect
the malignant opposition which he had had to overcome in
order to produce the great Encyclopaedia, was constrained to
reflect: 'The world does not profit from its advance into old age:
it does not change. It is possible that the individual perfects
himself, but the race becomes neither better nor worse in the
mass. The sum of evil passions remains the same, and the
enemies of the good and useful remain as numerous as ever.'[1]
Nevertheless, Diderot refused to believe that the scales really
were weighted against the forces of the good in any unalterable
fashion. The good, he was quick to add, always enjoyed one
vital advantage. 'The good man is susceptible of an enthusiasm
that the wicked man does not know.'
A voice like Diderot's may give way to despondency or even
to bitterness, but it does not go sour. In the case of Ibsen, however, the pendulum of the moral judgement oscillates frequently,
and the touch is less sure. The powerful and the conventional,
the pillars of society are attacked for their stupidity, their greed,
their intolerance; but it is suggested that those who struggle

---

[1] *Avertissement* to Vol. VIII of the *Encyclopédie*, 1751–65

against these evils, the Stockmans, the Gregors Werles are themselves chronically twisted in and by the conflict. The Christian ideal is the measuring rod by which social hypocrisy is tested; but in the end it is man himself whom Ibsen seems to spurn as unworthy of the challenge he has to meet. The aspiration is there, the example has been given us, but we are unworthy. While it may appear that man has only to heave himself to his feet with determination to take up the full weight of his cross, in life the burden is too great for him. He quails before the magnitude of the effort and despairs, or rather averts his gaze and passes by. The anguish in Brand's soul finds vent in a bitterness that is tainted by ironic self-pity.

> All of them have the craving in their hearts
> But the sacrifice frightens them.
> Their will is weak; their fear is strong.
> . . .
> It was not for us that He drained the cup of agony,
> Not for us that the thorn-crown scarred His brow;
> It was not for us that the lance pierced His side,
> Not for us that the nails burned
> Through His hands and feet. We are small and mean,
> We are not worthy. We defy the call to arms,
> It was not for us that He carried His cross.

But the matter can scarcely be left there. If we suppose that man carries within him the seeds of his own doom in an unrepentant egocentricity and competitiveness, we raise serious logical and metaphysical difficulties. To begin with, we are confronted by a root contradiction. On the one hand, it appears that we are so biologically constituted that the appetite for domination and power to obtain privileges for oneself or one's group at the expense of those with whom one is competing, is endemic and ineradicable in human nature. By definition, success in this struggle must be confined to a relatively small minority, since exclusiveness is a crucial element in the 'value' that is being sought. If all men alike were rich and powerful, leaders possessed of power and status, there would be no followers, no one to lead. But then the psychological motivation would dry up at the source, since the object of striving would have lost its savour. For such a system to work in any smooth, efficient, self-regulating way, it would be essential that human beings should be born into inherently different biological categories; viz. those whose basic motivation was to lead or to dominate, and those whose essential nature could only meet with full satisfaction by being dominated or led. In short, essential to such a hypothesis is the premise that there is no such thing as a common human nature. As Aristotle supposed, there is no uniform human nature. There is the nature common to the natural leader or citizen and the nature common to the natural slave. But it was precisely the supposition that we are bound by a common human nature, namely one that is inherently competitive and power-seeking, that led us into our difficulty. This is the first contradiction.

Alternatively, it might be suggested that this contradiction can be avoided, if we do not make the gratuitous supposition that the system was ever conceived as a rational whole, susceptible of an ordered and efficient harmony. In short, there is a common human nature, which entails permanent, endemic struggle between those who have succeeded in imposing their leadership on those who naturally resent this state of affairs and struggle to overthrow it. Nature is red in tooth and claw; the weak do go to the wall; conflict, tension and violence result but this is unavoidable. Resentment of the arrangements themselves, as distinct from resentment at the power of the particular ruling group of the moment, is irrational and derives from irrelevant rationalist hankerings. It is true that this traditionally recurring condition of conflict and violence has now in the course of evolution reached a stage where the destructive instruments in the power struggle will, when used, be no longer compatible with civilized life. For modern communities could not hope to survive another major power conflict or 'war'. On this hypothesis, no purely logical contradiction is involved. All that is necessary is for the mind to learn to adjust itself to the rationality of the idea that human life evolved, human civilization and culture struggled successfully to emerge, in order to perish amidst scenes of unimaginable horror and bestiality.

The acceptance of the idea that the struggle for inequality is endemic and ineradicable in human nature involves us either in a logical contradiction or in a metaphysical nightmare. And since this controlling idea is more or less accepted as an unquestioned axiom in the thinking of all 'realistic' men, intellectuals as well as 'practical' men, it is scarcely surprising if there should appear to be no firm foundation for 'knowledge' as to what is the right course of action for human beings to pursue. The alternative is that we examine the other hypothesis, namely that there is a common human nature and that the struggle for inequality is not endemic to it. All contradiction would then be resolved; for human beings would be then shown to be inherently rational, egalitarian, co-operative and loving beings, who would live peacefully and creatively. They would have the firmest possible basis for knowledge about the good. The problem that would then arise would be neither of a logical nor of a metaphysical character. There would be no logical contradiction, no metaphysical nightmare arising out of the necessity to accept the idea that the whole creation was a monstrous and diabolic joke. The difficulty would be how to explain how mankind has gone wrong; to diagnose the problem of evil and its source in historical conditions. This at any rate is a strictly empirical question which demands investigation, and is well within our capacities to undertake.

This issue has always been seen as central to the metaphysics of the reformist Left. The problem of error and evil looms large in the writings of all the Enlightenment thinkers. But in the eighteenth century there was a strong disposition to conceive of Nature in static rather than in evolutionary or dynamic terms. A mythical past was accordingly conceived in which natural man had lived according to the rational law in a primitive Arcadian paradise close to nature and in harmony with Nature's law. The problem of evil thus became the historical problem of discovering when and how man had come to take the wrong turning. Explanations were many and diverse, ranging from failure in linguistic ability to mirror correctly the world of experience to the emergence of 'the sinister interests', exploiting human credulity and moral weakness. But none of these explanations provided plausible grounds for believing in the possibility of human recovery of the right path. Once man had gone wrong, and had for long continued on the wrong path, it became increasingly improbable that he would be able to undo the accumulated legacy of wrongdoing in order to return to the original point of error. From the meliorist standpoint, both the

Hegelian dialectic and the Darwinian evolutionary hypothesis offered much stronger ground for optimism. Given that man was inherently rational and inhabited a rational universe, the problem lay in man's discovering through investigation and experimentation, through his own intellectual and moral development, the truth about his nature and relation to the world. There still remained, however, the depressingly powerful evidence of the constancy over very long periods of precisely the behaviour traits responsible for man's successive undoing, namely the urge to excel and dominate his neighbour. The question presents itself as central and inescapable: how rigid, how susceptible to modification is this disposition to inequality? This study accordingly begins with an attempt to establish a psychological base on which to theorize. While Freud is not the only important figure to have contributed to our psychological knowledge, it was he who pioneered the most significant revolution which has occurred in man's conception of himself. Moreover, no one has done more than he to shape the psychological assumptions of modern man. While he is still a highly controversial figure, it is also true that his authority is unrivalled. I begin then with a map of the mind as it appears in its new Freudian contours.

This map suggests to us how intimate is the connection beween individual character and the pressures and anxieties generated in the society in which the individual finds himself. Character formation is a subject that itself requires a knowledge of sociology and politics as an indispensable aid to understanding. And Freud's sociology and politics, though liberal, are essentially of his class and time. The task of therapy is confined essentially to enabling the individual to liberate himself from the unconscious Oedipean hold of authoritarian parental ties. Freud's political programme is confined to the modest social changes attendant upon increased mental well-being, not to instigating a fundamental change to equality in social and political relations. Indeed he remained deeply sceptical as to its possibility. At the same time he did not deny that human equality is a rational desideratum. It is an important source of the ruthless honesty which gave him his great strength of character. When Freud affirms his scepticism about the chances of human beings living in equality, he acknowledges this clearly to himself as pessimism. He comes to this conclusion reluctantly; he does not rejoice at the prediction. However, it is one thing to arrive sadly at the conclusion, held to be inescapable, that human beings are irretrievably irrational and immoral in their behaviour. It is quite a different thing to affirm that some inequality is not really inequality and is really a good thing. Here we return to the realm of moral self-deception and evasion, freedom from which constitutes a man's genuine authority – the quality which so pre-eminently stamps Freud. With one important exception: he is quite unable to grasp that equality is even desirable in the field of sexual relations. Where man and woman are concerned, above all in the intimacy of the marriage tie, Freud himself turns out to be little more than a Victorian paterfamilias, benevolent, courteous, loving even to a point, but always from within the protective shell of an unchallenged masculine primacy. In this context he does not affirm that equality is inherently difficult or impossible to attain. He affirms something very different: namely that equality is undesirable, is not a good thing. If it is not stated quite so nakedly, this is clearly the controlling belief.

Psychoanalysis, as a base for a sociology, with all its strength suffers from two deficiencies. First, because of Freud's blindness to the nature of inequality at the heart of the sexual relationship he left unexplored the sickness at the heart of this relationship, and so could not perceive the immense social consequences that flow from this. Serious distortion or repression in this relationship might well have the most far-reaching consequences both for human nature itself and the total culture that it produces. After all, it is this relationship which is the source of human life. It is not reasonable to suppose that disequilibrium and inequality at this juncture could escape adverse consequences for the development of character in children who inside the family receive their first and most powerful impressions. And secondly, psychoanalysis largely takes for granted the social values and class conflicts of the late capitalist era, and seeks to diagnose sickness and define therapy in the individual independently of them. The will to power and status, the social will, goes largely uncriticized by Freud. Consequently, the moral struggle between the individual and the pressures of the world's values is largely ignored by him. A man is psychoanalytically cured even though he yearns as deeply as ever for the social pre-eminence over his fellows that the prevailing culture deems to be the natural object of human striving.

The next step, then, is to put to the test these two criticisms of Freud's psychology. To test the significance of the hypothesis that inequality in the sexual and parental relationship necessarily corrupts raises obvious difficulties. Only professional analysts have their own case studies upon which to draw. Moreover, such material suffers from the disadvantage that the evidence is not public, and therefore does not admit of public verification of any kind. On the other hand, it is not easy to come across published sources such as letters and autobiography where the detail is sufficient or intimate enough to permit of anything more than intelligent guess work. My own attempt to solve the problem consists of a brief examination of the attitude of our society in the last century to the role of woman and in particular her relations with the male. This is followed by particular cases of the effects on character of sexual inequality in households where published sources are not inconsiderable, namely, the Barretts, the Mills and the Butlers – all well-known families. Although individual circumstance varies widely, a common pattern of personality disturbance is manifest. In each instance we observe the gradual development of symptoms of tension and stress in the character of the child growing to adulthood; and the symptoms are directly related to the power disequilibrium in the parental relations. Each is consistent with the central thesis that love is not possible where equality is absent. Moreover, the wielding of power and the consequent absence of love are destructive equally, although in different ways, to the characters of both parties to the relationship, the dominator and the dominated. To illustrate the second point, namely, the tension between the individual and his culture, I shall have recourse to works of fiction, which contain the insight of remarkable artists drawing upon their own intuitive psychological knowledge and observation of life. The cases of Frederick Dorrit, Ivan Ilych, Babbitt and Willy Loman reveal the way in which the gulf between the *is* and the *ought* in the greater society is mirrored in the character conflict of the individual. Each person is aware at some level of the truth of equality. But to affirm and live it is to struggle against the individual's own inbuilt character neurosis, rooted in the inequalities of the previous generation.

This weakness is further aggravated by the discovery that society too is apt to penalize the individual who affirms the truth. This it is which explains in part the strength of the pressure to conform. Thus each individual is powerfully induced to deceive himself about the significance of the moral law. He engages in self-deception in order to try to maintain the unity of his experience and the moral demands of his nature. The temptation is great to conclude that these latter can be evaded or ignored. And each individual accordingly comes to grief in moral aridity, ennui or actual suffering, even when, as in the cases of Dorrit, Ilych and Babbitt, the external conditions of their life are comparatively prosperous and successful.

In the greater society more than in the family the problem of power itself is thrust into the forefront of the discussion. Here we at once find ourselves faced by a curious paradox reminiscent of the paradox of human nature itself. Whereas in personal relations within the sphere of private family and social life the power nexus is generally recognized as a bad thing, in public life, in the administration of communal affairs and in relations between communities, power is regarded not as a bad thing, but as a good thing or at worst as a necessary evil. It is true that if the claims of power are pursued too nakedly and unashamedly, this is apt to produce signs of embarrassment even in the morally robust. Machiavelli is widely read, but he has never been exactly popular. At the other extreme, the morally sensitive will be found trying to argue that power is unrelated to force or even that force must be distinguished from violence. But common to practically all is the belief that power itself is a factor in human affairs that is morally neutral; that it may, in other words, be deployed for good or evil purposes, according to circumstance. Cavour it was who said something to the effect that he would be called a scoundrel by his friends and neighbours if he did in his private life those things which he frequently found himself called upon to do in his duties as a statesman on behalf of his country. Very few then or since appear to find anything very odd in this state of affairs. Still less do they relate it to the regularity with which they are visited by the scourges of war and poverty in the presence of great wealth. It is as though a man were to labour to fill a sieve with water. It would be difficult to conceive of greater irrationality than this; and yet so accustomed are we to it that few people seem conscious of the contradiction. For it is not a case of men seeing the better but following the worse. It is a case of insistence on a duality of mutually contradictory standards, protesting the while that each is equally mandatory upon the individual in its own proper sphere. In private life we ought to try to practise the ethic of Christianity of selflessness, and in our public life we ought with equal zeal to practise the ethic of *raison d'état* or national self-interest. Power carries along with it its own rights and duties. So while we strive in one direction in the private moral sphere, we labour in an opposite direction in the public political sphere. Though again, if the contradiction is stated so candidly as that, disavowals will be forthcoming. Much will be heard of our political responsibilities, and the need to prosecute the common weal, maintain the security of the state, and protect minimum welfare standards – phrases all with a strong positive content and apparent moral flavour. But thinly concealed behind such phrases lie the facts of power and coercion which have never been more naked and terrifying than today. This, then, constitutes the central topic of discussion in the middle section. My general conclusion is that the belief in the possibility of advancing human welfare through working to secure political power is itself the most important single illusion which stands in the way of advancing that welfare. It provides the individual with the most plausible and widely offered of all excuses to justify his failure to make the necessary changes to eliminate the contradictions within his own life.

So far the argument has been concerned with psychology or the nature of man followed by a discussion of the relation between morals and politics. The occasion of the first part might be summarized as an attempt to examine the plausibility of the cliché that 'you can't change human nature'. The second section might be considered relevant to that piece of folk-lore, which the sophisticated and privileged do little to discourage, that 'there's nothing you can do about it'. But one of the commonest symptoms of human *malaise* finds crude expression in the remark, 'There's no such thing as moral truth.' 'What is truth?' There is no reason to suppose that Pilate was jesting. Was it not really the rhetorical question of a sceptical man old in the ways of the world? Scepticism and relativism in theory of knowledge have been very influential in shaping men's attitudes. And never more so than today. Closely allied to this is the attitude which finds equally popular expression in the assertion that people who protest at common practice are behaving 'emotionally'. And the implication is plain that emotional behaviour is irrational. I conclude therefore with an examination of the status of metaphysical and moral beliefs, the role of reason and emotion in the formulation of them, and the part played by such beliefs in the determination of behaviour.

Scepticism finds itself reinforced from many quarters. Not least is the contradiction between the standards of private morality and public statecraft to which reference has already been made. This may take the form of denying a unitary system of values in a world where the facts will not square with such simplicity. Or the status of truth may be admitted but dismissed as irrelevant in the presence of more important considerations of power. Bolingbroke – and he does not lack apologists today – believed that 'things evidently false might deserve an outward respect, when they are interwoven into a system of government'. More frequently perhaps sceptics content themselves with appealing to the evidence of plurality and diversity of moral beliefs held by men even within the same culture as evidence of the view that there is no rational basis for a belief in absolute moral values. At best, it is suggested, appeal can be made to men of judgement and experience within a common field of experience within the same culture. Beyond that the only civilized thing to do is to accept difference good-humouredly and tolerantly as befits latitudinarian gentlemen.

Finally, this theoretical discussion about the status of belief is of direct practical relevance to the original question concerning the alleged impossibility of bringing about any really significant modification in human behaviour. The point that emerges from the psychological discussion is the failure to appreciate the importance of the consequences of sexual inequality on human character. The second point to be noted is that the importance of the status of belief has been inadequately appreciated as a determinant of human behaviour. In other words, where belief is genuine, sooner or later it must determine behaviour, even as the rudder of a ship determines its direction. If this is accepted, it then follows that the quality of genuineness of belief becomes

a factor of the first importance. Hume gives us a valuable clue
in this respect in his *The Natural History of Religion*.

> We may observe, that, notwithstanding the dogmatical, im-
> perious style of all superstition, the conviction of the religionists,
> in all ages, is more affected than real, and scarcely ever approaches,
> in any degree, to that solid belief and persuasion, which governs
> us in the common affairs of life. Men dare not avow, even to their
> own hearts, the doubts which they entertain on such subjects:
> They make a merit of implicit faith; and disguise to themselves
> their real infidelity, by the strongest asseverations and most
> positive bigotry. But nature is too hard for all their endeavours, and
> suffers not the obscure, glimmering light, afforded in those shadowy
> regions, to equal the strong impressions, made by common sense
> and by experience. The usual course of men's conduct belies
> their words, and shows, that their assent in these matters is some
> unaccountable operation of the mind between disbelief and
> conviction, but approaching much nearer to the former than to
> the latter.

Hume here notes the connection between men's beliefs and
their actions, but notes also that their words, even when spoken
sincerely, do not by any means necessarily correspond to their
real beliefs. This condition of the mind he diagnoses as 'an
unaccountable operation . . . between disbelief and conviction'
which not surprisingly is ineffective in determining behaviour.
There is thus no more effective way of inhibiting action or
behavioural changes at the source than by confusing a person's
sense of conviction. To produce intellectual confusion or to
undermine a person's confidence in his capacity to discern for
himself such truth as he needs to guide his behaviour is the most
effective way of rendering him impotent. And this is intuitively
understood by all those who work in the field of ideas and propaganda with the intent of maintaining in power those who
profit by their power. For the action of the mind when it expresses
itself clearly is itself a force which eludes and is felt to threaten
those who rely on the conventional weapons of power maintenance. 'We all complain of the senseless order of our life which
is at variance with our whole being, and yet we neglect to use the
unique and powerful instrument in our hands – the consciousness
of truth and its expression', wrote Tolstoy in *Christianity and*

Patriotism[1]. But in every generation there are many whose business it is to ensure that the potentially 'unique and powerful instrument' that we all possess is blunted at the source. It is very important to understand something of the ways in which this is done and to this end I shall examine the basis of conviction in reason and emotion.

---

[1] *The Kingdom of God* and Peace Essays, World's Classics, p. 534

2 The Psychoanalysis of Power

IN THE discussion of equality and power the hinge on which much of the argument turns is psychological. Protagonists take a different view about 'our common human nature', or of the degree to which it may be modified. Since psychology is the key to any political theory, we would expect to find any advance in psychology sooner or later reflected in the theory of politics. Hobbes erected an elaborate psychological scaffolding of his own devising; Locke drew on the observations of contemporary anthropologists; Bentham and Mill built on the findings of Hartley and the school of associationist psychologists. It seems odd therefore that in a period which has witnessed the psychological revolution pioneered by Freud, so little attention has been paid to these developments by professional political theorists. It is, accordingly, proposed here to examine in what way the insights of Freudian psychology are relevant to the discussion of the role of power and inequality in human affairs. Freud's findings have after all for good or ill decisively shaped our contemporary culture. Freud commands attention, and cannot be ignored, least of all in politics. Yet because of prejudice, and, more specifically, of a currently influential attempt by some behaviourist psychologists to discredit the psychoanalytic method, it is necessary to preface the discussion of the psychoanalytic implications for politics by a word on psychoanalytic method.

It is frequently asserted that the kind of evidence advanced by psychoanalysis does not admit of objective verification. In short, its claims to 'scientific' status are bogus. And since the term 'scientific' is one to which high prestige attaches, this charge effectively suggests that its findings are suspect. People who accept the truth of psychoanalytic 'evidence' are said to hold 'emotional convictions'. Irrationality is clearly implied. Without at this point raising the large question of the affective sources of 'conviction', it is relevant to speculate as to what the critic of psychoanalysis has in mind as an example of non-emotional conviction. This type of argument, with its appeal to the theory of knowledge, is the behaviourist's *tu quoque* to the analyst's insistence that acceptance or rejection of psychoanalytic hypotheses is equally irrelevant if made from outside the analytic experience, since either reaction would probably be a form of 'resistance'. The latter argument is only too likely to produce irritation in the sceptic. Any argument which takes less than seriously the actual content of what we have to say because of an alleged insight into motives unknown to us, appears to cast doubts upon either our integrity or our intelligence. Nevertheless, it is not possible for the analyst to take any other position; and he can only reply that it is open to everyone who is humble and patient enough, to undergo the analytic experience. This is objective, in that it is public, not private; and rests on objective psychic reality. It is true that the truth of many psychoanalytic statements cannot be demonstrated by any external or inter-subjective test. But, while this is a reason for caution, it is not a reason to dismiss them as romantic mythologizing. A simple illustration should make this plain. Having forgotten a name, I invite suggestions to help me to recall it. I reject them confidently one after another until the right name is pronounced. Everybody understands the confidence – the 'emotional conviction' – they feel that they are not mistaken that the forgotten name is Ponty-pridd and not Bridport. Naturally, it is impossible to demonstrate the truth of such 'knowledge'; yet few would be disposed to dismiss such a claim as nothing better than private prejudice. Psychoanalytic 'knowledge' is of this kind.

The other main line of attack challenges the therapeutic efficacy of psychoanalysts. Let a comparison be made between the proportion of cures effected in two groups of neurotic sufferers (defining both neurosis and cure in terms of functional efficiency), one exposed to psychoanalytic treatment, the other exposed either to no treatment whatever or merely to general practitioner nostrums. It will be found, it is suggested, that the proportion of cures is identical in both groups. The conclusion is then drawn that psychoanalytic treatment has no therapeutic value, although it may possibly console or divert. Now, no one, least of all Freud, has ever denied that in a considerable pro-portion of neurotic personality disturbances 'spontaneous re-

mission' occurs. In other words, given sufficient time, the patient
'gets better' anyway. He is able, that is, to resume his normal
personal and occupational function at his wonted level of
efficiency. Such a comparative yardstick is however a very crude
one. It has the merit that it is based solely on the observable and
measurable fact that an individual is now deploying certain skills
in an habitual fashion. But a human being, if he is to be understood, requires more than a purely ecological analysis. It can be
pointed out as a matter of logic that one important difference
must obtain between a patient cured by psychoanalysis and one
cured by 'spontaneous remission'. The former understands what
has happened to him, and why he is cured. In this knowledge
lies his immunization against the recurrence of his fear: the
principal source of fear is ignorance. The one effective remedy
is to learn to understand the causes of that which is feared.
Where the fear is of oneself there can be no more effective nostrum
than the Greek command to 'know thyself'. On the other hand,
the patient cured by spontaneous remission cannot understand
why or how he became ill or why or how he got better. However
competently he manages to function, he is never free from the
anxiety of living with the possibility of a return of unexplained
and frightening illness. It will be objected that the psychoanalytically cured patient's 'knowledge' is the illusion of an
'emotional conviction'. But this objection, even if true, would be
irrelevant to the truth of the proposition that there is no significant difference between the two control groups, the one cured
by psychoanalysis and the other cured by spontaneous remission;
since, in the one group the 'illusion' is real in that it succeeds
in giving its possessors the requisite confidence and freedom
from fear, whereas the members of the other group are equipped
with no such 'illusion'.

Before we can discuss Freud's view of political man and his
limits of manoeuvrability, it is necessary to summarize Freud's
individual psychology. Essential to Freud's sociology is his novel
topography or rather model of the dynamics of the mind. The
classical picture of the self was essentially simple; it ascribed to
the self the attributes of consciousness, rationality and morality.
Within the self lay the agencies whereby the individual experienced reality, derived his knowledge of it, judged and appraised
it. Within the self also was the rational agency which kept watch

and ward in the ceaseless task of controlling the irrational passions and appetites. The classical 'ego' was both rational and moral. Freud's map is quite different. It is more sophisticated and in some ways more convincing. But it has disturbing implications. The self is conceived as the resultant of dynamic tensions. On the one hand, there is the pressure of amoral impulse and appetite demanding an outlet from the instinctual and unconscious source of the 'id'. And sharply opposed to this is the force of cultural repression expressed through the 'super-ego' or 'conscience'. The function of the ego is to mediate between these two polarized forces; and a person's 'character' is the resultant of the equilibrium established by the ego. Reason is located in the ego, but it is a morally uncommitted reason. Or rather, its moral role is severely restricted. The role of reason is the prudential one of maintaining psychic stability. This it does by the effectiveness of the balance it achieves between the competing claims of appetite and conscience.

In Freud's picture reason is no longer the source of the moral judgement, since the moral judgement is deriving powerful impulse from unconscious sources. The instinctual reservoir of the id supplies not only the libidinal energy prompting the ego to seek gratification and pleasure; it also supplies the driving force of the super-ego in the inhibitory and cultural demands it makes upon the ego. Thus the feelings of guilt which play such a vital part in inhibiting or repressing libidinal desires are partly unconscious. Conscience in its origins is closely associated with the Oedipus complex which itself is wholly unconscious. The function of reason is no longer to ride and control the irrational passions in the interests of morality. Reason located in the ego, viz. the conscious intelligent self, is assigned the task of mediating between two hostile forces, each of which has its legitimate place and each of which is liable to wreak havoc if excessively indulged. Freud does not quarrel with the traditional view which regarded the appetites and passions as potentially dangerous. But he does suggest that our suspicion of appetite has been excessive. The novelty of this view lay in extending the area of suspicion to the revered source of all that is highest in man, the moral judgement itself. Not that Freud wishes to quarrel with any of the essential findings of the moral judgement. His suspicions derive from the conviction that inherent in the moral judgement is a harsh taskmaster, liable, if not carefully watched, to inflict lasting injury on the equilibrium of the mental economy.

Should this view of our mental dynamics be accepted? There would be a great danger in weakening the authority of the moral judgement. But such a danger is not necessarily entailed, if we accept Freud's picture. It must be admitted that unconscious guilt and compulsive moral demands can and do tyrannize over the personality. Freud enables us to understand how this comes about in a way that the classical picture of the psyche does not. In terms of the familiar iceberg metaphor, it is the id that is below the surface, and is the genuine source of psychic energy. And the id lies beyond good and evil. It knows neither morality nor rationality; it is blind to all values. The danger here is that if good and evil are shown to have a common psychic source, it might be inferred that the division between them is less sharp than had hitherto been supposed. Might not virtue appear to have been compromised? Moreover, Freud was extremely critical of the super-ego as a potentially ruthless source of inhibitory power. When we consider how ready men are to follow their desires and in particular to silence or ignore the promptings of conscience, it is not difficult to understand the apprehensions aroused by psychoanalysis. Freud himself, however, drew no such facile conclusion from his model of the mind. His own view is stated in *The Ego and the Id* in a discussion of the human capacity for rational, moral judgement. 'If any one were inclined to put forward the paradoxical proposition that the normal man is not only far more immoral than he believes but also far more moral than he has any idea of, psychoanalysis, which is responsible for the first half of the assertion, would have no objection to raise against the second half' (1927, pp. 75–6).

At the same time, we must be equally clear that psychoanalysis itself has no moral programme to recommend to the patient. Psychotherapy is conducted within a theoretical framework which presupposes a model of an ideal or 'normal' individual; and Freud's ideal construct of the 'norm' is not to be confused with a statistical norm. But Freud's therapeutic yardstick does take for granted the existing social and cultural context within which the individual finds himself. 'In the neurosis of an individual we can use as a starting-point the contrast presented to us between the patient and his environment which we assume to be "normal".'[1] There is a logical difficulty here. The therapeutic model is an ideal construct independent of statistical norms. Yet a crucial attribute of the model consists of the ability to function efficiently in the existing society, whose norms derive from the aggregate of ordinary, unanalysed men. Perhaps the answer is that Freud's ideal or 'cured' man, tied by no necessary moral commitment, is able to adjust without difficulty to his social context; but because, unlike unanalysed men, he has learnt to know himself, he is able to function more energetically and efficiently than they. He is more self-aware. He has resolved his inner tension. By the poise of his equilibrium he has maximized the efficiency of his psychic economy. He is not an inner-directed moral absolutist; but nor is he a Vicar of Bray. If he is inclined to suspect those who put their emphasis on the duty of self-abnegation, equally, he finds alien those who are unable to exercise adequate control over their libidinous impulses. A balanced, 'normal' self is one that is emancipated from unconscious conflict, freed, that is, from authoritarian Oedipean ties. A high value is placed on self-knowledge for its own sake, since it increases psychic efficiency, thus releasing energy for whatever ends we choose. In short, successful therapy increases the area of freedom of choice, without seeking to prescribe how that choice shall be exercised. '. . . after all, analysis does not set out to abolish the possibility of morbid reactions, but to give the patient's ego *freedom* to choose one way or the other.'[2]

Reason, so conceived, is virtually emptied of moral content, except in the limited sense that it should exercise prudence in maintaining psychic stability or viability. The healthy ego is stabilized by avoidance of repression and inhibition on the one hand, and of indulgence on the other. By exorcizing the censorship of taboo, reason enables the ego to cast out fear; by insisting on honesty and candour, it enables the ego to rid itself of the tensions inseparable from self-deception and evasion. When the rational gyroscope is off centre, it ceases to act as a built-in stabilizer; and the personality is afflicted with neurosis. But this to some degree is the case with (statistically) normal people who in aggregate constitute our existing sick society. Yet, at another

[1] *Civilization and its Discontents*, 1930, p. 142
[2] *The Ego and the Id*, 1927, p. 72n.

level, Freud is generally content to use ability to function in the society as a therapeutic test. Perhaps we need to take a closer look at Freud's definition of neurosis. What, in Freud's view, is the cause of error? How have we become sick? Wherein lies our offending? Basically, his answer follows from the foregoing analysis of the role of reason in therapy.

We are sick because in our weakness we offend against truth; we are weak and dissemble; we repress the painful. That which is for any reason hurtful to the ego, is promptly buried deep in the unconscious; because the ego in its naïvety believes that it is thereby disposing of the painful element. In fact, the reverse is true. Repressed, the painful thought continues to fester and accumulate energy. Ultimately it develops such a quantity of emotional excitation as to demand an outlet, which finds expression in neurotic symptoms. The concepts of 'repression' and the converse 'resistance' are vital for an understanding of the dynamics of neurosis. Forgetting is not a negative action but an active and significant decision taken by the ego, although this is not apparent at the level of consciousness. But the forgetting is never complete. The issue which has been evaded and buried deep continues its disruptive effects within the psyche. Thus neurosis may be defined as incomplete or partially successful amnesia. It is the task of therapy to liberate the psyche from unconscious conflict. This it does by bringing to the surface that which is too painful to contemplate. The patient's inevitable resistance to this threatened release from amnesia must be patiently worked through and ultimately overcome. Only in this way can he obtain the necessary insight into his compulsive clinging to his past. The resultant catharsis provides beneficial relief, and the patient is thus able to come to more realistic terms with himself. More light!

The problem of therapy is not, as preachers and moralists have for centuries supposed, a problem of the will. The real problem is one of knowledge. Exhortation or pious encouragement to more zealous aspiration is futile. Emancipation from the bondage of the traumatic depths of the psyche is only possible through an extension of the patient's self-knowledge. The symptoms dissolve when the repressed emotions are brought into the open where they may be consciously inspected. The psychic scar is then re-opened to permit of a fresh healing compatible with relief from the tension of guilt and anxiety. Rationality is still austerely conceived as cognition: in this instance, knowledge of internal psychic processes. Know thyself! Choose! Reason has not prescribed how to choose. The sick person is made whole without any predetermined moral commitment. Or almost without! For there is, after all, an important caveat. Sickness is so defined as to imply some moral deficiency. To diagnose neurosis is not a morally neutral, clinical statement. It contains a moral critique. The sick person is weak; he is afraid; he is unable to face the truth about himself and his situation; he is a slave to the pleasure principle. In short, simply in order to recover the ability to function confidently and efficiently in the particular social context prescribed by the 'sane' society, the patient must face, accept and overcome a weighty moral indictment of himself. If sickness is in part moral deficiency, cure must in part represent moral victory. This moral awareness is indispensable for adequate therapy. Nor is it likely suddenly to cease to operate. And so the vital question poses itself. Is it not inevitable that this new-found moral insight will continue to influence and shape the patient's moral evaluation of the culture within which he has to resume his life? Freud struggles hard to contain the concept of reason within a minimal definition, namely, the morally neutral one of rigorous psychic control in the interests of efficiency only. But the concept proves elusive. It constantly escapes from its master's self-denying ordinance, and demands a broader, more inclusive definition.

The assumption so far has been that therapy can be carried through to completion solely by an increase in self-knowledge and consequently of self-control. But this is only a part of the picture. Indispensable to a complete cure within the Freudian tradition is the phenomenon of 'transference'. Catharsis is not enough. Understanding is not enough. A further stage at the affective level must be worked through. Without dissecting the concept of 'transference' we cannot begin to apprehend the relation between reason and emotion at the roots of judgement and conviction. Therapy is, in Freud's expression, re-education in overcoming resistances. But reason, unaided, cannot of itself complete the job. In order that a cure should be complete and permanent, 'transference' to the person of the physician must take place. 'Conversion' is not simply a matter of the understanding; it is also a question of erotic acceptance. Love as well as reason is required of the successful patient. The human being's natural capacity to love derives, according to Freud, from the original primacy of emotions of dependence and submission. Love, in other words, is in its origins authoritarian. At the heart of every neurosis is to be found the Oedipus complex: the incestuous love of the child for the mother and the concordant jealousy of and resistance to the father. In order to resolve the tension of these conflicting emotions, the child has to learn to defer to paternal authority, and to curb the erotic desire expressed in a tender, compliant love for the mother. In this way culture becomes possible. Infantile love, thus conceived, is not a love between equal people, but a love based on authority. It is the task of maturity to outgrow this relation of subservience into the spontaneity of adult love, at once free and equal. The aim of therapy is to release the emotions and motives from the fetters of the prototype patterns of childhood.

> From the time of puberty onward the human individual must devote himself to the great task of *freeing himself from the parents.* . . . For a son, the task consists in releasing his libidinal desires from his mother, in order to employ them in the quest of an external love object in reality; and in reconciling himself with his father if he has remained antagonistic to him, or in freeing himself from his domination if, in the reaction to the infantile revolt, he has lapsed into subservience to him. These tasks are laid down for every man; it is noteworthy how seldom they are carried through ideally. . . . In neurotics, however, this detachment from the parents is not accomplished at all; . . .[1]

From the thraldom of unconscious parental bondage the patient can only be liberated by transferring the emotions of acceptance of paternal dominion to the person of the physician. The repressed emotions can then be brought to consciousness, and re-enacted before a sympathetic substitute father. In this way, the patient may finally learn to emancipate himself from libidinal ties of subservience, and to achieve a capacity for a mature, adult love, freely given and worthy of reciprocity. The

[1] *Introductory Lectures*, 1922, p. 283

aim of therapy is thus by the power of mature love to transform an immature love based on subservience into one based on freedom and equality. Since 'logical arguments are impotent against affective interests', the power of human love must be invoked to heighten the moral quality of the patient's own capacity for love. And yet psychoanalysis may not itself suggest that there is any specific moral programme which a 'cured' person would be obliged to accept. Reason, expressed in the 'science' of psychoanalysis, is for Freud, as for the positivists, morally neutral. Therefore the patient, restored to health, must be free to adopt any moral programme that is compatible with his renewed psychic efficiency.

So far we have considered man in his individual aspect. Man is also a social and political animal; and it is in this direction that the analysis must now be directed in order to elucidate the psychoanalytic contribution to the problem of the role of power in human affairs. Essentially Freud is a Hobbesian pessimist, but not entirely so. His pessimism, if constant, is reluctant; and is tempered by a wavering nostalgic sympathy for the liberal and socialist optimists. Freud's social contract is akin to that of Hobbes; but it is sustained by a mythology psychoanalytically rather than anthropologically inspired. Hobbes's natural man entered into the social contract in order to escape the consequences of universal distrust and egoism. Freud's natural man is driven to accept the inhibitions of culture and the coercion of the State by his remorse at the primal patricide and his discomfort at the uncontrolled sexual promiscuity resulting from it. Haunted by remorse at the original murder of the father, the fatherless brothers wearied of the anarchic consequences of their unrestricted libidinal conflicts; and sought to restore social discipline by accepting the authority of a substitute father. Political society and the status of government are thus explained in terms of unconscious (and in this sense, irrational) longing for the psychic security of paternal despotism. But the despotism, like Hobbes's Leviathan, has a neo-democratic base. The brothers chose this form of governance in contrast to the rule of the original father which was imposed from without. Government is therefore necessary for man, because of his inherent psychic weakness. Only under such tutelage, however harsh, can man find relief from remorse at the original patricide and thus assuage the crippling demands of his super-ego. Only in the State, too, can he set reasonable limits to the insatiable demands of his aggressive libido. The social relationship between men is, therefore, inevitably one of dominance and subjection. The anarchist who rejects this condition is guilty of a utopianism only possible to the psychoanalytically ignorant. But in practice, the harshness of the social nexus in the State is mitigated for Freud by the power of man's instinctive libido. The libido is also an emollient influence. Emotions are ambivalent, and are always liable to conversion into their opposites, if moved affectively in the psychic underworld of the id. The libido can be aggressive; but it can also soften the nature of the dependence on and subjugation by parent and parental surrogates.

Generally speaking, however, Freud does incline to the view that the ideal of the anarchists is excluded by fundamental psychic laws governing human behaviour. If one coercive institution or regime is overthrown, it will necessarily be succeeded by another. A condition of free social relations between equals is psychically impossible. The rebel against authority, however sincere his conscious motives, is himself unconsciously moved by the desire for power. There are two kinds of men: those who submit to power, and those who seek it for themselves. Those who seek to contract out of the struggle in order to eliminate power conflicts strive in vain. Moreover, they are deluded even as to the purity of their own motives. The strong obtain power; the weak and deferential unconsciously envy the strong whom they would like to replace. Men are weak, and so worship power. To rebel against the resultant political system is psychically futile. The real world is peopled by creatures unable to live outside the security of a coercive culture. These people may not inspire either liking or confidence; but they are our neighbours. And the first mark of the rational man is to observe accurately the character and intent of his fellow-men.

The bit of truth behind all this – one so eagerly denied – is that men are not gentle, friendly creatures wishing for love, who simply defend themselves if they are attacked, but that a powerful measure of desire for aggression has to be reckoned as part of their instinctual endowment. The result is that their neighbour is to them not only a possible helper or sexual object, but also a temptation to them to gratify their aggressiveness on him, to exploit his capacity for work without recompense, to use him sexually without his consent, to seize his possessions, to humiliate him, to cause him pain, to torture and to kill him.[1]

Freud's sombre picture has affinities with Dona Maria's vision of the status of her fellow-beings in Thornton Wilder's *The Bridge of San Luis Rey*.

She saw that the people of this world moved about in an armour of egotism, drunk with self-gazing, athirst for compliments, hearing little of what was said to them, unmoved by the accidents that befell their closest friends, in dread of all appeals that might interrupt their long communion with their own desires.[2]

Freud was markedly sceptical as to the rational and humane capacities of the mass of ordinary people. He was by no means free of all the prejudices of the European bourgeoisies. Although liberal in aspiration, not unsympathetic even to socialist indictments of existing property relations, he yet had no faith in the common man. Politically he was kith and kin to John Stuart Mill, the political theorist who commanded his greatest respect. Freud's thoughts on leaving the church he visited so often in Rome, San Pietro in Vinculis, are characteristic. After gazing in deep absorption upon Michelangelo's Moses, he would, he tells us, identify himself for a moment with the mob on whom the patriarch's eye had fallen – 'the mob which can hold fast no conviction, which has neither faith nor patience and which rejoices when it has regained its illusory idols.'[3]

The society of equals is unattainable, he claims, because it is against nature, and because of man's instinctual predisposition to aggression. '. . . nature began the injustice by the highly unequal way in which she endows individuals physically and mentally, for which there is no help.'[4] He disclaims any views on the economic merits of a communist society, which he is prepared to concede may be advantageous in terms of efficiency and equity. He even acknowledges that few things would

[1] *Civilization and its Discontents*, p. 85
[2] 1954 ed., p. 17
[3] *Collected Papers*, Vol. IV, p. 260
[4] *Civilization and its Discontents*, p. 88n.

be more beneficial than a change in men's acquisitive attitudes towards property – a diminution in their 'mania for owning things'.[1] But while he sympathizes with such aspirations, he insists that they are founded upon psychological illusion. Abolition of property would eliminate an indispensable instrument of the human instinct for aggression. The instinct was manifest long before man had acquired any possessions worthy of the name. And in the evolution of the individual, as in the evolution of the species, the aggressive instinct reaches far back into childhood. It is to be found in the nursery when the only possessions to be disputed are the child's own anal product. The aggressive instinct, evident in the will to subjugate the will of another to one's own purpose, lies at the root of every human relationship with the possible exception of a mother's love for her son.

It might pardonably be concluded from the foregoing argument that the first mark of a rational, illusion-free man in politics would be to subscribe to conservatism. But this would be too positive a conclusion to draw. Such a conclusion would give to reason a specific moral content. It would also leave out of account Freud's sympathy towards socialist and reformist aspirations. Freud insists that psychoanalysis is entirely apolitical. When asked whether he was 'red' or 'black' (Left or Right, in the contemporary Austrian terminology) he replied that he was flesh-coloured. In short, politically speaking he had contracted out – the only consistent thing for a psychoanalytic rationalist to do. From the standpoint of psychoanalysis, political activists, whether of the Right or of the Left, are alike motivated by unconscious psychic forces of an irrational character. The conservative activist seeking power wherewith to impose his dominion – the classical political personality, in fact – is diagnosed as one with an unconscious craving for deference, with a compulsive need to *command* respect and perhaps at least the outward semblance of regard. And the rebel, the Leftist in revolt against established authority, is one who unconsciously has never succeeded in reconciling himself to the ties of filial obedience, so that all authority tends to evoke in him the original prototype emotions of hatred for the father. This is to reduce all political conflict to the level of psychic conflict displaced from

[1] See *ibid*, p. 88. The phrase is Walt Whitman's

the private to the public sphere. It rests, of course, on the unstated premise that reality at any given time is endurable; and that our first psychic duty is to endure with resignation and the minimum of pain. 'To endure life remains, when all is said, the first duty of all living beings.'[1] It is, in short, a profoundly conservative metaphysic, and none the better for being unexamined.

Freud's political neutralism paradoxically emerges in his declared hostility to any form of ideological conviction. Granted his assumption that man has an innate disposition to aggression, it should follow that as libidinal feelings towards members of one's own group are intensified, in like measure are xenophobic feelings likely to be aroused. Men find themselves ill at ease when deprived of a natural outlet for aggression. Europeans ought accordingly to feel a measure of gratitude to the Jews, Freud observes ironically, for kindly furnishing Gentiles with convenient targets for destruction through so many centuries.[2] Any group cohesion or loyalty is bought at the price of intensified hostility to those outside the group. This is particularly the case where the ties binding the group together arise out of the common profession of a religion of love. The believer, the ideologue, the man of conviction who naturally wishes to persuade others to share his convictions, is therefore inherently suspect. He invites compassion, for, psychologically speaking, he knows not what he does. With his psychic liabilities overstretched, he is uniquely vulnerable. Belief and intolerance are inseparable bedfellows for psychic reasons. The tone is condescending. 'However difficult we may find it personally, we ought not to reproach believers too severely on this account; people who are unbelieving or indifferent are so much better off psychologically in this respect.'[3]

If there has been a marked decline in persecution, cruelty and intolerance within our culture in recent centuries, these softening influences may be traced to a corresponding decline in religious belief. Regrettably it is more than doubtful whether such progress can be maintained. For the evidence suggests that the libidinal ties binding together religious groups are merely

---

[1] *Thoughts for the Times on War and Death* (1915), *Collected Papers*, Vol. IV, p. 317
[2] See *Civilization and its Discontents*, p. 90
[3] *Group Psychology and the Analysis of the Ego*, 5th imp., 1949, p. 51

being diverted into socialistic channels. In this eventuality, communists will discover a profound need of the bourgeois as an object for their increased aggressive needs. We may, then, have to anticipate a renewed increase in ideological intolerance and cruelty. Psychoanalytically speaking, the ideal towards which we should strive is that of the non-believing, languid, antiseptic, liberal, 'flesh-coloured', moderate. Freud himself did not press the point, nor develop the full political implications of this viewpoint. Others, however, less scrupulous, were quick to fasten upon its polemical possibilities against the credentials of all forms of Left political revolt. Particularly in the United States has Freudianism been exploited to this end. On the one hand, political scientists have emerged with pretensions of knowledge of the irrationalities of the unconscious, prompting the political behaviour of ordinary uninitiated people. Claiming the status of qualified experts they prescribe the appropriate manipulative, therapeutic technique. On the other hand, it has become fashionable to dismiss political protest as displaced, regressive Oedipean conflict.

Politically then, Freud undoubtedly reinforced – and most powerfully – the conservative armoury in defence of the coercions of culture and institutions. At the same time he denied that he was committed to either side of the political conflict which divides society. While disclaiming any political aspirations, he has in fact proved a potent if not an original influence. In the sphere of morality, on the other hand, his contribution has been original as well as influential. How radical was Freud's break with the past is evident if we contrast Freud's model of the rational man with the classical or Christian model. That model, whether conceived in the mould of Prometheus' defiance of the immortal gods or of Jesus' supreme example of charity and compassion, represented the prophet, in revolt against a corrupt society, yet at the same time at one with and affirming solidarity with common people. It was the model of a radical and plebeian rebel. There could scarcely be a sharper contrast than that presented by Freud's prototype of the rational individual – cautious, prudent, resigned, self-exploratory, suspicious alike of altruism and enthusiasm, free from conflict, preoccupied with maintaining psychic poise rather than with political committal or individual involvement. For Christian and agnostic rationalist alike, the problem of man is a moral problem. How can men afflicted by moral insensitivity be brought to a condition of moral awareness? And how then can they be persuaded to translate the mandates of human obligation into everyday behaviour? From Plato and Augustine to Voltaire and Tolstoy, classicist and Christian, agnostic and deist would not have quarrelled with such a formulation of the essential human challenge. Yet it was this way of presenting the question that Freud stood on its head. In one sense, Freud insisted, man has gone astray not because of his moral inadequacy, but because of an excess of morality. Absorption in moral problems, anxiety of conscience lest there be a dereliction of duty, instead of denoting the worth of aspiration, becomes a symptom of possible sickness inviting diagnosis.

Freud's treatment of the notion of 'conscience' leaves moral aspiration itself compromised. So far from being the 'stern daughter of the voice of God' or the still small voice of duty, the promptings of conscience may be diagnosed as guilt feelings occasioned by repressing instinctual desires from the id that we would do better to acknowledge and accept. Instead of representing awareness of a sinful nature, the voice of conscience appears, turned inside out, as the punishment for holding compulsively to unrealistic ideals. Unlike the aggressive instincts which are psychically original to man, the moral urge to curb those instincts at the instigation of the ego-ideal is secondary and derivative, or, as Freud puts it, 'partly a reaction-formation against the instinctual processes in the id'.[1] On this analysis, man's pathetic aspirations to raise himself above his lower aggressive nature are largely foredoomed. The super-ego, being distinct from the rational ego, draws its energies in part direct from the unconscious instinctual forces of the id. It is therefore as liable to dominate the personality with its ruthless demands as the id itself. The scales would appear to be weighted most unfairly against men. If we are morally insensitive on account of a poorly developed super-ego, then our aggressive impulses against our fellows will be free to flow unconfined. If, on the other hand, we have a well-developed super-ego and accordingly strive to perfect ourselves in the interests of peace

[1] *The Ego and the Id*, p. 82

and brotherly love, we fall foul of the possibly worse tyranny
of our guilt reactions.

'It is remarkable that the more a man checks his aggressive
tendencies towards others the more tyrannical, that is aggressive,
he becomes in his ego-ideal.'[1] Freud again is intent upon under-
lining the paradoxical nature of his view, which turns the conventional view inside out. It is illusory to urge men to exert
themselves morally to curb their aggressive, anti-social impulses.
For, to the extent that a man succeeds in bringing his aggression
under control, he displaces the aggression which, denied the
one outlet, turns round upon the self. Moral aspiration feeds
upon itself, and exerts a cumulative crippling influence upon the
personality. This pattern is discernible in the dynamics of even
the ordinary person's comparatively limited moral sensitivity.
'But even ordinary normal morality has a harshly restraining,
cruelly prohibiting quality.'[2] But it is to the lives of the saints
that we must look, if we are to reveal the full potential sadism
of the ego-ideal as it turns its aggressive energies destructively
upon the ego. 'That is, the more righteous a man is the stricter
and more suspicious will his conscience be, so that ultimately
it is precisely those people who have carried holiness farthest
who reproach themselves with the deepest sinfulness.'[3]

Both in what he wrote and, more effectively, by the way in
which he lived, Freud demonstrated his strong sympathy with
the moral aspirations of men. Nevertheless, his moral teaching
had two unfortunate consequences. It served to encourage men
in a supposition to which they are very ready to lend a willing
ear, namely, that moral aspiration is severely restricted by
psychobiological factors. Secondly, it implied that 'conscience',
when investigated scientifically, has no claim to be considered
as an objective ethical index. Freud, in short, encouraged moral
defeatism; and discredited the authority of the inner voice.
Freud's sceptical pen makes a frontal assault upon our idealized
image of the 'inner-directed man' of the Protestant tradition,
wrestling with his conscience, striving after righteousness, eager
to discover and to fulfil his duty however 'strait the way and
narrow the gate'. The will to be good, as distinct from the social

[1] *ibid*, p. 79
[2] *ibid*, p. 80
[3] *Civilization and its Discontents*, p. 109

will to power, becomes a source of embarrassment. The will to power itself is a mark of psychic realism. The conscience-ridden man stands in need of therapy in order that he may learn to know what is the unconscious guilt tormenting him. He needs to acquire a more tolerant attitude towards himself and his failings. He has to recognize that what he may regard censoriously as vice or sin may be inherent in the nature of man. Freud believed that mankind was heir to an ineradicable social legacy of unconscious guilt. This followed from Freud's theory of the primal act of parricide and the resultant remorse, combined with his Lamarckian belief in the inheritance of acquired mental traits. Hence the persistence of irrational religious longings in man. It might of course be argued that the universality of these guilt feelings testifies to the objectivity of the voice of conscience protesting against evil. But this was not the inference that Freud drew. The force and persistence of the primeval taboo, 'thou shalt not kill', suggested to Freud how deep-rooted is the instinct to aggression and murder in the nature of man. The inference therefore is not that our fundamental moral standards are universal and unchanging, and that our duty is to follow the dictates of conscience when such laws are violated. It is rather the recognition that killing is natural to man. Regrettable though this is, nothing is gained by refusing to recognize and accept the fact. Through psychoanalysis and Freudian anthropology we may discover why we feel haunted by guilt; and so achieve a maturity in which the need for the consolations of religious belief, the illusory therapy of the childhood of the race, will be outgrown.

Nor is Freud willing to distinguish between the moral tradition of Christianity and the institutions of Christendom which claim to be the guardians of the tradition. Such a distinction is vital, for example, to an understanding of the hostility of the Enlightenment to religion. The Churches, with their centuries-old experience in adjusting the moral imperatives to the daily waywardness of men, might presumably have gained Freud's respect. But his hostility to the Church is as relentless as to the Christian ethic itself. Freud would agree with Dostoevsky, for instance, that men are tenacious in clinging to authority and to the cult of religious ritual because of their irrationality and moral weakness. But realist though he is, Freud is quite unable to share Dostoevsky's resigned acceptance of the necessity for religious belief and its institutional sanctions. Man is weak certainly, agrees Freud; he is neurotic and therefore stands in need of religious support. But we should not take pride in the fact. Man should be exhorted to grow up, to reach adulthood, to embrace honesty, to live fearlessly, to dispense with illusory consolations. Just as his revered Moses denounced the children of Egypt for their backsliding, so the prophet Freud denounces organized religion for exploiting human weakness. His stand in this field is consistent with his prophetic role in therapeutic medicine; but contrasts strangely with his advocacy of resignation and 'realism' in the field of morals and politics.

Freud is signally unappreciative of the prophetic and critical role of the religious tradition at its noblest. This is partly attributable to his reluctance to distinguish this aspect of religion from the preoccupation of the Church militant with secular power. But it derives even more from a suspicion that Christian ethical currency is itself in need of deflation. The command 'Thou shalt love thy neighbour as thyself' is interpreted quite literally; and subjected not without malice to analysis by Freud. After overcoming our initial incredulity on coming across such an extraordinary injunction for the first time, we may consider it on its merits. As an ethical imperative it fails on two counts. Firstly, if we were to love all men indiscriminately, we would debase the value of our discriminatory love for those who merit it and are accordingly very close to our hearts. Secondly, love imposes upon the one who loves weighty obligations which it is only appropriate to strive to fulfil when the object is worthy of such sacrifice. And many, perhaps the majority, of men are not worthy of our love. The maxim must also be rejected as psychologically unrealistic: again, on two grounds. In making demands so severe by calling for such an inflation of love, too little consideration is shown for the comfort and stability of the ego. And secondly, this injunction underestimates the strength of the instinctual urges of the id. It is impossible. It is even unworthy. Its chief function is to encourage self-righteousness. ' "Natural" ethics, as it is called, has nothing to offer here beyond the narcissistic satisfaction of thinking oneself better than others.'[1]

Moreover, it is an injunction which the exponents of morality

---

[1] *Civilization and its Discontents*, p. 140

cannot themselves afford, since its adoption would inevitably put the defenders of the good at a fatal disadvantage in the struggle with the bad. Freud quotes approvingly the well-known French aphorism frequently deployed against abolitionists of capital punishment, 'Que messieurs les assassins commencent!' To turn the other cheek, to return good for evil, to love our enemies, is simply to put 'a direct premium on wickedness'. Freud had a very immediate, down-to-earth assessment of the consequences of being on the losing side where power was concerned. Given his opinion of the probable behaviour of his neighbour if in a position of power, he believed with the common man in the wisdom of anticipating an opponent's strength by building up his own. He was in any event resigned to the inevitability of war. 'But war is not to be abolished,' he wrote in 1915; 'so long as the conditions of existence among the nations are so varied, and the repulsions between peoples so intense, there will be, must be, wars.'[1] This he believed also for psychoanalytic reasons. He was convinced of the primitive origin of the aggressive instincts, to be curbed by cultural repression only at a severe price in psychic tension. Peace time is not a normal condition. Rather does it represent a strained achievement of necessary but expensive 'civilized hypocrisy'. When we live at peace with our neighbours within the state, and with our neighbours of other states, we are liable to be living beyond our natural psychic means. Our psychic economy is eventually stretched to breaking-point; the bow snaps back, and war provides the necessary periodic psychic 'blood-letting'.

Estranged by cultural demands from his native instincts, man needs relief from the resulting tension. Individually he may have recourse to the analyst to relieve his neurotic symptoms; collectively he has recourse to war, a perfect natural outlet for his. repressed aggressive impulses. The analogy is not precise; since it ought to be less difficult for the community to contain its repressed aggressive impulses than for the individual to repress the sexual demands of his libido. But the structure of the problem is the same in each case.

They [members of society] are consequently subjected to an unceasing suppression of instinct, the resulting strain of which

[1] *Collected Papers*, Vol. IV, p. 316

betrays itself in the most remarkable phenomena of reaction and compensation formations. . . . That the greater units of humanity, the peoples and states, have mutually abrogated their moral restraints naturally prompted these individuals to permit themselves relief for a while from the heavy pressure of civilization and to grant a passing satisfaction to the instincts it holds in check.[1]

Freud does not deny that some men are in fact congenital pacifists; he was himself pacific by nature and considered this a hallmark of maturity. But he held that this quality was confined to the few and beyond the reach of the many. Here again we meet Freud's basic assumption that an unbridgeable gulf separates the moral and intellectual capacity of the minority from that of the untutored and unanalysed multitude. The ancient aspiration of men in a Christian culture to rely upon the power of the will to be good he considered an illusion. The will is fundamentally divorced from the good, drawing its energies direct from the reservoir of the id. Only a sophisticated minority, therefore, can achieve the equilibrium of tension necessary for consistently civilized behaviour.

There is, however, in Freud's writings another and more optimistic strain, which he normally inhibits as a suspect super-ego symptom. But he occasionally permits himself the luxury of cautious hope. Freud always insisted that our human nature was capable of greater good as well as of greater evil than we are wont to assume. The power of the intellect in most human beings may be disappointing. Confidence, at any rate, shrinks when reason is in conflict with stronger instinctual propensities. But human intellectual aspiration can never be dismissed as impotent. Weak it may be; but it is an insistent weakness, of peculiar significance. 'The voice of the intellect is a soft one, but it does not rest till it has gained a hearing. Finally, after a countless succession of rebuffs, it succeds.'[2] And elsewhere he indulges the quiet hope that, if we are patient, there may yet be some fruits to be garnered from social protest, and improvement may take place. 'We may expect that in the course of time changes will be carried out in our civilization so that it becomes more satisfying to our needs and no longer open to the reproaches we have made

---

[1] *Thoughts for the Times on War and Death*, 1915, *Collected Papers*, Vol. IV. p. 299–300
[2] *The Future of an Illusion*, 1962 ed., p. 49

against it.'[1] Although there are no more than hints thrown out here and there, we can yet find in Freud the raw material of an alternative viewpoint fundamentally at variance with his own characteristic scepticism and insistence on 'realism' and freedom from 'illusion'.

For instance, at one point in the essay, *Thoughts for the Times on War and Death*, Freud sharply rejects the familiar argument that the immoralism of *raison d'état* is inevitable. The moral problem, as it confronts the individual, is not analogous, he believes, to that which confronts the State. It is as disadvantageous, he points out, for the private individual as it is for the State to eschew evil in the interests of morality. The State is rarely in a position to indemnify an individual for the losses he sustains as the price of his moral behaviour in an immoral society. Yet, with no more excuse than has the individual, the State proceeds on its Machiavellian course. Under the guise of inter-state conflict, it fatally relaxes such moral ties as bind states together. The inevitable result is the corruption of existing moral standards in the individuals who make up the warring states. For conscience is not an autonomous ethical index, reliably reporting the voice of God, but simply the dread in each individual of the rebuke of the community. When that sanction is withdrawn, and the community, so far from exercising any reproof, itself sets the example of evil, it is not surprising if large numbers then surpass themselves in the violence, rapine and cruelty they commit. Responsibility lies with those who withdraw the customary inhibitory sanctions, designed to curb the predisposition to violence.[2]

This raises the whole question of the sources of the formation and advancement of the cultural super-ego of the community itself. Whence is derived that authority which, when projected from the community and assimilated within the individual super-ego, becomes the voice of individual conscience? It originates, Freud argues, in much the same way as does the individual super-ego itself. 'The super-ego of any given epoch of civilization . . . is based on the impression left behind them by great leading personalities, men of outstanding force of mind, or men in whom some one human tendency has developed in

[1] *Civilization and its Discontents*, pp. 92–3
[2] cf. *Collected Papers*, Vol. IV, p. 294

unusual strength and purity, often for that reason very disproportionately.'[1] These rare individuals are generally recognizable also by the ridicule, ill-usage or persecution and martyrdom that they frequently undergo at the hands of their unappreciative contemporaries. Even as men revolted against and did to death the primal father, so are they liable to treat their greatest benefactors. Subsequently they seek to appease their remorse for their evil deeds by deifying their victim of yesterday. Jesus is merely the best known of such examples – if indeed his entire life does not belong to mythology, Freud feels it necessary to add.

Thus it appears that some men *are* able to direct their libidinal energies towards their fellows. This they do by a diversion of the original instinct for genital love into channels where the original aim is inhibited. In this way the tumultuous and passionate sexual aims of the average man are diverted from the vulnerable target of specific individuals and sublimated into a stable and enduring tenderness towards all men equally. For the single-minded absorption in one individual, precariously exposed to loss of affection and suffering, is substituted a calm, generalized love of humanity. The more egocentric satisfactions of romantic love are exchanged for an 'inner feeling of happiness', a tranquil serenity usually associated with religious feeling. Whatever Freud's scepticism concerning the objective ethical value of this kind of altruistic love, *agape* as distinct from *eros*, he does not deny its power to influence behaviour in the rare instances where it occurs. Nor is he altogether able to deny its essential nobility. 'From one ethical standpoint, . . . this inclination towards an all-embracing love of others and of the world at large is regarded as the highest state of mind of which man is capable.'[2]

And what is the secret of the remarkable influence which such individuals succeed in exercising over successive generations of men? Why is it that they play so important a role in influencing the voice of individual conscience and thus in developing and maintaining the super-ego of the entire culture? Because of the peculiar power of human love, where it is sublimated to transcend the clamorous egocentric appetites of the libido.

---

[1] *Civilization and its Discontents*, pp. 136–7
[2] *ibid*, p. 70

And in the development of mankind as a whole, just as in individuals, love alone acts as the civilizing factor in the sense that it brings a change from egoism to altruism.[1]

This is the other side to Freud at variance with the sceptical pessimism so ingrained and generally ascendant in his thinking.

Freud's position in intellectual history is secure as one of the very few who permanently altered the outlines of man's self-knowledge. With Darwin and Marx he has largely shaped the basic assumptions of contemporary sociology. Whether he exaggerated the extent to which man is morally crippled by his existing psychobiological inheritance is still an open question. He did perhaps underestimate the flexibility of character or the ability of most men to modify their actual behaviour. The rapidity and extent of his own influence in changing men's attitudes on education, child nurture, mental health, art, is a striking testimony to what can be achieved by the research and example of one man. Freud wrought better than he perhaps knew. He revolutionized our mental world. At the same time, while appreciating Freud's intolerance of the illusions with which men console and deceive themselves, his 'realism' is not entirely free from undertones of quiet satisfaction. When Machiavelli writes in similar vein, not far beneath the surface lies a quiet malicious pleasure in the brutality of the 'realism'. In Freud it is not so. Yet it is hard to avoid the feeling that there is a little misplaced pride, a sorrow that is not quite genuine, in the protestations of the incurability of the sinfulness of the world. The dryness of Freud's inimitable irony on occasion slightly oversteps the bounds of the permissible in human candour. If he never speaks ill of virtue, he sometimes comes close to suggesting that our concern that it should prevail is a trifle excessive. What we really demand of him is consolation; but he is too old, too wise in the ways of the world, too weary, too sceptical to be taken in by any such frailty. There is a faint note of presumption, almost unconscious patronage. Fortunately it is rare; but it exists.

Remarkable also in a man of the stature of Freud, who consciously identified with Moses' prophetic role, is his under-estimation of the radical critic in influencing the practice of the

---

[1] *Group Psychology and the Analysis of the Ego*, p. 57

world. He did less than justice to this element in the Western religious tradition. It may be that this failure of vision was inseparable from the insistence that the reasonable man's responsibility does not include necessary commitment to a specific moral programme. Any possible gain in critical detachment is purchased at the price of the persuasive strength of moral conviction. He writes impressively enough, 'And now it may be expected that the other of the two "heavenly forces", eternal Eros, will put forth his strength so as to maintain himself alongside of his equally immortal adversary.'[1] It is difficult to resist the comment that Freud is not God. This sociological observation would be more impressive if Freud had made it quite clear that it was the manifest and binding duty of all rational men, himself included, to commit themselves unreservedly in the cause of eternal Eros. But this he could not bring himself to do. At heart he always remained sceptical of what could be accomplished by the mere will to be good. Exhortation to strive to perfect thyself, to aspire and strenuously endeavour, was for him a vain hope, because he suspected it to be a mask to conceal striving for mastery and power.

---

[1] *Civilization and its Discontents*, p. 144

3 Power corrupts . . .

EVERY POLITICAL theory is based on a psychology. Consequently, when a figure as important as Freud succeeds in revolutionizing our psychological assumptions, the effect on political attitudes is bound to be considerable, whether the source of the influence is acknowledged or not. Politically uncommitted, Freud has in fact strengthened the intellectual forces of both the Left and the Right. The Left he encouraged by sharing their meliorist aspirations as well as by confirming their conviction that human behaviour, if not human nature, is capable of modification. But the Right also drew comfort from his prevailing mood of scepticism and pessimism with its insistence on the fact that aggressive impulses and the urge to dominance were inherent in man; and that accordingly egalitarian, anarchical aspirations to unseat the role of power in human affairs were foredoomed. On balance, it is Freud's pessimism which has been most influential in politics.

Freud, it is true, taught that the essential challenge confronting men was how to attain adult capacity for love based on equality whilst emerging from the authoritarian, Oedipean ties of childhood. But he was not confident that the majority of men would ever be likely to prove capable of travelling very far along this path. In politics if not in religion, he believed that men could not achieve the self-discipline and co-operation for stable social life without recourse to an authoritarian father-substitute in the shape of a coercive Government. And further he doubted the very possibility of putting an end to war because of man's allegedly inherent aggressive impulses. It will be argued here that Freud was unduly pessimistic in the limits he set to the possibilities of human development in the direction of co-operative equality and peace. It will further be argued that Freud's failure of insight at this point lay in his inability to challenge the accepted view of the relations which ought to obtain between man and woman. Freud's view governing the

45

nature of the ideal sexual relationship did not differ essentially from the prevailing view among people of his class and time. It was a view which rejected equality as undesirable, although this would rarely be stated quite so bluntly. Since the sexual relationship is the most important of all human relations, in that it is the source of life itself as well as of subsequent child nurture, an error at this point is bound to distort the total picture of man's psychic possibilities. The assumptions of masculine primacy are so deep-seated in our culture that the real point is frequently not taken even today. For example, the story, no doubt apocryphal, of Mrs Sylvia Pankhurst trying to console one of her fellow-suffragettes in Holloway Prison by urging her, 'Put your faith in God. She will help you', is guaranteed to cause amusement in any audience. But people are rarely conscious that there is anything odd about a culture in which such a story does seem irresistibly funny.

Even the most radical and perceptive of self-critics is apt to leave some part of his character unexamined. Freud was no exception. His values were generally subjected to rigorous scrutiny, but not always; with the result that sometimes beliefs that were little more than contemporary class prejudices were made the foundation of what purported to be scientific hypotheses. Erich Fromm, in a not unsympathetic study of Freud's personality, *Sigmund Freud's Mission*, has given a number of significant instances of views which reflected either personal prejudice or limitations of character. For instance, Freud asserted that only the psychoanalytically ignorant could share the anarchist's belief in the possibility of creating a society based on co-operation instead of on command and obedience. Fromm points out that Freud was himself a rebel, as distinct from a revolutionary in character, in the sense that he never succeeded in overcoming his own attachment to authority and a concomitant wish to dominate others. He cites, as an example of this, Freud's determination to fashion 'politically' an instrument wherewith to disseminate his gospel. 'Is there any other case of a therapy or of a scientific theory transforming itself into a movement, centrally directed by a secret committee, with purges of deviant members, with local organizations in an international superorganization?'[1] The question is hyperbolic as well as

[1] *Sigmund Freud's Mission*, 1959, p. 82

rhetorical, and is clearly hostile in intent; but the point as to Freud's own will to power is taken.

Similarly, Fromm correlates Freud's scepticism concerning the moral command to 'love one's neighbour as oneself' with Freud's own aloofness in his relations with people, and a lack of warmth and intimacy in close personal relations. Fromm presents him as a Puritan, esteeming highly discipline and emotional restraint in order to sublimate energy to create and foster civilized achievement. Hence also his class sympathies and pessimism regarding democratic values, since he believed only an esoteric intellectual group would be able to make the necessary pleasure sacrifice. Himself a man of the professional middle classes, he reflected the bourgeois will to social success, the prestige of ownership and power. He lacked the values of solidarity and communal loyalty characteristic of the working class, whose emotional life he recognized as more spontaneous and unsophisticated than that of the middle class.

Freud's hostility to political egalitarianism had as its logical counterpart a cherished prejudice concerning the inequality of the sexes. Here again, Fromm insists, the connection is plain between Freud's own unexamined prejudice and the error in his psychoanalytic theories concerning the specifically female emotions. 'There must be inequality', Freud is reported to have remarked in a conversation with Dr J. Worthis on the subject of the relations between the sexes. And since this inequality must prevail, 'superiority of the man is the lesser of the two evils.' There is no reason to doubt that this aptly summarized Freud's own relations with his wife. The adored Gretchen of courtship is wooed tenderly and ardently in order to be raised subsequently to the respected position of matriarchal *Hausfrau*. The husband remains devotedly loyal, but distantly so in terms of emotional involvement. Fromm attributes Freud's inability to establish relations of genuine warmth and intimacy with the opposite sex to his own sexually inhibited feelings and a weakly developed sexual drive. This lack of closeness was the source of his failure to understand the nature of feminine psychology. His theories on this subject, Fromm goes so far as to assert, were no more than 'naïve rationalizations of male prejudices, especially of the male who needs to dominate in order to hide his fear of women'.

It is not my concern to explore Freud's psychoanalytic theories concerning women or the deficiencies in those theories. What is relevant is the connection between Freud's view of the relations between the sexes and his view of the relations between large groups such as social classes. Convinced affectively as well as intellectually of the inferior status of women he could not attain an adequately tender or complete relationship with a woman. Given this emotional inadequacy, the ego drive to power, already strong in Freud, received further nourishment. In one of his intellectual bent, it found expression in an excessive worship of reason as the sole instrument of truth destined to liberate mankind from the crippling prejudices of 'common sense'. It was the source of Freud's outstanding quality, his immense courage and faith in himself; but it was dearly purchased. For it led him to a thinly veiled contempt for those, the vast majority of mankind, who allow their surface emotional preoccupations to prevent the sublimation of their creative energies. How otherwise could men hope to penetrate with their reason beneath the surface of things and bring under control the anarchical world of nature? In short, Freud at heart never was nor could be a democrat. A typical child of the European Enlightenment, he shared Voltaire's aristocratic faith in reason without Tom Paine's parallel faith in the potential capacities of the common man. This ambivalence in the Enlightenment tradition and in Freud personally is very evident in Freud's attitude to John Stuart Mill, the prototype of nineteenth-century rationalism. Freud greatly admired Mill. One writer (Imre Hermann) has even attributed Freud's anti-revolutionary and conservative politics to the influence of John Stuart Mill. More probable is Ernest Jones's view that he was simply drawn to Mill by an affinity of outlook and a distrust of simple or superficial political solutions. Freud himself expressed his admiration in terms of their common penchant for rationalism. J. S. Mill was, he said, 'perhaps the man of the century who best managed to free himself from the domination of customary prejudices'.

He first became familiar with Mill's writings in 1880 at the age of twenty-four, when he translated into German the twelfth volume of Theodore Gomperz's edition of J. S. Mill's collected works, containing essays dealing with the labour question, the enfranchisement of women, and socialism. Mill, like Freud, put great faith in the power of human reason untrammelled by emotion; he was liberal and tolerant; he placed the highest value on human liberty; he distrusted the emotions and power of the untutored 'masses'. He suffered from only one serious defect in Freud's eyes. He lacked a sense of humour in his inability to put into proper perspective the relations between the sexes. The relevant passage in one of Freud's letters is worth quoting at length:

On the other hand, . . . he lacked in many matters the sense of the absurd; for example, in that of female emancipation and in the woman's question altogether. I recollect that in the essay I translated a prominent argument was that a married woman could earn as much as her husband. We surely agree that the management of a house, the care and bringing up of children, demands the whole of a human being and almost excludes any earning, even if a simplified household relieve her of dusting, cleaning, cooking etc. He had simply forgotten all that, like everything else concerning the relationship between the sexes. That is altogether a point with Mill where one simply cannot find him human. His autobiography is so prudish or so ethereal that one could never gather from it that human beings consist of men and women and that this distinction is the most significant one that exists. In his whole presentation it never emerges that women are different beings – we will not say lesser, rather the opposite – from men. He finds the suppression of women an analogy to that of negroes. Any girl, even without a suffrage or legal competence, whose hand a man kisses and for whose love he is prepared to dare all, could have set him right. It is really a still-born thought to send women into the struggle for existence exactly as men. If, for instance, I imagined my gentle sweet girl as a competitor it would only end in my telling her, as I did seventeen months ago, that I am fond of her and that I implore her to withdraw from the strife into the calm uncompetitive activity of my home. It is possible that changes in upbringing may suppress all a woman's tender attributes, needful of protection and yet so victorious, and that she can then earn a livelihood like men. It is also possible that in such an event one would not be justified in mourning the passing away of the most delightful thing the world can offer us – our ideal of womanhood. I believe that all reforming action in law and education would break down in front of the fact that, long before the age at which a man can earn a position in society, Nature has determined woman's destiny through beauty, charm and sweetness.

Law and custom have much to give women that has been withheld from them, but the position of women will surely be what it is: in youth an adored darling and in mature years a loved wife.[1]

The patronizing tone towards woman is quite unconscious; it bespeaks the period. The irony could hardly be greater. Mill is singled out as the man above all others of his epoch who succeeded in surmounting contemporary prejudices; and then rebuked for his supreme achievement in unmasking the most disastrous of prejudices to which Freud succeeded in clinging his life long. It was Freud's intellectual insight and courage that so clearly illuminated the influence of nurture upon character through the genuinely original conception of the Oedipus complex. It was his tragedy that he was prevented by endemic sexual prejudice from being able to complement this insight by an understanding of the importance of equality for the establishment of a sane relationship as the basis for human nurture. This point has the most far-reaching implications for adult social and class relations, and is far from being generally conceded even today. I propose therefore to try to illustrate it in circumstantial detail within the historical context of Mill's own lifetime and Freud's childhood. This will be attempted in five sections: (1) a brief account of the general climate of opinion in the early and mid-Victorian period governing the relations between the sexes and the rights of women; (2) a case study drawn from original sources to illustrate the remarkable power of the Oedipean ties to cripple human freedom in such a cultural climate, namely the well-known Browning-Barrett courtship; (3) a case study from original and primary sources where the effects of inequality in marital relations can be studied at close quarters, namely in Stuart Mill's own family background; (4) Stuart Mill's original and inadequately appreciated analysis of the character distortion produced by sexual inequality in his *The Subjection of Women*; (5) a portrait of Samuel Butler's childhood to illustrate the corrosive effects on the moral judgement of inadequate liberation from parental ties.

(i) *Woman's Role*

I shall here attempt a brief but illustrative sketch of the con-

---

[1] Ernest Jones, *Sigmund Freud: Life and Work*, Vol. I, pp. 192–3

ception of woman, her role and function, her feminine identity as generally conceived by both men and women in early- to mid-Victorian England.

Attempts to generalize upon this theme suffer from the fact that our knowledge is limited to a minority of Victorian women of the middle class. Very little is known of the anonymous army of the wives and mothers of the Victorian working class beyond the fact that their lot was by modern standards harsh. The average expectation of life for the typical working-class mother after she had reared her family was not more than twelve years.[1] Thousands of poor women died prematurely through excessive child-bearing and prolonged drudgery, even where they were not the victims of actual brutality. The lot of many middle-class women, if not comparable, was nevertheless not a happy one. One way of gaining some idea of the conception of woman's rights is to take the marginal case of behaviour towards women that would today be considered intolerable, and yet was not so regarded then. The most obvious instance is that of a woman's rights in respect of her children. To separate a mother from her young children for any reason other than the mother herself constituting a danger to the children would strike us as brutal. Yet the cases of Mrs Norton and of Mrs Besant are merely the two best-known instances (on account of the independent fame of those two women) that come to mind as evidence that majority opinion in this country a century ago was not so sensitive. Mrs Caroline Norton, the beautiful and gifted Sheridan grand-daughter, was married at the age of nineteen to George Norton, brother of Lord Grantley. Three children were born of the marriage; and after a series of violent quarrels, Norton separated from his wife and deprived her of the custody of the children. Mrs Norton possessed a ready and eloquent pen, was a woman of great vitality and some influence, and determined to secure the redress of her wrongs. Thanks to her tireless exertions the Infant Custody Bill finally passed on to the Statute Book in 1839. The mother's feelings in the interim period of abortive negotiations to allow her access to the children may be imagined. The following paragraph is taken from a modern biography, descriptive of the scene at the Grantley

---

[1] O. R. MacGregor, *Divorce in England*, 1957, p. 98; cf. R. M. Titmuss, British National Conference on Social Work, *The Family*, 1954, p. 12.

mansion, where in 1837 Mrs Norton had contrived to gain illicit entry.

> When Lord Grantley came in, he found Caroline sitting with one child in his nightdress on her knee, and the others near her. A most terrible scene then took place. She was ordered to leave, and when she refused, her brother-in-law pulled and shook her so violently she threatened to indict him for assault. He rang for the servants. Two men came, and oblivious of the screams of the now terrified children they seized the boy on his mother's knee by the arms and legs and dragged him from her. She feared they would break his limbs and made no struggle. The other children ran shrieking away and Lord Grantley ordered them to be pursued and locked up. Thus Caroline was parted from her boys in an atmosphere of brutality and violence, so that her very presence must, in their minds, have been associated with inexplicable anger and retribution. After this she fell seriously ill, . . .[1]

Of course, contemporary opinion did not condone behaviour of this kind on the part of the Nortons. But to deplore a brutal episode was not to infer that such an event might argue certain basic defects in current ideas of marital relations. It is true that as early as 1791 Mary Wollstonecraft had written her passionate (if stilted) *A Vindication of the Rights of Women*. But when Mrs Shelley offered her support to Mrs Norton in her distress, Mrs Norton was considered by her relations to be risking her reputation by associating with the daughter of the notorious Mary Wollstonecraft. Again, Thomas Love Peacock had in 1818 written of women in *Nightmare Abbey*: 'The fault is in their artificial education, which studiously models them into mere musical dolls, to be set out for sale in the great toy-shop of society' (1947 ed., p. 4). But Peacock represented contemporary opinion no more than did Mary Wollstonecraft. The publicity attracted by Mrs Norton's struggle with the existing law, the publication of her *English Laws for Women in the Nineteenth Century*, the passing into law of the Marriage Act of 1857 establishing a Divorce Court, the lifelong efforts of professional feminists of the stamp of Harriet Martineau, finally Mill's own massive frontal assault, all combined to begin to make some small impression on educated opinion. But the depth of the resistance

[1] A. Acland, *Caroline Norton*, 1948, p. 112

to be overcome was demonstrated at painful sacrifice by the harrowing experience of Mrs Besant in the 'seventies in a case receiving widespread publicity.

Annie Besant's unfortunate youthful marriage to a clergyman of narrow, doctrinaire outlook, preoccupied with outward conventional forms, did not survive the conversion of that vigorous young woman to agnosticism. While the Rev. Frank did not wish to make a window into men's souls, he did insist on his lawful wedded wife's outward conformity. Given the integrity and independent spirit of Mrs Besant, the result was her expulsion from home. Accordingly in 1873 a legal separation was obtained, the daughter going with the mother, the son with the father. In 1877, in a case deliberately brought to test the law under which a Bristol bookseller had been imprisoned for selling an illustrated edition of Knowlton's *Fruits of Philosophy*, a pamphlet giving elementary contraceptive information, Bradlaugh and Mrs Besant were put on trial. With the details and outcome of this famous trial, a major landmark in the birth control movement in this country, we are not here concerned, except to draw attention to the publicity and the emotions aroused by the case. For it led to a personal tragedy which Mrs Besant could scarcely have foreseen when she undertook her crusade. Because of her notoriety as the principal accused in the case, application was made to the High Court to deprive her of the custody of her daughter on the grounds that she was not a fit and proper person to trust with the care of the child. Although her moral qualities as a woman and her exemplary behaviour as a mother were beyond question, the application nevertheless succeeded. The grounds of the judgement were that an agnostic, declining to give religious instruction to the child, was unfit for parental responsibilities. The child was accordingly removed from the mother, in the latter's own words in her *Autobiography*, 'shrieking and struggling, still weak from the fever, and nearly frantic with fear and passionate resistance'.

Such cases were extreme and comparatively rare, but they reveal the extent of the changes that have taken place in attitudes towards women and their rights in the vital field of their relations with their own children. Significant too was the widespread conviction at this time among women of rare gifts and culture of their own inferiority to men. It is interesting to recall that Mrs

Sidney Webb (then Beatrice Potter), whatever the reasons that prompted her, signed an anti-suffragette manifesto, although she subsequently repudiated this judgement. Large numbers of Miss Martineau's female contemporaries disapproved of her professional and forthright agitation for woman's status. Even Elizabeth Barrett considered Miss Martineau's proposal to admit women as members of the Commons to be a 'retrograde' measure, although her reasons were doubtless not altogether representative – viz. that the work of Parliament could best be carried out by 'second-rate minds'.[1] Speaking with rather less ambivalence she wrote in an earlier letter, '. . . let us say and do what we please and can . . . there *is* a natural inferiority of mind in women – of the intellect . . . not by any means, of the moral nature – and that the history of Art and of genius testifies to this fact openly.'[2] The only exception she was prepared to admit was 'that wonderful woman George Sand'. Mrs Norton herself, for all her suffering and struggle for remedial legislation, had no patience with a more general movement to champion the rights of women; and accordingly received scant respect from Harriet Martineau. The following passage is taken from Mrs Norton's correspondence:

> The wild and stupid theories advanced by a few women, of 'equal rights' and 'equal intelligence' are not the opinions of their sex. I, for one (I, with millions more), believe in the natural superiority of man, as I do in the existence of a God. The natural position of woman is inferiority to man. Amen! That is a thing of God's appointing, not of man's devising. I believe it sincerely, as a part of my religion. I never pretended to the wild and ridiculous doctrine of equality.[3]

Reference is made elsewhere to Frederic Harrison's reaction to Mill's *The Subjection of Women*, and the strong language he used in discussing it. This might appear surprising from such a militant positivist; in fact, Harrison's initial reaction to the book was favourable. His final judgement was the fruit of his *wife's* persuasion. After describing how he received a copy of the book from Mill's own hand, he continues:

[1] *The Letters of Robert Browning and Elizabeth Barrett*, 1913 ed., Vol. II, p. 281
[2] *ibid.*, Vol. I, p. 116
[3] Jane Gray Perkins, *The Life of Mrs Norton*, 1909, quoted pp. 149–50

I was keenly impressed by its picture of the legal disabilities of
women and of the domineering tone then too common in men of all
classes; but my wife has ultimately convinced me that bad laws
and bad manners can be mended, and have been mended in these
last thirty years, without any radical revolution in the political
functions and the domestic equality of the two sexes.[1]

This positive and widespread reluctance of the allegedly op-
pressed class, the women themselves, to complain of their fetters;
their apparent support of the existing pattern of sexual relations
and conventions, constituted a weak link in Mill's argument
which critics like Sir James Fitzjames Stephen were quick to
fasten upon. He writes:

> It is true that the actually existing generation of women do not
> dislike their position. The consciousness of this haunts Mr Mill
> throughout the whole of his argument, and embarrasses him at
> every turn. He is driven to account for it by such assertions as that
> 'each individual of the subject class is in a chronic state of bribery
> and intimidation combined,' by reference to the affection which
> slaves in classical times felt for their masters in many cases, and
> by other suggestions of the same sort.[2]

And Stephen is right here. These particular arguments adduced
by Mill are not very convincing.

Whatever their sufferings under the existing order, women, it
seemed, were indifferent to female emancipation. The emphasis
so far has been confined to the legal rights of women. Almost as
harrowing a picture emerges if we look at the conditions of
their domestic life. Miss Nightingale was, of course, a very
unusual woman; doubtless, few would have chafed as much
as she from the frustrations of domesticity. On the other hand,
many must have suffered without being aware of it. They would
have known nothing else and would not have dared to question
the accepted pattern. The following is Miss Nightingale's
account in 1852 of a typical day in the life of a girl in an upper
middle class home of the time.

> Morning: 'sitting round a table in the drawing-room, looking
> at prints, doing worsted work and reading little books.'

---

[1] Frederic Harrison, *Autobiographic Memoirs*, 1911, Vol. I, p. 302
[2] James Fitzjames Stephen, *Liberty, Equality, Fraternity*, 1873, p. 205

Afternoon: 'taking a little drive.'

Evening: 'the accumulation of nervous energy, which has had nothing to do during the day, makes them feel every night, when they go to bed, as if they were going mad. The vacuity and boredom of this existence are sugared over by false sentiment.'[1]

This recalls a similar account of frustration by Beatrice Potter (Webb) in her girlhood in the 'eighties, although she was more fortunate than Miss Nightingale in the intellectual opportunities available to her (cf. *My Apprenticeship*). The reason why *The Journal of Marie Bashkirtseff*, published in England in 1890, made such an impact on so unlikely a personality as Mr Gladstone, for instance, consisted in its effective exposure of the false sentiment in the notion of gentility in a young girl's upbringing. The simplicity and passion with which Miss Bashkirtseff expressed her immense vitality, her shameless, aggressive longing for fame, romance and power, was like a gust of cold wind into the drapery-laden heaviness of the Victorian drawing-room.

In Miss Nightingale's case, the intense emotions aroused by the prospect of a lifetime amid the cups and saucers, the needlework and the draperies caused her to decide to reject marriage with the man of her choice, Richard Monckton Milnes.

I have an intellectual nature which requires satisfaction [she wrote] and that would find it in him. I have a passionate nature which requires satisfaction and that would find it in him. I have a moral, an active, nature which requires satisfaction and that would not find it in his life. Sometimes I think I will satisfy my passional nature at all events, because that will at least secure me from the evil of dreaming. But would it?[2]

I know I could not bear his life, that to be nailed to a continuation, an exaggeration of my present life without hope of another would be intolerable to me – that voluntarily to put it out of my power ever to be able to seize the chance of forming for myself a true and rich life would seem to me like suicide.[3]

But despite her painful struggle to achieve her mission in life in face of all the obstacles that a prejudiced family could put in

---

[1] quoted by Cecil Woodham Smith, *Florence Nightingale*, Penguin Books 1955, p. 74

[2] quoted, *ibid.*, p. 62

[3] quoted, *ibid.*, p. 63

her way, Florence Nightingale, herself an aristocrat to her finger-tips, had no sympathy with the egalitarianism of the women's rights movement.

'I am brutally indifferent to the wrongs or the rights of my sex,' she wrote in 1858.[1] When in 1860 she was asked by John Stuart Mill to support the movement to establish equality of access for women to the medical profession, she declined. Women, she felt, already had more professional opportunities than they knew how to use profitably.[2]

The position of women, then, at the time Mill wrote his book, was one of inferiority in legal status and in the prevailing attitudes of men. Fitzjames Stephen spoke for the large majority of upper middle class males at the time. After reviewing a series of typical questions such as are bound to arise in the running of any domestic household, he says:

> On these and a thousand other such questions the wisest and the most affectionate people might arrive at opposite conclusions. What is to be done in such a case? for something must be done. I say the wife ought to give way. She ought to obey her husband, and carry out the view at which he deliberately arrives, just as, when the captain gives the word to cut away the masts, the lieutenant carries out his orders at once, though he may be a better seaman and may disapprove them. I also say that to regard this as a humiliation, as a wrong, as an evil in itself, is a mark not of spirit and courage, but of a base, unworthy, mutinous disposition – a disposition utterly subversive of all that is most worth having in life.[3]

The accepted relation between man and wife was one of subordination, of authority and obedience. And this was accepted as right and inevitable by the vast majority of women. Those few, like Mrs Shelley or Harriet Martineau, who deliberately sought to challenge this idea, were judged eccentric, if nothing worse, by the very people whose 'rights' they sought to vindicate.

Sometimes tragic cases arose where inability to recognize the symptoms of aggressive masculine 'superiority' could lead to prolonged misery within the marital relationship. Witness the extraordinary case of Effie Gray, the object of the 'affections'

---

[1] quoted, *ibid.*, p. 245
[2] *ibid.*, p. 363
[3] *Liberty, Equality, Fraternity*, pp. 217–18

and wooing ardour of John Ruskin. The latter's outrageous egotism would be comical, if the symptoms could be divorced from their tragic genesis and their ultimately disastrous consequences. The point, however, is that symptoms obvious to us were far from being appreciated as such by Miss Gray and her relatives, conditioned to accept the prejudice of masculine ascendancy. Their awakening came only after Effie's intense suffering had made the truth unmistakable. Ruskin's was an extreme, pathological case; he was himself the victim of a demoniacally possessive mother and his monomania culminated eventually in the breakdown of his moral and intellectual faculties. But this merely serves to underline the extent to which young women were schooled to regard as normal the subordinate or even subjugated role cast for them by the husband. This is illustrated by Ruskin's letters during his courtship protesting the lengths of his devotion to Effie Gray.

In a letter to his fiancée some five months before his 'marriage' – it was never consummated – he was scarcely able to contain his transports at the prospect of how useful his future bride would be to him in his architectural investigations, if she will learn to share his tastes and be willing to serve them in a humble capacity. 'For you will have often to wait for me', he tells her, 'while I am examining cathedrals, by the *hour* – you may do it at the Inn – but in most cases – when it is not cold, I imagine it will be in the church – that you may see what I am about – see me getting my coat all white over, and creeping into crypts on my hands and knees. . . .' She will soon find that unless she makes up her mind to inform herself in this subject, one cathedral will appear much the same as another, so that in her own interest she will be well advised to acquire some technical knowledge if she does not wish to 'be tired of sauntering up and down aisles – hearing fat priests chanting dull bass discords – or watching old women mutter over their beads'. The only alternative is that 'you will have to pass many an irksome hour' for after all he has his profession to pursue: '. . . while for a certain time of the day – I shall always be entirely *yours* – to go and be with you where you choose – yet for another part of the day, and that – usually the largest – you will have to be *mine* – or to sit at home.' Nor does this inestimable prospect exhaust her possibilities of usefulness. He complains of the badness of the common run of available translations from the German. 'There, at any rate is one thing, my love, in which you will often and often be of use to me. I can read translations of German books *now*, and when I come to a bit that I want to comment upon – I shall ask you if it be rightly translated and get you to give it me better from the original.' At such a picture of married bliss as this conjures up he is quite unable to contain his transports. 'Ah – how happy it will be,' he exclaims.[1] Why does such a person wish to marry, it might well be asked? Ruskin's egoism was of the galloping variety. He could discuss without any sense of incongruity the function of marriage in relation to the one subject of absorbing interest – himself. He deeply regretted that fortune had not permitted him to engage himself to his fiancée long ago, he tells her, since 'it would at any rate have saved me from much loss of health' (p. 64). It is unnecessary here to pursue further the distressing story of Ruskin's sexual relations and his ultimate collapse as his intellect finally gave way under its combined emotional burdens.

In this section an attempt has been made to uncover something of the prejudicial effects of an unbalance in the relations between the sexes so far as the adults themselves are concerned. There follows an account in some detail of a celebrated instance of what may be the consequences for the children of a profound disturbance of the Oedipean ties of the parent-child relationship in such a culture.

(ii) *The Case of Elizabeth Barrett*

Where parental affection and in particular an unpossessive tenderness are lacking, the adverse psychological effects on the emotional development of the child are today well enough understood among the general educated public. But it is necessary to differentiate between abstract intellectual awareness and a direct imaginative apprehension of the way in which such parental deficiency has harmful effects. There can be few better case studies, in which the process can be observed at close quarters, available in our literature than in the correspondence

---

[1] *The Order of Release*, The story of John Ruskin, Effie Gray and John Everett Millais, Told for the first time in their Unpublished Letters, Edited by Admiral Sir William James, 1947, pp. 60-1

of Elizabeth Barrett with Robert Browning. It might be objected
that few women are so unfortunate as to be given over to the
tender mercies of such a domestic tyrant as Mr Barrett. This
may be true, but we would do well to remember that Mr Barrett
was not in any way regarded as pathological by those who knew
him. It should also be remembered that Elizabeth Barrett was
a woman of exceptional strength of character and intellect, and
that she was a woman of forty when her relations with her father
were put to the test by her love for Robert Browning. The agony
of her struggle, as she sought to release herself from the paternal
despotism without violating her filial duty, she herself has
portrayed in unforgettable terms in her letters to Browning
before the elopement. While no one would claim that Miss
Barrett belongs to the first rank as a poet, it would be hard to
deny her such status in the epistolary art.

Edward Moulton Barrett, father of Elizabeth, was a very
wealthy widower, legatee of large Jamaican estates, himself the
son of a woman who was abandoned by her husband before the
boy was two years old. His childhood seems to have oscillated
between an excessively indulgent mother and an excessively
harsh schooling. Towards his own large family he apparently
behaved with generosity and 'kindness' so long as it was recognized that no one should challenge his own imperious will. Not
least among his requirements was the clearly understood taboo
on marriage so far as his three daughters were concerned. Hence
the dilemma confronting Elizabeth, the invalid daughter,
when at the age of thirty-nine she fell in love with the young
man, whose admiration for her poetry prompted him first to
write and then to visit her at Wimpole Street. The struggle which
then went on within her is exposed in all its pathos and intensity
in the letters to Browning. It provides a vivid illustration of the
extraordinary difficulty experienced by even the grown adult
in attempting to see the parent objectively as he must appear to a
distinterested spectator. So great is the need to preserve intact
the child's image of the loving and infallible parent, so entrenched is the fear of violating a moral culture epitomized in
the fifth commandment of the decalogue, that the child continues in adulthood habits of evasion and rationalization in
order to preserve the illusion of filial affection on the one side and
paternal love on the other. For the child a conflict of these

dimensions is so painful that it is certain to be repressed. And the wound thus veiled may well, with the passage of time and the accretion of further repressed material, develop a dynamism of its own, capable of reducing the personality to impotence in its dealings with external reality. In the case of Miss Barrett, Robert Browning arrived on the scene in time to act as a kind of catalyst helping her to see her relationship in its true light. Because her existing relation with her father, which she accepted without conscious resentment at the start of the Browning correspondence, was an absolute bar to a union with Browning, Elizabeth Barrett was obliged to face up to her psychic dilemma. In this sense she was fortunate, since a more compliant and less irrational father might have been wise enough to consent to the marriage without relaxing his inner hold over his daughter's need for his approval. Elizabeth Barrett was compelled to look her problem in the face or give up her love for Browning. It required all her courage and all Browning's gentle and intuitive wisdom to pull them through. As the drama mounts to its climax, the tension of the situation grips the reader very powerfully. It springs precisely from a consciousness of how even is the balance between the forces of paternal domination and the child's longing for the protection of her lover. The equilibrium is always precarious, the outcome never certain. In the event, the daughter triumphs and by a dramatic elopement exchanges the harsh servitude of the father for the gentle dominion of the poet. For Elizabeth Barrett had long since been put beyond hope of attaining a marriage of two independent beings living on terms of complete equality.

Miss Barrett was gradually helped to enlightenment by the patience and understanding of Browning in an embarrassing and explosive situation. But the struggle was one of great mental anguish. We are fortunate that she who suffered it was also possessed of rare literary gifts. The correspondence began in January 1845 and concluded with the elopement in September 1846. In the 1913 edition, the letters extend to over 1,100 pages. The correspondence was admittedly prolific, yet in the space of little more than eighteen months Elizabeth Barrett made greater discoveries about herself and made more progress towards emotional maturity than many people, much less severely crippled by paternal ties than she, succeed in making in a lifetime. The correspondence begins with a vivid self-portrait untouched by self-pity of a lonely creature, confined within the world of her own imagining, owing nothing to the delights of social intercourse, but a world with its own riches notwithstanding. 'You seem to have drunken of the cup of life full, with the sun shining on it. I have lived only inwardly; or with *sorrow*, for a strong emotion.' Hers was a lonely country life, she says, a world of books and dreams, of poetry and reveries, a quiet, sheltered world, a gentle succession of domestic rounds and the somnolence of summer.

> And so time passed, and passed – and afterwards, when my illness came and I seemed to stand at the edge of the world with all done, and no prospect (as appeared at one time) of ever passing the threshold of one room again; why then, I turned to thinking with some bitterness . . . that I had stood blind in this temple I was about to leave – that I had seen no Human nature, that my brothers and sisters of the earth were *names* to me, that I had beheld no great mountain or river, nothing in fact. I was as a man dying who had not read Shakespeare, and it was too late![1]

The friendship advanced rapidly, and within seven months they had succeeded in establishing a close understanding. The peculiar nature of Elizabeth's relation with her father, which Browning must have quickly discovered for himself, began to force its way into overt discussion. Elizabeth's analysis betrays an uneasy and embarrassed constraint; she concedes the painful fact of her father's dominance, but tries to explain it away on the grounds of her own willing acceptance of the position. She clearly feels a strong measure of guilt in consenting to discuss the matter at all even with one so intimate and sympathetic. She confesses in retrospect to feeling 'uncomfortable' at having broken her silence on this matter in conversation with him, and seeks to justify herself in her disloyalty by an appeal to necessity – 'only that you could not long be a friend of mine without knowing and seeing what so lies on the surface.'[2]

There follows a humiliating attempt to argue that her servitude is not really servitude, since she had grown accustomed to it and has no desire to exert a 'will' of her own. Moreover, the com-

---

[1] *The Letters of Robert Browning and Elizabeth Barrett*, 1913, Vol. I, pp. 43–4
[2] *ibid.*, Vol. I, p. 174

pensations have been and are many. The very variety of the
arguments employed testifies to the fact that the self-deception
is only partially successful. 'Every now and then there must of
course be a crossing and vexation – but in one's mere pleasures
and fantasies, one would rather be crossed and vexed a little
than vex a person one loves . . . and it is possible to get used to
the harness and run easily in it at last . . .'[1] Also she has enjoyed
freedom in the private, non-*overt* world which she and the other
children had fashioned for themselves beyond the reach of
paternal coercion – the side worlds in which thought could be
concealed, 'carpet work,' 'literature' where Elizabeth in
particular had found her opportunity for self-realization and
'real liberty which is never enquired into'. And if in truth
obedience has been required of her in small matters as in great,
she has felt this to be no hardship, since the course demanded
of her has never conflicted with her own sense of 'right and
happiness'. In fact, when you have never lived otherwise than in
fetters, you are not able to recognize the fetters for what they are.
You learn to adjust your wants to the goad in order to preserve
the precious illusion of freedom. Moreover, honesty compels her
to confess something of the full bitterness she has experienced
in being compelled to indulge in evasions, concealments,
disingenuousness, yes, let it be admitted, cowardice itself, to
protect the integrity of the self from the intrusions of the father.
The spectacle too of her brothers being constrained '*bodily*'
by their financial dependence upon their father is so painful to
her that she feels the need to confess it. But she senses the rebuke
to her father implicit in these remarks wrung from her by her
emotional distress. She is flooded with guilt, and hastens to
withdraw from the position into which she seems to have
manoeuvred herself. Is she not bound by paramount ethical duty
to honour and love her father? The denial of his tyranny by any
subterfuge is too flagrant a fault to be permitted; then the fault
cannot lie with him. At all costs it must lie elsewhere; at all costs
she must preserve intact the illusion of a *really* loving father,
however harsh the reality. There are few more moving pages in
letters than the inner torment of Miss Barrett's desperate protestations of her love for her father in the teeth of all the evidence
that in no human breast could love have survived such a tyranny.

[1] *ibid.*

But what you do *not* see, what you *cannot* see, is the deep tender affection behind and below all those patriarchal ideas of governing grown up children 'in the way they *must* go!' and there never was (under the strata) a truer affection in a father's heart . . . no, nor a worthier heart in itself . . . a heart loyaller and purer, and more compelling to gratitude and reverence, than his, as I see it! The evil is in the system – and he simply takes it to be his duty to rule, and to make happy according to his own views of the propriety of happiness – he takes it to be his duty to rule like the Kings of Christendom, by divine right. But he loves us through and through it – and *I*, for one, love *him*![1]

The further evidence that is produced of his virtue is significant. He did not reproach her in the matter of the one great offence of her life, the guilt of which still deeply encumbers her. There follows an account, distorted by disproportionate guilt, of the tragic accident in which her brother lost his life whilst sailing off Torquay. Because she knowingly used her illness as a weapon against her father in order to keep her brother as a companion during her seaside convalescence, she insists with morbid relish on her responsibility for her brother's death. 'Morbid relish' may seem a harsh phrase to describe suffering so genuine. It is a description of her state of mind, not a suggestion that she was insincere in her belief that she had fully deserved her bitter self-reproaches.

Browning seems intuitively to have understood the need to bring all his tact and patience to bear on the large problem concealed from the beginning in their relationship. He behaved throughout with rare self-restraint under trying and embarrassing provocation. He was very sensitive to the unusually harrowing conflict of loyalties to which his beloved was subjected. In his situation a lesser man would easily have exploded in wrath and contempt for a potential father-in-law so preposterously behaved. Nevertheless, there were limits even to Browning's stock of patience. As time slipped by, he increasingly came to realize that if he was to win a bride, she must be led to face the disagreeable truth about the nature of the hold exercised over her by her father. We may judge by the gentle but firm way in which he set about this, not only of the love he bore her, but also of his realization of the danger to their own relation-

---

[1] *Letters, op. cit.*, p. 175

ship if he tried to break this distorted but intimate parental tie. In March 1846, some fourteen months since Browning's introductory letter of appreciation to a fellow-craftsmen, he found himself for the first time compelled gently to remonstrate with 'Ba' concerning her view of her father. It was in all probability from that moment that, consciously at least, her emancipation began. After protesting his determination to see with her eyes in matters of a family nature, he nevertheless continues:

> ... what I see I will *never* speak, if it pain you; but just this much truth I ought to say, I think.... That a father choosing to give out of his whole day some five minutes to a daughter, supposed to be prevented from participating in what he, probably, in common with the whole world of sensible men, as distinguished from poets and dreamers, consider *every* pleasure of life, by a complete foregoing of society – that he, after the Pisa business and the enforced continuance, and as he must believe, permanence of this state in which any other human being would go mad – I do dare say, for the justification of God, who gave the mind to be *used* in this world –where it saves us, we are taught, or destroys us – and not to be sunk quietly, overlooked, and forgotten; that, under these circumstances, finding ... what, you say, unless he thinks he *does* find, he would close the door of his house instantly; a mere sympathizing man, of the same literary tastes, who comes good-naturedly, on a proper and unexceptionable introduction, to chat with and amuse a little that invalid daughter, once a month, so far as is known, for an hour perhaps – that such a father should show himself '*not pleased* plainly', at such a circumstance ... my Ba, it is SHOCKING! See, I go *wholly* on the supposition that the real relation is not imagined to exist between us.[1]

The weight of suppressed emotion suffuses the whole passage with a degree of near-incoherence not at all characteristic of Browning's informal epistolary style. The whole subject is intensely painful to him, and after this single outburst, he announces his intention of never again recurring to it, that she might not misunderstand his entire silence henceforth.

Four months later, Elizabeth is in open revolt against her father's domination, although she dare not allow him to see it. But still the resentment is mixed with a good deal of guilt,

---

[1] *ibid.*, pp. 530–1

expressed in continued attempts to convince herself that her father is in reality a lovable man. On the one hand, his old terms of endearment – 'my love', even 'my puss' – cause her consciously to shrink from him as from so many knife-wounds. 'Anything but his *kindness*, I can bear now.'[1] But then she feels the immediate need to expiate this by cataloguing his virtues. He is upright, a man of conscience; though obdurate, not a man of stone. But it is doubtful if she even deceives herself when she assures Browning that if he really understood her father, he would respect him and even perhaps eventually come to love him. So great has been her own devotion to him that only his inability to love her openly has prevented his continuing to the end not only his role as father but as king over her. 'So the night-shade and the eglantine are twisted, twined, one in the other, . . . and the little pink roses lean up against the pale poison of the berries – we cannot tear this from that, let us think of it ever so much.'[2] She is clearly no longer under any illusion as to the lethal nature of the roots which bind her to her father. But still to be contended with is the fear he inspires. She is able to reconcile herself to open defiance by eloping with Browning but only on the strict understanding that after the shock of the thing is over, they must be 'humble and beseeching . . . and try to get forgiven'. In contemplating the shock of such defiance, she wonders whether it might not be better after all to break it to him first. But this she knows is not a genuine alternative, in view of the certainty that he would use his power to deprive her of all further freedom, and to sever completely her relations with Browning. Even more fatal is the objection that her new-found, still faltering courage freezes within her at the prospect conjured up by his fearsome anger. '. . . I should have fainting fits at every lifting of his voice, through that inconvenient nervous temperament of mine which has so often made me ashamed of myself. . . . I shut my eyes in terror sometimes. May God direct us to the best.'[3]

Her acute fear of her father remains unweakened right down to the final moment of escape. Witness, for example, the small episode of a hot thundery August day, in 1846, when Browning

---

[1] *Letters, op. cit.*, Vol. II, p. 341
[2] *ibid.*, pp. 341–2
[3] *ibid.*, p. 342

during one of his visits to Elizabeth was compelled by the storm outside to delay his departure from Wimpole Street. After his departure, just before dinner, Mr Barrett visited his daughter. One is left to imagine the tone in which he inquired as to whether she had been clad in her dressing-gown since the morning, and whether it was true that 'that man' had been there the whole day. Far from brushing aside these impertinences, Elizabeth sought by soft answer to excuse herself and turn away his wrath. Her own comment on the episode is revealing:

> Brief enough – but it took my breath away . . . or what was left by the previous fear. And think how it must have been a terrible day, when the lightning of it made the least terror.[1]

On another occasion an admiring reference by her father to some flowers given to her by Browning sufficed to unnerve her. 'I could scarcely answer', she writes, 'I was so frightened.'[2]

But if the terror inspired by her father's anger remained unabated, the courage with which to combat and conspire against it steadily increased. For her love was fortified by a growing awareness of the real nature of the ties that had held her in sick subjection. Right up to the last moment she was capable of writing: 'I am paralysed when I think of having to write such words as . . . "Papa, I am married; I hope you will not be too displeased." ' But she is in fact no longer paralysed, since the dammed-up passion has forced the dykes and found another outlet. She can afford to say, 'Ah, poor Papa!' She is not only within five days of freedom; she has succeeded in penetrating to a remarkable extent into the nature of her father's 'love' for her. For a moment her honesty and ability to question the childhood image of her father push her to the very brink of understanding the Oedipean ties which bind him to her. She writes:

> Once I heard of his saying of me that I was 'the purest woman he ever knew,' – which made me smile at the moment, or laugh I believe, outright, because I understood perfectly what he meant by *that* – viz – that I had not troubled him with the iniquity of

[1] *ibid.*, p. 385
[2] *ibid.*, p. 450

love affairs, or any impropriety of seeming to think about being married.[1]

Again we see the intensity of the effort required to acknowledge to herself this picture of her father in his true colours. For the criticism is instantly followed by remorse, by the longing that will not be stifled to be taken back within the warm shelter of father's forgiveness. Her pain sears the page on which she writes and we still shrink from the awful implications of ties so strong that they withstand even the tyrannical monomania of a Barrett.

> But we will submit, dearest. I will put myself under his feet, to be forgiven a little, . . . enough to be taken up again into his arms. I love him – he is my father – he has good and high qualities after all: he is my father *above* all. And *you*, because you are so generous and tender to me, will let me, you say, and help me to try to win back the alienated affection – for which, I thank you and bless you, . . . Surely I may say to him, too, . . . 'With the exception of this act, I have submitted to the least of your wishes all my life long. Set the life against the act, and forgive me, for the sake of the daughter you once loved.' Surely I may say *that*, – and then remind him of the long suffering I have suffered, – and entreat him to pardon the happiness which has come at last.[2]

The pendulum of ambivalence still swings her emotions towards her father, but now as liberation dawns and the conflict comes more and more into the open, the oscillations of mood are much swifter. Truthful analysis of her father, of which she is now capable, is immediately productive of guilt, but even in the expression of it, the phrases become double-edged. The will to live, to love, to be free, force the truth even through the guilt of affirmation of filial love. Her vindication of her father becomes noticeably feebler, the very words she uses are silently transmuted into her own apologia; and before she has completed the thought, she is asking him to *pardon* her happiness. When the very defence she still feels obliged to make of her father turns into an indictment, she is almost free. She has little or no illusion any more. His answer to her plea for pardon – what will it be? She knows it, and answers the unformulated question without

---

[1] *Letters, op. cit.,* p. 551
[2] *ibid.,* pp. 551–2

equivocation but from the deep wells of crushed affection. 'And *he* will wish in return, that I had died years ago!' Nor was she in any way wrong in her prophecy. Despite all her pleas, all her contrition, he never did forgive her. The relationship was broken for ever.

(iii) *John Stuart Mill's 'Mental Crisis'*

From the age of fifteen when he first was introduced to Bentham's writings, Mill tells us, the stability of his character, the object of his strivings and consequently the foundations of his happiness all derived from his determination to expend his energies in securing the reform of the world. This sufficed until the age of twenty when he experienced a memorable and painful mental upheaval. In conscious intellectual terms this crisis presented itself as an unalterable conviction that even the realization of all his reform projects would not in fact promote his own happiness. The goal of all his strivings had failed to provide the emotional satisfaction he demanded; and he accordingly fell into the melancholia associated with a sense of the futility of human existence. 'I seemed to have nothing left to live for.'[1] The love of humanity, of intellectual elevation, of moral excellence as goods in themselves had ceased to give meaning to his life. This mental anguish persisted for long without any alleviation, and was aggravated by his acute loneliness. For he had no one in whom he could confide without fear of reproof or ridicule. Despite his sufferings, a mind as inquisitive as Mill's could not fail to try to analyse and explain a phenomenon so deeply disturbing to his equilibrium and peace of mind. His analysis, though necessarily confined to the evidence of conscious introspection, was acute and is worth considering. For if it does not provide the explanation which Mill took it to be, it helps to throw light on Mill's own state of mind at the time, as well as on his earlier upbringing.

According to the hedonistic, associationist psychology in the principles of which Mill had been educated, human desires and aversions determining conduct are themselves determined by their associations of pleasure and pain. Accordingly the task of education consists of the attachment of adequate applications of praise and blame, pleasure and pain, to the

---

[1] John Stuart Mill, *Autobiography*, World's Classics edition, p. 113

salutary and insalutary objects of human desire respectively. In this way our behaviour and in particular the feelings sustaining the behaviour are artificially induced. Thus precariously rooted in the early stages of development, they are liable to disintegration if subjected to premature corrosion as by the habit of analysis. This Mill thought to be his own case. Given a severe education in the habits of rigorous logical analysis from a very early age, he was of the opinion that his feelings had not been permitted sufficient time to attach themselves ineradicably to the socially valuable objects of human striving. While he still acknowledged intellectually the desirability of securing certain social reforms, his sentiments were no longer harnessed to the task. He was emotionally indifferent; and the life of the reformer, which alone he considered intellectually acceptable, had lost its savour. In short, life itself had become intolerable to him: '...I did not think I could possibly bear it beyond a year' (p. 119).

Mill's instinctive reaction to his distress was an attempt to analyse its hidden causes in order to understand and face the truth about himself. His diagnosis was that he was suffering from an excess of analysis and a deficiency of feeling. On the one hand, his education had 'made precocious and premature analysis the inveterate habit of my mind' (p. 117); on the other hand, 'The fountains of vanity and ambition seemed to have dried up within me, as completely as those of benevolence' (p. 118). The conclusion seemed irresistible that the analytic habit and the emotional void were linked as cause and effect. He accordingly associated his 'recovery' with his attempt to redress the balance of his interests. He tried to cultivate the emotional side of his nature through the wonders of Nature and by reading Wordsworth's poetic tributes to Nature's splendour. Mill is too candid, however, to pretend that he did effect a recovery as distinct from the alleviation of his symptoms. The cloud over his life gradually disappeared: 'and though I had several relapses, some of which lasted many months, I never again was as miserable as I had been' (p. 120). If he never again was 'as miserable', illness, nervous habits, spasmodic outbursts of irrational behaviour remained a permanent feature of his life. Mill's great achievement lay in his intellectual honesty. He was capable of grasping that his inner unconscious conflict was closely connected with the development of his moral and political beliefs. He was also able to understand something of the nature of his conflict. In both respects he stood head and shoulders above his contemporaries.

Mark Rutherford, for instance, whose candour enables the reader of his *Autobiography* to share his experience of a 'mental crisis' similar in nature and symptoms to that of Mill, affords us a contrast of mature insight and rustic simplicity. Reared in the chill and gloom of an eastern county conventicle, Rutherford evinced all the timidity of the repressed and self-taught. There was also present the arrogance of neglected and unappreciated aspirations. After preaching his first sermon to the congregation of his parish, the contrast between his own intellectual eloquence and the stolidity of an indifferent congregation is too much for his precarious equilibrium. In his loneliness and despair he experiences his first nervous collapse:

> I was overwrought, and paced about for hours in hysterics. All that I had been preaching seemed the merest vanity when I was brought face to face with the fact itself; and I reproached myself bitterly that my own creed would not stand the stress of an hour's actual trial. . . . all support had vanished, and I seemed to be sinking into a bottomless abyss. I became gradually worse week by week, and my melancholy took a fixed form. I got a notion into my head that my brain was failing, and this was my first acquaintance with that most awful malady hypochondria. . . . For months – many months, this dreadful conviction of coming idiocy or insanity lay upon me like some poisonous reptile with its fangs driven into my very marrow, so that I could not shake it off. It went with me wherever I went, it got up with me in the morning, walked about with me all day, and lay down with me at night. I managed somehow or other to do my work, but I prayed incessantly for death; . . .[1]

Mill himself cannot match the force with which Rutherford recaptures in tranquillity the powerful sufferings of yesterday. Rutherford realized that his experience was important in his psychic life – he could scarcely have failed to do so, since he frankly admits: 'I have never been thoroughly restored' (p. 37). But when it comes to suggesting a remedy for his symptoms, his performance is puerile. 'What enabled me to conquer, was not

[1] *The Autobiography of Mark Rutherford*, 8th ed., 1900, pp. 36–7

so much heroism as a susceptibility to nobler joys, . . .' (p. 39) and '. . . the first thing to be aimed at is patience – not to get excited with fears, not to dread the evil which most probably will never arrive, but to sit down quietly and *wait*.'[1] But he does escape the trite when his description of his emotions in his depressive phase suggests a clue to the diagnosis. For instance, he remarks later in the book when describing another attack of 'that horrible monomania':

> A main part of the misery . . . lies in the belief that suffering of this kind is peculiar to ourselves. We are afraid to speak of it, and not knowing, therefore, how common it is, we are distracted with the fear that it is our own special disease.[2]

This observation is both shrewd and relevant.

That Mill should have outdistanced his contemporaries in the quality of introspective literary analysis is not surprising. What is odd is that our own contemporaries, writing in a post-Freudian culture, provide analyses considerably less acute even than Mill's own. Mr M. St John Packe, for instance, in a remarkable biography is singularly unsure of himself in handling Mill's 'crisis'. After invoking a medieval monastic analysis of *accidie* as an apparently serious explanation and an uncomfortably facetious reference to the months of the east wind when, according to Voltaire, Englishmen hang themselves by the dozens, the author invites the reader to put the episode into a proper perspective, that of a mental storm in a teacup, so to speak.

> Still, as he enshrined the whole in a lengthy chapter under the momentous heading 'A Crisis in my Mental History', most commentators have attached a good deal of importance to it, and as his account was indefinite, they have naturally made their own interpretations according to their various proclivities.[3]

We are then treated to a brief excursus on the various explanations which have been proffered, in which a short but invaluable essay by an American analyst is discussed on the same plane as Bain's and Leslie Stephen's 'overwork' hypothesis and an

---

[1] Rutherford, *op. cit.*, pp. 39–40
[2] *ibid.*, p. 98
[3] M. St John Packe, *The Life of John Stuart Mill*, 1954, p. 79

American lady's theory that Mill's deficiency was 'the bread of life'.

The facts of Mill's parental background and educational milieu are well known. My purpose here is simply to marshal the facts directly relevant to an understanding of John Stuart's personal problems. By reviewing the characters and domestic relations of the Mills Senior it is hoped to throw into relief the factors mainly responsible for the inner tensions built into the character of John Stuart.

James Mill is himself a major figure in British intellectual history, and accordingly much discussed in his own right as Bentham's foremost coadjutor. My subject here, however, is not James Mill the utilitarian, but James Mill the father of John Stuart. He was born in 1773 of poor Scottish parents, the father being a village shoemaker by trade, whose personal characteristics appear to have been conventional, steady, industrious, and devout enough to have aroused little comment. Of much greater influence was the mother, according to all accounts. Although no more than conjectural, the rumour itself is not without interest that her father had owned land which he had lost as a result of joining the wrong side in the '45 rebellion. Whether or not Isabel Fenton's family had in fact 'come down in the world', it is clear that she herself resented the low social status of her husband, and sought to compensate vicariously through her eldest son for the disappointment of her own pathetic pretensions. She was, according to Bain, a woman who was resented by her neighbours for the air of superiority which she assumed. She rejected porridge as a plebeian dish, and insisted on tea and butter. The family name of Milne was changed to Mill, a name less common in that part of the world. And if the neighbours thought she had ideas above her station in her ambition that her son should be called *Mr* Mill, they appear to have so far conceded her claims as to consider none but their best china worthy of her social calls. The mother's consuming passion was James's career, to which end she harnessed not only her own energies but the claims of all other members of the family. The picture that emerges of the family's 'self-sacrifice' or, more truly, of the deficiencies in the mother's love for her children, is not a pleasant one. We have a glimpse of James, the scholar, undisturbed in a study improvised by curtaining off one part of the cottage room. His meals, prepared specially by his mother, he took apart from the rest of the family. The younger brother was put to work in the father's shop, the daughter helped her mother in the house and tended the cow. The role of James is described by Bain as follows:

> ... James Mill neither assisted in his father's trade, nor took any part in the labour of the field, whereby he might have been less dependent on his parents. He saw what was going on, contracted an interest in farming, but his own sole occupation was study.[1]

The poverty was doubtless real enough, but it can have been as nothing compared with the unhappiness and resentments generated by a family life so deeply unbalanced. The mother died prematurely of consumption, as did the son William, while the father was paralysed as well as bankrupt.

James, however, with his native abilities backed by so much extraneous conviction of his destined importance, continued to rise in the world. Under the patronage of the Stuart family, after whom his own first two children were named, he succeeded in getting to Edinburgh University. But after disappointment of clerical patronage he left Scotland at the age of twenty-nine to seek his fortune in London. He did not have to wait long for success in metropolitan journalism. Although he appears to have afforded such financial assistance as he was able to his stricken relatives, he nevertheless deliberately turned his back henceforth on his Scottish origins. Even the accent was carefully eliminated; and although he shared so much of his mental life with his eldest son, John Stuart was unable to learn anything of his father's origins or early circumstances. The self-made man, who has come up the hard way, with a past of which he is ashamed, even though it is redolent of nothing worse than social obscurity, is not an unusual figure in Victorian England, in fact or fiction. Josiah Bounderby, the grasping, brass-fronted manufacturer of *Hard Times*, the canting and pompous Bulstrode, the banker in *Middlemarch*, come immediately to mind. We are apt to forget that similar burdens of repressed emotions were carried by many of the literati and intellectuals, whose aggressiveness and single-minded determination had brought them to

[1] *James Mill: A Biography*, 1882, pp. 6–7

renown. Their advancement only intensified their sensitivity
to the social stigmas of humble birth in such a preternaturally
class-conscious society. The portrait of James Mill here presented
is far from being the whole of the man; Mill was a man of lofty
purpose, sincerely intent throughout his life upon the promotion
of the public good. But his personal character bore the marks
of his early conditioning.

His primary characteristic was his dour will to succeed and a
harsh, unimaginative, proud manner in his dealings with other
people. Bain compares him with Pitt. Will was uppermost in
him, and his emotions were harnessed to the fierce demands of
his ambition to win his way in the world by intellectual power.
Intellect he overvalued as the indispensable means of his own
rise. He was a firm believer in government by an aristocracy of
merit; and having by his own efforts attained his rightful place
in that society of the upper intellectual middle class, he sedulously aped its manners. 'He was', says Bain, 'scrupulously
attentive to the manners and refinement of good society. He
dressed carefully; being what is termed a "natty" man. His
fine figure was not thrown away. . . . In spite of all that is said of
his arrogant manner, he made his way in society, and gained
over people his superiors in rank.'[1] His view of life was austere
and compounded of a large measure of duty. The emphases fell
upon discipline and struggle and self-immolation to secure self-
advancement. His advice to his son James, studying in 1835
at Haileybury for the Indian Civil Service, is characteristic.

> I was much pleased to see you had the highest mark in everything
> last month. You must strive hard to have the same in the remainder.
> The difficulties you are in about the fate which awaits you in
> point of honours can only be met by your utmost exertions. He
> who works more than all others will in the end excel all others.
> Difficulties are made to be overcome. Life consists of a succession
> of them. And he gets best through them, who has best made up
> his mind to contend with them.[2]

That the aim of excelling all others might be a sterile aim did
not occur to Mill. His gospel was essentially the gospel according
to Samuel Smiles, although reinforced by a much superior

[1] Bain, *op. cit.*, p. 425
[2] quoted by Bain, *ibid.*, p. 397

intellect. That the difficulties of life, of which we are seemingly
doomed to an endless succession, might be the product of deficiency of character and an inadequate philosophy were impious
thoughts incapable of penetrating Mill's complacency. His own
merits had been amply confirmed by the position he had won
by his own unaided efforts. The adjectives which Bentham permitted himself on one occasion to use of his friend should not
perhaps be allowed to influence unduly our judgement. Any
friend of Bentham must have experienced difficulties in dealing
with his own peculiarities of temper. Nevertheless, the choice of
such terms as 'domineering', 'oppressive', 'overbearing' in
describing the character of a long-standing and close friend,
has its relevance.[1]

It was not in the nature of things that such a man could be
capable of a happy marriage. He in fact married at the age of
thirty-three a woman ten years his junior, the beautiful daughter
of a Yorkshire widow of not inconsiderable means. Bain's laconic
account of the arrangement is revealing of the delicacy required
to handle the more painful aspect of his subject:

> Mrs Mill was not wanting in any of the domestic virtues of an
> English mother. She toiled hard for her house and her children, and
> became thoroughly obedient to her lord. As an admired beauty,
> she seems to have been chagrined at the discovery of her position
> after marriage. There was disappointment on both sides: the
> union was never happy.[2]

Having married her for her beauty, James proceeded to father
nine children upon her while never attempting to conceal his
contempt for her lack of intellectual interests. He no doubt
conducted himself for the most part correctly, indeed righteously,
but without love; for of love he had none to offer. In a letter
to an acquaintance on the occasion of his marriage, he made
pointed reference to his confidence that his friend's choice will
not have led him to be deceived, 'because you are past that hey-
day of the blood when the solid qualities are apt to be overlooked
for the superficial.'[3] Where people know each other well, they
run less risk of subsequent disappointment, he adds sententiously

---

[1] cf. Bain, *op. cit.*, p. 463
[2] *ibid.*, p. 60
[3] *ibid.*, p. 156

but ruefully. Mill was of course neither the first nor the last to fail to realize that what Hamlet termed that 'hey-day in the blood' in its intensest form may bespeak no more than the isolation and loneliness of an individual whose need for love is equalled only by an inability to give it. Often the greater the degree of egocentricity, the deeper the conviction that few can hitherto have prostrated themselves so unreservedly on the altar of love.

In marriage the claims Mill unconsciously made for himself were in marked contrast to the unquestioned subservience he demanded of his wife. Although we do not know a great deal about Harriet Burrows, her lot as Mrs Mill could not have been very different from the role so brilliantly portrayed by Robert Graves of Mary Powell as 'wife to Mr Milton.'[1] She is generally described as inoffensive, kindly, good-natured, good-tempered. The most serious criticism Francis Place permitted himself to make was that she was 'not a little vain of her person, and would be thought to be still a girl.' Mrs Grote's contemptuous reference in a letter to Lady Amberley tells us more about Mrs Grote and incidentally James Mill than it does about Mrs Mill.

'He married a stupid woman "a housemaid of a woman" & left off caring for her & treated her as his squah but was always faithful to her.'[2] There is general agreement among the different witnesses to the unfortunate *malaise* in the Mill household that the source lay in Mrs Mill's intellectual shortcomings. Even John Stuart's third sister, Harriet, in her spirited defence of her mother in a letter of 1873, did not dispute that this was the cause of the marital discord that did so much to paralyse the springs of affection within the home:

> Here was an instance of two persons, as husband and wife, living as far apart, under the same roof, as the north pole from the south; from no 'fault' of my poor mother most certainly; but how was a woman with a growing family and very small means (as in the early years of the marriage) to be anything but a German Hausfrau? How could she 'intellectually' become a companion for such a mind as my father?

[1] The Milton home on the edge of St James's Park, afterwards 19 York Street, was occupied by James Mill before it passed into Hazlitt's tenancy.
[2] *Amberley Papers*, Vol. I, p. 421

Harriet could not have known that James Mill had been reared by his mother to consider it a woman's privilege to serve the interests of the male to whom she was attached. Mill would not have thought of it quite like that perhaps. But ingrained in his character was the notion of his own male primacy. How could it have been otherwise? Any woman capable by training and native endowment to have acted as a genuine intellectual companion to James Mill would have repelled his sexual proclivities. He could not have done other than marry a woman who would not satisfy his needs, since in the first place he had learnt to conceive of marriage in no other light than as the final coping-stone to his otherwise successful career. And secondly because his emotional nature required the subservience that was incompatible with any form of real companionship. Harriet, whose letter we have just quoted, vaguely sensed the nature of her father's personal handicaps when she wrote elsewhere of him, '*His* great want was "temper" . . . though I quite believe circumstances had made it what it was in our childhood, both because of the warm affection of his early friends, and because in the later years of his life he become much softened and treated the younger children very differently.'

Independent testimony confirms the peculiarly harsh behaviour of which James Mill was capable towards his wife even in the presence of guests. When John Stuart spoke in *The Subjection of Women* of men reserving the sulkiest, most selfish and violent sides of their character for the benefit of those who shared their hearth and home, he must have spoken from first-hand knowledge:

> The one really disagreeable trait in Mill's character, [writes Bain, friend as well as biographer,] and the thing that has left the most painful memories, was the way that he allowed himself to speak and behave to his wife and children before visitors. When we read his letters to friends, we see him acting the family man with the utmost propriety, putting forward his wife and children into their due place; but he seemed unable to observe this part in daily intercourse.[1]

And this is confirmed by the comparison the young Henry Solly could not refrain from making with his own parents when

---

[1] Bain, *op. cit.*, p. 334

visiting the Mills. After describing James Mill as a man stately and courteous of manner, he continues: 'but accustomed as I was to my father's behaviour to my mother, and that of other gentlemen whom I had observed in similar relations, I could not help being rather pained at his manner occasionally to Mrs Mill.' Mrs Mill herself he describes as sweet-tempered, pleasant and fond of her children but 'not much interested in what the elder ones and their father talked about.'[1]

This, then, was the family setting in which James Mill proposed to give his eldest son an education appropriate to the heir of the utilitarian tradition after his own and Bentham's demise. Mill believed that the child's desires and aversions could be conditioned by associations of pleasure and pain to any required end. Since the end was proclaimed as an axiom to be the greatest happiness of the greatest number, John Stuart was to receive a rigorous discipline in which he would learn to associate his own happiness with the 'duty' of promoting the moral elevation of mankind. The humourless and doctrinaire thoroughness with which this educational programme was prosecuted was subsequently described by John Stuart himself in his *Autobiography*. The total isolation of the child from the potentially 'corrupting' influence of playmates, the meticulous and unflagging discipline, the extraordinary range of language and historical literature in the curriculum from the earliest years, together constituted a measure of paternal fanaticism unique in educational annals. Indeed, many readers of the *Autobiography* have been so aghast at the picture of such severe intellectual labour undertaken by a precocious and prematurely forced child that they have felt no need to look further for the explanation of John Stuart's subsequent mental distress and failures of health. John Stuart himself had no hesitation in rejecting this explanation, relying on the ancient saw that 'hard work never killed anyone' – a piece of folk-lore which, properly interpreted, modern psychology has done nothing to undermine. It was not the educational programme nor the content of the regimen that destroyed Mill's childhood and wrought such permanent harm, so much as the fiercely fanatical spirit of domination that lay behind it. It was not the means adopted, but the spiritual poverty of a father who, however sincere, could conceive the right on his part to

[1] quoted by Packe, *op. cit.*, p. 76

shape and determine another's character to serve as his own instrument. Objectively, James Mill saw in his educational experiment on his son the union of his paternal love and his benevolent concern for the public welfare. But subjectively, he sought by this means simultaneously to find satisfaction for his appetite for power and in his son a substitute for the companionship he could not find with his wife. To this end he exercised severe discipline over others, and immense patience and energy on his own account. John Stuart could scarcely have developed his outstanding intellect and strong character, had there not been some measure of genuine affection for his son in James Mill's make-up and also some awareness of the true nature of education. This was perceived by his daughter, Harriet, in her lament of the authoritarian relationship which existed between the other children and their father. 'My father could not teach us as he had done John by companionship', she wrote. This picture is also confirmed by Henry Solly, who observed that while James Mill was 'not unkind' to his children, he took little notice of them with the exception of John.

The details of a day in the Mill family have been bequeathed to us by Francis Place who visited them when they were staying at Ford Abbey as guests of Bentham in 1817. The father rose between five and six, and proceeded to compare the proofs of his current writings with John. At seven, the two sisters arrive, and as soon as the proofs are done, John is free to teach them until breakfast at nine. The meal over, a full three hours are given up by the father to hearing the three children's lessons and readings until one o'clock. Place comments on the 'excessive severity' of James Mill, though for the rest he is lost in admiration of such discipline and single-minded devotion. 'No fault, however trivial, escapes his notice; none goes without reprehension or punishment of some sort.' And he presents a gloomy picture of their plodding wearisomely away over their books at 3 p.m. without having had their dinner and destined to continue without food until six o'clock, and all because of a mistake in one word. John was inculpated with the others, since he had condoned their error. Such methods applied by a temperament such as James Mill's meant that his relation with his children was predominantly one of fear. After he went to India House, the only time the children had any contact with him was in the evening on his return, and then, in Harriet's words, 'we were always in disgrace over the hated Latin.' John Stuart himself in his *Autobiography*, although seeking to soften the criticism, does not deny that, so far as the elder children were concerned, fear was the predominant element in their relations with their father. Bain's evidence is even more chilling. In discussing James Mill's constitutional irritability, unrestrained at home, he goes on to say that 'even in his most amiable moods, he was not to be trifled with.' There follows the grim indictment: 'His entering the room where the family was assembled was observed by strangers to operate as an immediate damper.'[1]

These shortcomings of the Mill household have long been public knowledge. But the real point has been missed. The general tendency has been to use the evidence as a stick with which to beat Utilitarianism, and to expose its sterile inadequacies as a creed. This, we are left to infer, is the husk to which vital human affections and humour may be reduced if we follow the mechanical and unimaginative precepts of utilitarianism. The aridity of which the critics have complained was assuredly there. But much is to be attributed to a psychology as shallow and mechanistic as associationist hedonism. The most effective satire on Stuart Mill's education we owe to Dickens. It was the element of cold calculation introduced into the relation of the parental pedagogue with the child that outraged Dickens. Dickens's cold anger when under complete control could be deadly. The reader should savour in full the masterly fifteenth chapter of *Hard Times* in which Mr Gradgrind embarks upon the delicate task of discovering whether Louisa, his loved and meticulously moulded daughter, is amenable to the proposal to betroth her to Mr Bounderby. The following extract is a short but perfect illustration of Dickens's power of economy in irony:

'What do I know, father,' said Louisa, in her quiet manner, 'of tastes and fancies; of aspirations and affections; of all that part of my nature in which such light things might have been nourished? What escape have I had from problems that could be demonstrated, and realities that could be grasped?' As she said it, she unconsciously closed her hand, as if upon a solid object, and slowly

[1] Bain, *op. cit.*, p. 334

opened it as though she were releasing dust or ash. 'My dear,' assented her eminently practical parent, 'quite true, quite true.' 'Why, father,' she pursued, 'what a strange question to ask *me*! The baby-preference that even I have heard of as common among children, has never had its innocent resting-place in my breast. You have been so careful of me, that I never had a child's heart. You have trained me so well, that I never dreamed a child's dream. You have dealt so wisely with me, father, from my cradle to this hour, that I never had a child's belief or a child's fear.' Mr Gradgrind was quite moved by his success, and by this testimony to it. 'My dear Louisa,' said he, 'you abundantly repay my care. Kiss me, my dear girl.'[1]

Given the atmosphere and tensions in the home, how did John consciously react to his father and mother? James, we know, singled him out from all his other children, and devoted a great deal of time and energy to his eldest boy, not attempting to conceal the fact that he considered him more important than any of the others. He also treated the boy in some measure as his intellectual equal, and within the bounds of a severe parental discipline offered him genuine companionship. Again, the father's contempt for the mother's attainments and interests was not concealed; and the son must quickly have learnt from his father the inferior status of the mother. Given the severity of the father, a possible compensatory and excessive attachment to the mother might have occurred. She was kindly and indulgent to her children, who constituted her principal interest in life. On the other hand, she deeply resented her status of inferiority, the more so that she had before marriage been an admired beauty in a domestic world where such feminine values loomed large. Her wounded vanity, her resentment, her deep marital unhappiness, her bewilderment and acceptance of her intellectual inferiority, her financial cares in the early days of the marriage, her labours and preoccupations with the perennial burden of bearing and rearing nine children, together must have constituted a crippling burden on her limited psychic strength. There could not have been much time or energy to give the uninhibited maternal tenderness to her individual children which they needed to mitigate the consequences of the father's aloof severity.

[1] Collins' Classics edition, p. 137

I have attempted to reconstruct the characters of John Stuart's father and mother, to portray their mutual relations, so as to convey something of the emotional atmosphere and domestic tension in which the boy grew to manhood. This was necessary to understand the problem of the younger Mill's breakdown at the age of twenty. Reference was made earlier to Mr Levi's article on the sources of Mill's mental crisis, published in the *Psychoanalytic Review* (1945) and to Mr St John Packe's cavalier treatment of it. Professor Hayek, in his edition of Mill's correspondence with Mrs Taylor, is appreciative of the Levi article but adopts a cautious attitude as to the validity of the interpretation. He also subscribes to the 'overwork' theory rejected by Mill himself.

> That one of the main causes of the acute dejection, from which he emerged only gradually over a period of years, was, in addition to overwork, the struggle to emancipate himself from the complete intellectual sway which his father had held over him, one may readily believe without subscribing to the full to the psychoanalytical interpretation given of it recently in an interesting study.[1]

Levi's paper is somewhat condensed and addressed to an audience primarily of psychoanalysts. My purpose here is to seek to make the Levi analysis, so far as it goes, better understood by students of Mill and politics.

Levi's hypothesis can be summarized very briefly. John Stuart, it is argued, developed so much resentment against his father that at the unconscious level he hated him sufficiently to desire his death.[2] A desire so repellent to Mill's moral values must have been ruthlessly repressed; and the consequent inner conflict proved in adolescence too much for his conscious mental equilibrium. Perhaps a root difficulty for the sceptical is the supposition that individual character can exercise so direct an environmental influence, almost as if character defect were contagious, so to speak. People are more willing to suppose that

---

[1] *John Stuart Mill and Harriet Taylor: Their Correspondence and Subsequent Marriage*, by F. A. Hayek, 1951, p. 31

[2] Levi draws attention to John Stuart's own observation that the reading of Marmontel's Memoirs in which the author recounts the death of his father on the threshold of his own manhood led to a feeling of relief of tension and depression on John Stuart's part.

character can be inherited than 'grafted' by living persons in this way. The former is the more comfortable hypothesis, so far as the notion of individual responsibility is concerned. Explanation in terms of hereditary transmission is less mortifying to our self-respect than explanation which connects our character defects with those of our children. To spell out the mechanics of the transmission of the neurosis is not the same as the ability to recognize the process at work in any given case. Freud, writing of the sources of neurosis, says:

> On appearance it looks as if we then had an inherited condition to deal with, but closer inspection shows the effect of powerful infantile impressions. As a mother, the neurotic woman who is unsatisfied by her husband is over-tender and over-anxious in regard to the child, to whom she transfers her need for love, thus awakening in it sexual precocity. The bad relations between the parents then stimulate the emotional life of the child, and cause it to experience intensities of love, hate and jealousy while yet in its infancy. The strict training which tolerates no sort of expression of this precocious sexual state lends support to the forces of suppression, and the conflict at this age contains all the elements needed to cause lifelong neurosis.[1]

Concerning the attitude of the parent Mills to sexual problems and the sexual education of children the evidence is negative. There is no positive evidence that such matters were not discussed in the Mill household. But (a) a *ménage* free from severe inhibition would have been unusual in his class at this time; (b) we can reasonably infer from James Mill's Scottish Puritan upbringing that unforced discussion of such a topic would be very difficult even if he did not impose an absolute taboo, and (c) – most conclusive – we know how much difficulty John Stuart experienced even as an adult in broaching even indirectly any topic concerning his relations with the opposite sex. There is no reason to suppose that the sexual culture of the Mill household was substantially different from that in which Charles Kingsley was reared with such unfortunate consequences. He describes it in the thinly veiled autobiographical novel, *Yeast*: 'All conversation on the subject of love had been prudishly avoided, as

[1] Freud, *Collected Papers*, Vol. II, 1924, p. 97; from *'Civilized' Sexual Morality and Modern Nervousness* (1908)

usual, by his parents and teacher. The parts of the Bible which spoke of it had been always kept out of his sight. Love had been to him, practically, ground tabooed and "carnal" ' (Ch. I, p. 3). This, after all, was the normal condition of domestic education in nineteenth-century England, at any rate in the middle classes.

The struggle to see those who first gave us our impressions of the human form and character in all their frailty and imperfections constitutes the first profound crisis of the discovery of the self and the soul's awakening. The difficulty is that whereas we are amply documented concerning John Stuart's feelings towards his father, his feelings towards his mother can only be inferred indirectly. Positive evidence concerning this crucial relationship is unfortunately lacking. The dominant role assumed by the father at the expense of the mother is evidence of an adverse emotional background for the child, whose emotional needs can be met only if father and mother each play their respective roles adequately. The fact that we know so little about Mill's relations with his mother is significant, particularly since Mill is both introspective and communicative by nature. The *Autobiography* makes no mention of his mother, whereas up to his marriage the same document features his father consistently as the central figure. Further, we know from the correspondence recently published by Hayek that Mill's relations with his mother were seriously and adversely affected by his marriage to Mrs Taylor. Moreover, he was seriously ill the year that his mother died, as well as the year in which his father died. If we look at John Stuart's relations with his father rather than with his mother, it is not because they are more important but because there is direct evidence. His father does seem to have occupied a more prominent place in John Stuart's conscious thoughts than did his mother.

The ties between John and his father were always close. Some intellectual comradeship there was, but no warm mutual affection. How could there be with a doctrinaire pedagogue, frost-bound in duty, the man of whom Bentham himself had written, 'He comes to me as if he wore a mask upon his face',[1] conscious of his inner rectitude and of the boy's good fortune in having such a father. As James told his son at the age of thirteen, to protect him from the pitfalls of vanity over his

[1] quoted by Bain, *op. cit.*, p. 463

remarkable intellectual accomplishments, the credit belonged
not to himself 'but to the very unusual advantage which had
fallen to my lot, of having a father who was able to teach me,
and willing to give the necessary trouble and time'.[1] What
impresses most about the character of James Mill in his relations
with his gifted first-born is his unwavering egocentricity. When
in 1812 Bentham wrote to him offering in the event of Mill's
death preceding his own to undertake the guardianship of
John Stuart, promising to take him under his own roof 'and
there or elsewhere, by whipping or otherwise, do whatsoever
may seem most necessary and proper, for teaching him to make
all proper distinctions, such as between the Devil and the Holy
Ghost, and how to make Codes and Encyclopaedias,' the irony,
if such it was, was quite lost on James Mill. Not in the least
disquieted by the prospect thus opened up for his six-year-old
son, he replied, 'I take your offer quite seriously, and then we
may perhaps leave him a successor worthy of both of us.'[2]
Indeed, he confessed to Bentham that such fear as he had of dying
stemmed largely from his anxiety lest this great task should be
left unaccomplished. 'Should I die, one thought that would
pinch me most sorely' would be leaving the poor boy's 'mind
unmade'.[3]

To ensure that his mind should not remain 'unmade', the
child was cut off from all contact with other boys to avoid their
'corrupting influence' and 'the contagion of vulgar modes of
thought and feeling'.[4] How did the child react in this peculiar
situation? To the end of his life John Stuart respected, and
continued to be influenced by, his father's intellect, scholarship,
iron self-discipline, and apparent self-denial in the pursuit of the
public good. But the warmth and spontaneity of the personal
relationship were irremediably impaired. It remained an acknowledged failure. There is the direct evidence of the *Autobiography*. Even more revealing is *The Subjection of Women*, where he
acknowledges that the master-pupil relationship, however
benevolent, is fundamentally incompatible with the affection
and candour reciprocally required of father and son:

---

[1] *Autobiography*, World's Classics edition, p. 29
[2] *The Letters of John Stuart Mill*, 1910, Vol. I, Introduction, p. xvi
[3] Leslie Stephen, *The English Utilitarians*, Vol. III, 1912 reprint, p. 3
[4] *Autobiography, op. cit.*, p. 30

As between father and son, how many are the cases in which the father, in spite of real affection on both sides, obviously to all the world does not know, nor suspect, parts of the son's character familiar to his companion and equals. The truth is, that the position of looking up to another is extremely unpropitious to complete sincerity and openness with him. The fear of losing ground in his opinion or in his feelings is so strong, that even in an upright character, there is an unconscious tendency to show only the best side, . . . (pp. 44–5).

In the *Autobiography* it is the perfectly genuine admiration for his father which is uppermost, and which John Stuart was naturally anxious to make the most of in presenting to posterity a portrait of his father, whom he felt to have been posthumously neglected by educated opinion.[1]

Nevertheless, his intellectual honesty did not allow him to suppress strongly felt criticism, which in turn prompted him to defend his father's character. Yet it is the defence which furnishes the most damning indictment. The filial urge is strong, but so also is the sense of injury. We are reminded of Elizabeth Barrett's pathetic efforts to justify her father. James Mill's principal deficiency as a father according to John Stuart was his lack of tenderness. Conscious of the gravity of this charge, the son hastens to add that he does not believe this deficiency to have been in his father's nature. Rather his father was by temperament and English phlegm unable and even ashamed of showing his emotions. Nevertheless, he shrewdly adds, absence of demonstrativeness in matters of affection and feeling is apt to starve the feelings themselves. If, for whatever reason, we habitually refuse to show our feelings, desuetude will eventually compel us to raise the question as to how real are feelings that are unable to address themselves to the person arousing them. As if aware that what he has given with one hand he has taken back with the other, he hastens to add the excuse of his father's constitutional irritability as well as the irksome nature of sole responsibility for his children's education. Given his father's determination to do the best he could for his children, and his longing to feel in return an affection which they could not give him, it would be difficult to deny him our compassion. In later life his manner softened

---

[1] cf. his entry in his diary for 12 January 1854, *Letters of John Stuart Mill*, Vol. II, Appendix A, p. 358

sufficiently to enable him to enjoy a different relation with his younger children, who accordingly loved him 'tenderly'. '... if I cannot say so much of myself, I was always loyally devoted to him', Mill adds with unconscious pathos.[1] The reasons for this admission he has already avowed – what lies unstated between the lines is the pain the statement must have cost him – the elder children could not give him affection, because they 'must have been constantly feeling that fear of him was drying it up at its source.' This leads him to discuss and, somewhat oddly to the modern ear, to defend the role of fear in education. He does not number himself among those who believe that boys can be persuaded by gentler means to apply themselves assiduously to tedious but necessary educational tasks. However, the caveat is entered that if fear becomes the main element it will be fatal to genuine education. For when fear

> predominates so much as to preclude love and confidence on the part of the child to those who should be the unreservedly trusted advisers of after years, and perhaps to seal up the fountains of frank and spontaneous communicativeness in the child's nature, it is an evil for which a large abatement must be made from the benefits, moral and intellectual, which may flow from any other part of the education.[2]

In John Stuart's mental crisis at the threshold of manhood, the one man to whom the son could not look for help was he who had sought to do most for him and to whom he owed most, namely his father. What John could not then know, and never fully did know, was that this in itself was a large part of his psychic *malaise*. Recollected in the tranquillity of age, the harshness of this experience has been allowed to mellow. Yet even then emotional undertones are still present.

> My father, [he writes] to whom it would have been natural to me to have recourse in any practical difficulties, was the last person to whom, in such a case as this, I looked for help. Everything convinced me that he had no knowledge of any such mental state as I was suffering from, and that even if he could be made to understand it, he was not the physician who could heal it.[3]

---

[1] *Autobiography, op. cit.*, p. 44
[2] *ibid.*, p. 45
[3] *ibid.*, pp. 114–15

For the sources of spontaneity within him had long since dried up. As he sadly says of himself, he never was a child. To apprehend this imaginatively we need again to have recourse to Dickens. Where is John Stuart's own case better stated than in the picture Dickens presents us of Mr Gradgrind confronting his crushed and dutiful Louise on the threshold of *her* adulthood?

> As he now leaned back in his chair, and bent his deep-set eyes upon her in his turn, perhaps he might have seen one wavering moment in her, when she was impelled to throw herself upon his breast, and give him the pent-up confidences of her heart. But, to see it, he must have overleaped at a bound the artificial barriers he had for many years been erecting, between himself and all those subtle essences of humanity which will elude the utmost cunning of algebra until the last trumpet ever to be sounded shall blow even algebra to wreck. The barriers were too many and too high for such a leap. With his unbending, utilitarian, matter-of-fact face, he hardened her again; and the moment shot away into the plumbless depths of the past, to mingle with all the lost opportunities that are drowned there.[1]

Whether such wavering moments occurred in the childhood of John Stuart, there is no means of knowing. What we do know is that the relationship had a canker at its heart, and the consequences for the son were severe.

Miss Barrett, it will be recalled, tried to convince herself that if we are sufficiently inured to running in harness, and have known nothing else, we are not conscious of the harness, since our own wants coincide with those imposed by it. At the conscious level there is much truth in this, although the mere ability to make this analysis is sufficient indication that the illusion of freedom is at an end. And unconsciously, it is impossible for a growing child not to resent sooner or later the imposition of another's will, however benevolent. Moreover, as Elizabeth Barrett perceived, her own case was much alleviated by the fact that the most important part of her mind, on her own valuation, was beyond her father's reach or desire to reach. So long as she conformed to the external requirements of his will, she was at least fancy-free: the life of the mind was her own. In Mill's case the reverse was true. It was precisely his son's

---

[1] *Hard Times*, Collins Classic ed., pp. 134–5

mind that James Mill was at such pains to secure. His persistent fear was lest he should die with his son's mind left 'unmade'. Under these circumstances, given, too, the intellectual vigour of such a talented child, the conflict with the father was bound to make itself increasingly felt. The harness would begin to chafe in adolescence. Indeed, we do not have to infer this resentment; the evidence is there. At the age of fourteen John was permitted, as a brief respite from the closed family circle, to make an extended visit to Bentham's younger brother, Brigadier Sir Samuel, and Lady Bentham, who lived in the south of France. Although far from home, his habit of work was by now ingrained as is revealed by the meticulous account of the apportionment of his time that he kept in his diary. Moreover, his father was constantly kept informed by letter of the progress he made. Outwardly, the harness at this point appears to have been still something of a necessary crutch. But inwardly, resentment must already have been at work. More than twenty years later, Mill wrote to Comte of the happiness of those days he had spent in Montpellier (Comte's home town): 'It was also there that for the first time I found a friend, that is to say a friend of my own choice, as opposed to those given me by family ties.' Again there is the small but revealing episode of John's loss of his watch at the age of sixteen, when staying with the Austins. The letter to his father is significant. The confession comes at the end after an account of his studies, a visit to Yarmouth, an analysis of local politics and a political sermon. The watch, he says, although lost out of doors, could not have been stolen, and the fault therefore must be his own. He minimizes the loss to himself, but only to emphasize the more his own carelessness which warranted a greater punishment. 'It must, however, vex you – and deservedly, from the bad sign which it affords of me.'[1] What should have alarmed any discerning eye in such a confession is the evidence of an exacting perfectionism reinforced not simply by the desire to please but also by fear.

Such self-abasement over such a trifle must have occasioned unconscious humiliation and resentment against the father who was the source of it. But consciously he felt only guilt at his own shortcomings when measured against his father's perfection, as the letter shows. Nor are we without evidence that this tiny

[1] Bain, *John Stuart Mill: A Criticism*, 1882, p. 28

episode left the unconscious scar that has been inferred. As Mr St John Packe shrewdly observes, when on his father's death Mill received Ricardo's watch as an heirloom, he promptly gave it to his brother.[1]

But the strongest piece of evidence of the intense conflict with the father has been uncovered by Mr A. W. Levi in a passage quoted from Mill's earlier manuscript of his *Autobiography*, and omitted by him from the final draft as too frank for publication. Commenting on an evil common to sons of 'energetic fathers', namely that the child's own strength of will is apt to suffer from constant exposure to the supervision of a strong paternal will, he wrote, 'I was so much accustomed to be told what to do either in the form of direct command or of rebuke for not doing it that I acquired a habit of leaving my responsibility as a moral agent to rest on my father and my conscience never speaking to me except by his voice.' These are indeed bitter words; the revolt is open; and it is scarcely surprising that Mill in his maturity decided to exclude them from the published version of his *Autobiography*. In the light cast by this passage upon the sorrows of his youth, the vivid passage in *The Subjection of Women* touching upon the emotions inherent in the transition from boyhood to the responsibilities of manhood must be seen as a *cri de cœur*:

> Was it not like the physical effect of taking off a heavy weight, .. ?
> Did he not feel twice as much alive, twice as much a human being,
> as before? (p. 181).

This, then, is the background to Mill's mental crisis at the age of twenty, when he was overtaken by a mood of acute and prolonged depression, accompanied by mental obsession. His despair with himself, his philosophy, his purpose in life, never left him for more than a moment. 'I carried it with me into all companies, into all occupations. Hardly anything had power to cause me even a few minutes' oblivion of it. For some months the cloud seemed to grow thicker and thicker.'[2] At the same time his conscious mood was suffused with a vague sense of guilt. His own description provides a significant and apt comparison,

---

[1] cf. *Life*, p. 51
[2] *Autobiography, op. cit.*, p. 114

'the state, I should think, in which converts to Methodism usually are, when smitten by their first "conviction of sin" ' (p. 113). He emphasizes too his strong sense of isolation, the fear from having no one to whom he could turn for understanding of his plight, least of all to his father. For behind his distress lay the long years of childhood's emotional isolation, when his only playmates were his brothers and sisters, to whom themselves he had always stood in the relation of monitor and pupil. His childhood must have known in even fuller measure the solitude and secret sorrow to which de Quincey bore eloquent testimony:

> Deep is the solitude of millions who, with hearts welling forth love, have none to love them. Deep is the solitude of those who, under secret griefs, have none to pity them. Deep is the solitude of those who, fighting with doubts or darkness, have none to counsel them. But deeper than the deepest of these solitudes is that which broods over childhood under the passion of sorrow.[1]

And in the midst of his forlorn, intelligibly self-pitying state, there often occurred to his thoughts the words of Macbeth to the physician. Again, it is perhaps not without significance that he does not quote Macbeth, leaving the reference oblique, although he readily quotes Coleridge's lines beginning 'A grief without a pang . . .' as exactly illustrative of his emotional state. For Macbeth went unerringly to the heart of the matter:

> Canst thou not minister to a mind diseased;
> Pluck from the memory a rooted sorrow; . . ?

Can there be any further doubt as to the nature of Mill's rooted sorrow? The nature of the conflict with the father is clear beyond doubt; what lurks in much greater obscurity is the wound in the relation with the mother, a wound which went so deep that Mill could not bring himself to make a single reference to her in the published version of the *Autobiography*.

(iv) *The Subjection of Women*

To understand Stuart Mill's unusual insight into the sources of human character as well as the limitations of his outlook, it is

---

[1] *Autobiography of Thomas de Quincey*, 1950 ed., p. 32

necessary to look further than the evidence of the *Autobiography*. Already in 1838 he had sufficiently emancipated himself from the pure milk of Benthamism to note the inadequacies of the hedonistic calculus as a measuring rod. It would do well enough to detect the moral error in such acts as murder, arson or pillage, but it was far too blunt an instrument to serve as a moral yard-stick of intimate human relations of a family or sexual character, which Mill rightly saw as 'facts in human life which are liable to influence the depths of the character.'[1] In his mature work we see how far he advanced his understanding of close personal relations and their influence on character. *The Subjection of Women* was written in 1861 and published in 1869. Most of his work bears the stamp of his own time so clearly that it has been superseded by subsequent research or changed perspectives. *On Liberty* endures because it memorably restated an abiding truth; but *The Subjection of Women* was ahead of its time, and to some extent is still so. It was bitterly assailed by contemporaries; and of all his work of abiding value it has suffered most neglect.

On its first appearance it was attacked by an anonymous reviewer in *Blackwood's Magazine*, of which the following extract is a fair sample: 'His intense arrogance, his incapacity to do justice to the feelings or motives of all from whom he differs, his intolerance of all but his own disciples, and lastly, in natural consequence of these qualities, his want of playfulness in himself and repugnance to it in others, all combine to create something like antipathy.'[2] Sir James Fitzjames Stephen's comment, 'a work from which I dissent from the first sentence to the last',[3] was doubtless to be expected.

> There is something – I hardly know what to call it; indecent is too strong a word, but I may say unpleasant in the direction of indecorum – in prolonged and minute discussions about the relations between men and women, and the characteristics of women as such. I will therefore pass over what Mr Mill says on this subject with a mere general expression of dissent from nearly every word he says.[4]

But even Professor Bain, friend and biographer of Mill,

---

[1] *Mill on Bentham and Coleridge*, ed. F. R. Leavis, 1950, p. 71
[2] *Blackwood's Magazine*, Vol. CVI, July-December 1869, p. 320
[3] Bain, *op. cit.*, p. 131
[4] Fitzjames Stephen, *Liberty, Equality, Fraternity*, 1873, p. 206

commented incredulously, 'he leads us to suppose that the relations of men and women between themselves may work upon a purely voluntary principle.'[1] Twenty-three years after Mill's death, Frederic Harrison, the distinguished positivist, in an appreciation of Mill in *The Nineteenth Century*[2], appeared to find difficulty in restraining himself on this painful subject: 'The subjection of women is a mere hysterical sophism in itself. The remedy proposed to cure it is rank moral and social anarchy.'

Mill was obviously touching a hypersensitive nerve. Why was this? At one level, the explanation is obvious enough. Much of Mill's argument demonstrates the potential equality of women with men in vocational and professional terms in order to open the gates of employment to them on the same terms as men. This side of the case led directly in the political field to the whole suffragette campaign. The prolonged and frequently bitter struggle finally overcame all resistance; and the main aims were attained. The right of women to compete with men in virtually every form of employment not exclusively dependent on physical strength is no longer a matter of serious controversy. Nor is there need to speculate what might be achieved by women given equality of opportunity in education. The facts are there for all to see. Mill's book has dated by the very success of his arguments. This part of the book, trite though it may now seem, remains an eloquent testimony to the climate of opinion in which Mill was required to argue. That he in no wise exaggerated the power and prejudice of contemporary masculinity is evidenced by the anonymous *Blackwood's* reviewer:

> In the world, as we and all mankind that has preceded us have known it, women under no conceivable circumstances can have the law on their side but by the permission of men; therefore they seem to us to act wisely by owning a natural law of subordination, and submitting to 'subjection' as a Bible word. . . .[3]

Mill's choice of title was deliberate and went to the heart of his subject. He was not just discoursing upon the ancient theme of the attributes of the sexual category. He did believe that the

---

[1] Bain, *op. cit.*, 1882, p. 130
[2] *The Nineteenth Century*, September 1896, p. 501
[3] *Blackwood's Magazine, op. cit.*, p. 316

blanket label of sex was used to conceal and stifle at birth the richness and diversity of human creativity. But he was also challenging at the deepest level the very notion of 'woman', in her social and personal roles. Frederic Harrison was right, when he noted:

> *The Subjection of Women*, however, is not a simple sermon against male arrogance. It is a systematic effort to recast the whole form of our domestic, social, and political life, and, as such, it must be judged.[1]

The *Blackwood's* reviewer clearly thought he had disposed of the matter by observing: 'He exactly corresponds to the lunatic who proved logically that all the rest of the world was insane. It is nothing to him that mankind from the beginning has seen the matter in another light.'[2]

The reviewer was right in grasping the extreme radicalism of Mill's position. Doubtless there is also a strong *prima facie* case of error where a man claims to be the only member of the regiment who is in step; although, if the rule were infallible, no advance in human knowledge or ethical understanding would ever have been possible. Mill had in fact made a profound and revolutionary discovery at the heart of our society. The force of the resistance he touched off only confirms this. But the implications of what Mill had grasped went deeper than even he realized.

The insight was weakened by its polemical force. To make an impression on such a stolid wall of prejudice, it was necessary to evoke strong emotions. It became a dearly cherished Magna Charta which young girls kept under their pillows for years to come in many parts of the world. But the polemic gets in the way of the vision. The institution of contemporary marriage, which is his real subject, he dissects admirably up to a point. But beyond that point he cannot go because of his emotional commitment, the *parti pris* of a modern Galahad taking up the cudgels on behalf of an outraged class of people, viz. one half the human species. No doubt social therapy required a militant attempt to break through the armoury of male arrogance. But the temp-

---

[1] *The Nineteenth Century, op. cit.,* p. 501
[2] *Blackwood's Magazine, op. cit.,* p. 309

tation is to overlook the complicity of the other sex; and thus to fail to see that the real problem is a cultural one in which both sexes are corrupted in different but equally crippling ways.

The book's strength lies in its awareness that the quality of the marital relationship has effects which ramify into every aspect of the life of society. The thesis is that the existing marital relationship is one of subordination of the female to the male; that such a relationship is morally indefensible; that this moral defect is the *fons et origo* of all the moral deficiencies of the greater society; and that until it is remedied and put on a basis of complete equality, it will be vain to look for any appreciable measure of human advancement in other spheres. 'We have had the morality of submission, and the morality of chivalry and generosity; the time is now come for the morality of justice.'[1] Existing sexual relations are an anachronistic survival in a society whose needs are no longer met. The consequences of this relationship are then traced for the male, the female and the children of the union.

The portrait of the male in particular is exceptionally well done, wholly convincing, and the unflattering verisimilitude of the portrait so near the bone that few male readers could have failed to recognize something of themselves. This itself would explain some of the hostility the book aroused. Mill drew from life; the portrait is of the bourgeois Victorian male. The lot of women delivered over to that large number of men who are 'little higher than brutes' is a conjecture that evokes in him a scarcely repressed shudder. This aspect of the question, touching on unplumbed depths of human misery, strikes him as so appalling as to require no further argument.[2] He proceeds to dissect the more subtle effects of bourgeois marriage upon the males of the society in which he was himself nurtured. Here he could speak from first-hand knowledge.

No doubt there are families which exemplify the ideal to which the institution is supposed to conform. But such families, working by the light of sympathy and self-forgetfulness, are rare exceptions. Much oftener the pattern of family life stems from the fact that the husband is the linchpin of the institution. All other members derive such rights as they may enjoy from the fact

---

[1] *The Subjection of Women*, 1869, pp. 79–80
[2] *ibid.*, pp. 64–5

that they are felt to reflect the man's own interests and become extensions of his own personality, so to speak. Under these conditions, the family, far from being a civilizing institution inculcating gentler *mores*, is a 'school of wilfulness, overbearingness, unbounded self-indulgence, and a double-dyed and idealized selfishness, *of which sacrifice itself is only a particular form*' (pp. 66–7, my italics), 'a school of despotism, in which the virtues of despotism, but also its vices, are largely nourished' (p. 81). The corrosive effect upon the character of the male of this universal assumption of his primacy over the female is brilliantly portrayed. Power and privilege corrupt heads of families as they corrupt all privileged groups or persons. Men require no encouragement in the art of learning self-adulation. Whereas respect for society and fear for our standing in the eyes of others inhibit the worst forms of male behaviour in public, these checks cease to apply in the privacy of the home. It is here that the man feels free to vent his power over those entrusted to his care without the restraints associated with public shame. 'Even the commonest men reserve the violent, the sulky, the undisguisedly selfish side of their character for those who have no power to withstand it' (p. 66). Further, this egocentric assumption that the male is more important than those who are dependent upon him is self-perpetuating. The male child in the family subject to the *patria potestas* feels the brunt in his own person, but he is quick to detect that his subjection is temporary only. For one day he too will become eligible to join this privileged class of male adults. The seeds of superiority consciousness and consequent corruption are thus sown very early in the mind of the male child. Since his entire culture is saturated in assumptions of male superiority, he is permeated with its implications from his earliest days. If he does not quickly sense it for himself, he will be infected by his school-mates with the idea that he is of greater consequence than his sisters, before long than his mother, and then by process of development than of the woman whom he will eventually honour by marriage.

'Is it imagined', asks Mill rhetorically, 'that all this does not pervert the whole manner of existence of the man, both as an individual and as a social being?' (p. 150). He is corrupted as any despot or hereditary monarch is by the heritage of absolute power over his subjects. The vassal may be abased by his servitude; but the lord's character is even more gravely affected in its moral wholeness by the power to hold in servitude. The harshness of this relation inside marriage is normally concealed by the emollient influence at work in our society and by the intimacy of the marriage tie. But the kind of emotion that is not based on freedom and equality is a spurious 'love of freedom'. However close the intimacy, when it is combined with overlordship it can only be productive of a sentiment that is not 'the genuine or Christian love of freedom'. Mill's insight into character is perspicacious enough to grasp that the love of freedom on the lips of many a libertarian is often a veiled expression of 'an intense feeling of the dignity and importance of his own personality' (p. 82). This must be so, where the libertarian in his personal family life is a despotic father and husband. Nor is this a trite observation. It is still not the practice to submit the authenticity of the libertarian's public claims to this kind of test. But Mill did not push the analysis further to inquire in what way the assumption of greater right by one person in relation to another necessarily corrupts the wellsprings of spontaneous affection. That marital and paternal 'love' are not compatible with the concept of *patria potestas* Mill grasped, though not very surely. But he was far from grasping its full consequence.

If marriage grounded on the principle of authority and subordination corrupts the male, what are its consequences for the female? *The Subjection of Women* is primarily a plea for equality; indeed, although Mill is best known for *On Liberty*, he has not been excelled in the cogent persuasiveness of his statement of the egalitarian case.

> ... the only school of genuine moral sentiment is society between equals [p. 79].... But the true virtue of human beings is fitness to live together as equals; claiming nothing for themselves but what they as freely concede to everyone else; regarding command of any kind as an exceptional necessity, and in all cases a temporary one; and preferring, whenever possible, the society of those with whom leading and following can be alternate and reciprocal [p. 81].... What is needed is, that it [the family] should be a school of sympathy in equality, of living together in love, without power on one side or obedience on the other [p. 82].

The vindication of this plea is seen in the corruption of the one who wields command and the violation of right in the one compelled to submit. The picture Mill presents of woman and the effect upon her of her marriage role is accordingly an impassioned plea for liberty. His intense sympathy with this subject irradiates the more memorable passages of the book. At the same time it affords him a penetrating insight into the manner of female adjustment to her marital situation.

He observes that most people experience difficulty in realizing that others are as sensitive to grievance as they themselves are. The need for law arises in the first instance from the frequency with which the individual seeks to make an exception to the general rule in his own case. While people are quick to resent injustice in their own person, their powers of imagination and sympathy are rarely adequate to the task of apprehending that others feel much the same way as they themselves do when subjected to like injustice. The love of freedom, of unimpeded scope to realize the self's goals, is inherent in all people and in all nations, unless it is utterly crushed by the instruments of coercion and fear. What nation would voluntarily exchange its freedom for guarantees of increased prosperity and efficient administration at the hands of some other nation? What man would consent to submit himself to another's complete control for whatever gain? Let him recall his own childhood tutelage and recall the joy with which he embraced manhood and the chance to be responsible for his own life at last. 'Was it not like the physical effect of taking off a heavy weight, or releasing him from obstructive, even if not otherwise painful, bonds? Did he not feel twice as much alive, twice as much a human being, as before?' (p. 181). What consummate egoists men must be to remain blind to the fact that women must react just as they themselves would, if denied this basic freedom? Women are also human beings; and as such must experience frustration and resentment by living in a permanent state of tutelage to men, a state in which the husband is the legal successor to the father, her first keeper. Mill admits that this resentment may not be visible on the surface. Women are schooled by convention, long discipline and a sense of inevitability to suppressing and concealing such emotions. They may not even recognize them as such. Given the power of the existing ideal of woman's feminine role over the imagination, such emotions may well be rigorously repressed. Nevertheless, Mill insists, weakness, when deprived of liberty, cannot yield to power without psychic tension. The resentment is merely driven underground with harmful effects upon the character. As he puts it, 'the internal principle remains, in a different outward form.' The energies, dammed up in this way, will seek some other outlet. In the absence of freedom, that outlet will be the quest for power. 'To allow to any human beings no existence of their own but what depends on others, is giving far too high a premium on bending others to their purposes. Where liberty cannot be hoped for, and power can, power becomes the grand object of human desire . . .' (pp. 181–2).

To have discerned the relation between woman's subordinate social role and the depth of the female craving for power was no mean analytic feat on Mill's part. The question then arises: what form does the urge to power take? Mill unfortunately does not realize how important this question is. He dismisses it very briefly in terms which anticipate Tolstoy's fulminations against the ingenuity with which woman bedecks her sexuality to captivate and dominate the male (cf. *The Kreutzer Sonata*). This frustration of the desire for liberty and its sublimation into the channels of power is, according to Mill, the explanation of woman's interest in coquetry, sartorial elegance and pre-occupation with physical beauty, and all the social evils which allegedly result. Mill's rather arid asceticism here finds expression in phrases like 'mischievous luxury and social immorality'. Nevertheless, the passage concludes with a statement of the principle of equality, of which only a nature so generous and disinterested as Mill's would have been capable: 'The desire of power over others can only cease to be a depraving agency among mankind, when each of them individually is able to do without it: which can only be where respect for liberty in the personal concerns of each is an established principle' (p. 182).

What Mill did not see, indeed *could* not see (since had he done so, he would have been a different person), was that one of the commonest channels for a married woman's appetite for power is to be found in her relations with her children. This is the most obvious source of relief and compensation for a mother who is disappointed of self-realization, and whose energies cannot flow freely outwards on equal terms with others. This is the relationship which is the obvious target for corruption by emotions soured and starved in the marital and social roles by the principle of female subordination. The children can so easily become living objects for the receipt of 'affections' compounded of disappointed pride or crushed self-respect or rejected love. Under what more innocent cloak than maternal love could such bruised and thwarted emotions find a seemingly more legitimate release? Had Mill been able to take this further analytic step, he would have let in a flood of light upon his own personal conflicts. His own resistances were far too powerful to permit him to do so. Hence also his inability to elucidate the problem which Fitzjames Stephen rightly saw to have embarrassed Mill throughout the book, namely, that women themselves were generally indifferent where not actually hostile to his crusade on their behalf.

Mill's explanations that the individual woman dare not resist because she is exposed to the retribution that might follow from her lord; that generations of women have been educated by men to conceive as their primary role the duty of submission, to live through others, to be pliant and yielding, are by no means irrelevant. But they do not get to the root of the matter. They might account for women's apparent indifference to pleas for equality. But why are women's fear and resistance often as strong as men's, or stronger, if they feel the existing relation to be genuinely threatened? When healthy and sound emotions are denied a valid outlet, it is not normally the case that they continue to beat against the barrier impeding them until they have overcome it. Thwarted in one direction, they seek to find substitute expression through whatever outlets are available. As Mill correctly sees, the female who is denied by birth the normal freedom permitted to persons born as males will seek power as a surrogate. The fact that this form of object identification is incompatible with psychic health, genuine human affection and development to full maturity, can only be revealed by deep and prolonged analysis. Because power has developed as a necessary compensation in maintaining the balance of the existing psychic structure, the individual feels a threat to her ability to express her desire for power as a threat to her fundamental emotional stability. In other words, women, denied the rewards of psychic freedom, develop a strong interest in preserving such opportunities for psychic power as they have been able to forge for themselves.

(v) *Samuel Butler: The Reluctant Son*

The final case study concerns Samuel Butler, a classic example of a son imprisoned within the bonds of paternal affection. Many men have to suffer a power over them which they resent. But it is given to few to be able to nourish and sustain such resentment through a lifetime, and then to bequeath it posthumously as a literary legacy to posterity. Butler hated his father from earliest childhood, and took his revenge in the unforgettable portrait of Theobald in *The Way of All Flesh*. This celebrated quarrel has attracted its full share of attention and has been generally well enough understood. But I do not believe that the weakness of Butler's moral judgement has been clearly seen to connect with his childhood experience at the hands of his parents. I shall rely largely, though not entirely, on the evidence of *The Way of All Flesh* (Everyman edition). For while the portrait of Theobald Pontifex almost certainly distorts and exaggerates the defects of Canon Butler, there is little doubt that on the plane of psychological reality Theobald is an accurate portrait of the Canon as experienced and felt by his son.

In one aspect at least Samuel was admittedly just to his father. He presents Theobald as himself the victim in his own childhood of a tyranny comparable to that which he in his turn was to inflict on Ernest. 'Before he was well out of his frocks it was settled that he was to be a clergyman. . . . The boy's future destiny was kept well before his eyes from his earliest childhood. . . .' (pp. 25–6) Theobald's very profession must have represented an unconscious reminder of the full brunt of his own father's power. Even marriage he stumbled into half against his will, under the joint pressures of his own inexperience and another's need. For the woman who chose him is a characteristic daughter of a Victorian parsonage, for whom marriage offers both a profession and an urgently needed escape from domestic boredom. Theobald, with all his deficiencies, ponderous, complacent, self-centred, is the means of her deliverance. To hold his allegiance she is more than ready to give in return a submissive and uncritical adulation of her lord. In this way the bonds of marital stability are forged, but at a price for herself and her offspring not within her capacity to foresee or compute. For while Samuel was quick to fasten on the egregious vanity concealed within his mother's compensatory fantasy life, at no point does he reveal an awareness that her daydreams constituted the only outlet for the frustration involved in her total subordination to the will and wishes of her husband. Emotionally he must of course have sensed this, and that is doubtless why the full measure of his venom is reserved for his father.

The real nature of the relations between his parents is skilfully brought out in the description of the commencement of the honeymoon. Christina is genuinely scared of having to take command of the dinner arrangements at the hotel where they are to break their journey, and tearfully begs to be excused. Theobald reacts out of instinct to this crossing of his desires on a matter as important as his stomach by falling into a prolonged sulk – a weapon which to his gratification turns out to be entirely successful. His bride capitulates entirely: Theobald has begun to savour the first fruits of domestic power and finds them sweet. This modest experience is sufficient for his essentially timid soul to become alive to the possibilities inherent in successful self-assertion. 'He had conquered in the first battle, and this gives great prestige. How easy it had been too! Why had he never treated his sisters in this way? He would do so next time he saw them; he might in time be able to stand up to his brother John, or even his father' (p. 51).

Christina remained at all times a loyal and devoted wife, and expected her children in their turn to find their highest duty in obedience to her lord. Although, as even Butler grudgingly admits, his mother was fond of him, such warmth as there originally was could not survive the atmosphere generated by the unquestioning obedience to the head of the household. By flattering his vanity and humouring his every whim, by urging her children to regard him in this light also, she sought to maintain intact her own position. She was no doubt genuinely surprised and hurt to find that her son for his part did not seem to acknowledge the gratitude he ought to have felt, nor find his first duty in studying his father's happiness. While he did not fear his mother as he did his father, he detected within her breast the same determination to make him feel guilty for his inability to accept his mother's uncritical picture of her own and his father's virtues. There was the same unwillingness to recognize that he was an autonomous being with the right to develop independent wishes and feelings of his own. She felt a genuine affection for him nevertheless, and so 'it was long before she could destroy all affection for herself in the mind of her first-born. But she persevered' (p. 77).

Allowing for the bitterness, Butler is shrewd enough to see that the root of the conflict with his parents lay in his struggle to protect his own individuality from the imperiousness of their wills. He understands clearly enough that behind the maternal or paternal solicitude lurks their own will to power, which finds expression in a concern lest the offspring should develop along lines with which they are unfamiliar or of which they actively disapprove. 'It is this', he says, 'that is at the bottom of the whole mischief' (p. 93). Such behaviour springs in part from the personal characters, partly from studied policy. What Butler did not perceive is that it also springs directly from deficiencies in the marriage relation itself. The whole subject aroused in him too great an aversion for sympathetic consideration of the nature of the problems involved. His childhood experience of both the marital and parental institutions was such as to leave him with a passionate lifelong determination to steer well clear of either. The Victorian family as depicted by Butler is essentially an unholy alliance between an overbearing but petty patriarch and a vain adulatory consort for the purpose of deceiving their offspring as to the real nature of their parents and of a society composed of them and their like. 'It would have been better perhaps if she had not so frequently assured her husband that he was the best and wisest of mankind, for no one in his little world ever dreamed of telling him anything else, and it was not long before he ceased to have any doubt upon the matter' (p. 60). And in the letter to her children before her confinement, to be delivered only in the event of her death, which Butler was unkind enough to print verbatim, Christina wrote of her spouse: 'You know . . . how he has devoted his life to you and taught you and laboured to lead you to all that is right and good. Oh, then, be sure that you *are* his comforts. Let him find you obedient, affectionate, and attentive to his wishes, upright, self-denying, and diligent; let him never blush for or grieve over the sins and follies of those who owe him such a debt of gratitude . . .' (pp. 91–2). Butler was not of a forgiving disposition, but clearly he had much to forgive.

The reaction of the child Samuel in this family constellation was predictably ambivalent. It was peculiar in the intensity of the ambivalence. On the one hand, he feared a power which he felt at such close quarters, and whose pervasiveness he came to understand more fully the older he grew. This power he respected, wished to identify with, and on occasion deploy against others weaker than himself, even as it had been used against him. On the other hand, he deeply resented, hated and feared this power, against which he strove and rebelled all his life long. But because he had smarted so much under it, he had learnt to fear it deeply; so although his revolt was bitter and sustained, it was also timid and covert.

A reading of *The Way of All Flesh* gives a new awareness of how stupidity and self-centredness backed by 'religious' authority can contrive a remarkable tyranny for creatures as vulnerable as children. The scene where Ernest's father requires him to pronounce 'Come' correctly is unforgettable. Calmly and deliberately Theobald raises the temperature of intimidation until the climax of the inevitable beating is reached. The episode has an authentic ring. Only a very great artist could have devised such a scene and Butler himself was the least imaginative of writers. The parents knew what was best for their children. They could not connect policies and values which they saw as reflections of their own rectitude with the egoism and promptings of personal convenience of which they were unconscious. The atmosphere of the Sabbath in particular, of children mumbling prayers, hymns and confessions to the watchful eye and ministering hand of a pompous and admonitory father, furnishes an even more damning indictment of that institution than that given by Dickens in his picture of the childhood of Arthur Clennam in *Little Dorrit*. The children, white and sickly; the family doctor hovering in attendance; the dosings with calomel; the prayers and hymns, the daily beatings: it is a memorable picture. And what made it worse was, as Butler carefully observes: 'All was done in love, anxiety, timidity, stupidity, and impatience' (p. 79). How, he asks, was it possible for any child to grow up in such an atmosphere without being stunted and warped in the process? If both physically and emotionally they

were pale and puny specimens, this is correctly diagnosed as a
condition of deprivation. Their complaint was *homesickness*.
'They were starving, through being overcrammed with the
wrong things.' And Nature accordingly took her revenge.

The child reacted through the twin emotions of fear and
anger; and the seeds of a lifelong character conflict were well
and truly laid. On the one hand, he craved affection, felt that his
parents' picture of his own shortcomings must be the correct
explanation of his failure to merit that affection, and suffered
guilt accordingly. This side of Ernest led to his own self-contempt
and distrust coupled with a powerful desire to identify with
strong people who wielded authority over others and were highly
regarded by their fellows. The evidence for this is strong and
comes through again and again:

> [Ernest] hated and despised himself for what he, as much as
> any one else, believed to be his cowardice. He did not like the boys
> whom he thought like himself. His heroes were strong and vigorous,
> and the less they inclined towards him the more he worshipped
> them. All this made him very unhappy. . . [p. 112].
>
> Much as he feared and disliked his father (though he still knew
> not how much this was), he had caught much from him; if Theo-
> bald had been kinder Ernest would have modelled himself upon
> him entirely, . . [p. 129].
>
> He held himself much too cheap, and because he was without
> that physical strength and vigour which he so much coveted, and
> also because he knew he shirked his lessons, he believed that
> he was without anything which could deserve the name of a
> good quality [p. 138].

He longed to be loved, but this was ruthlessly denied him. So
bruised and repelled, emotionally and spiritually starved, he
turns inwards in self-distrust, timidity, guilt and anxiety, ready
to acknowledge avidly and humbly any crumb of recognition
or acceptance that may be thrown his way. But accompanying
this was a deep resentment destined to consolidate itself into a
lasting hatred, from which emotion sprang in part his hyper-
sensitivity where issues of justice were involved. The whole book,
in addition to the countless controversies in which Butler the
adult involved himself, is a monument to that side of his nature
which flared up at regular intervals into open revolt. The conflict
was of explosive proportions.

What is interesting and remarkable is the degree to which Butler proved capable of analysing the true nature of his own unconscious conflict. It would seem more than probable that, had he lived sufficiently long, Butler might well have duplicated the love-hate relationship which he enjoyed with Darwin on the subject of evolution by a parallel one with Freud on the subject of psychoanalysis. Certainly when the date of Butler's authorship of *The Way of All Flesh* is taken into account, Butler's understanding of the mechanism of unconscious conflict seems unusual. The point is never developed, but it is made repeatedly clear that Butler knew something of the process whereby his own energies were drained by unconscious conflict. Although parental power seemed rather less forbidding the older he became, nevertheless the watchful eye, the protective hand never ceased to hover anxiously above him, depriving him of any real sense of freedom. Is it to be wondered at, he asks, if the boy 'wore often an anxious, jaded look when he thought none were looking, which told of an almost incessant conflict within?' (p. 168). Even more pointed reference is made to the nature of unconscious conflict, the mechanism of resistance, and its purpose to protect powerfully repressed knowledge. It occurs in the account of the bullying of Ernest by his parents over the matter of his schoolfellows' peccadilloes. He is subjected to unremitting pressure to divulge which of the boys at Roughborough indulge in smoking, drinking and swearing. The parental probe continued until they 'were on the point of reaching subjects more delicate than they had yet touched upon. Here Ernest's unconscious self took the matter up and made a resistance to which his conscious self was unequal, by tumbling him off his chair in a fit of fainting' (p. 162).

The nature of the conflict has already been indicated. Butler himself spells it out quite clearly on more than one occasion. Part of him accepted the picture of the world as presented to him by his parents. The parents were both powerful and virtuous and therefore their power represented legitimate authority. If Ernest resented and feared that power, that must be because he, Ernest, unlike his parents, was not virtuous but naughty, and therefore merited the loss of affection of which he was all too painfully conscious. The wrath that was brought down upon his luckless head represented no more than his just deserts for resenting a power over him which was designed only for his own good. In short, part of Ernest wished to identify with Authority, to have it on his side, and to enjoy its privileges, blessings and securities. Deprived of these things, Ernest felt very insecure indeed. Moreover, he suffered agonies of inferiority and guilt: inferiority, because he despised himself for his fear of the power under which he suffered; guilt, because of his feelings that the parental power was good, and it was he who was naughty for resenting it.

> I have said more than once that he believed in his own depravity; never was there a little mortal more ready to accept without cavil whatever he was told by those who were in authority over him: he thought, at least, that he believed it, for as yet he knew nothing of that other Ernest that dwelt within him, and was so much stronger and more real than the Ernest of which he was conscious [p. 113].

Thus far the picture of his own emotional life is identical with the picture he has already sketched of his father's psychology; but in his father's case the unease occasioned by resistance was much weaker than in his own case, and the sparks scarcely had time to smoulder before they were finally snuffed out for ever. Theobald acquiesced, and became a tyrant in his turn. Speaking of his father's weak-kneed attempt to escape his enforced clerical destiny, Butler writes:

> No one believed in the righteousness of the whole transaction more firmly than the boy himself; a sense of being ill at ease kept him silent, but it was too profound and too much without break for him to become fully alive to it, and come to an understanding with himself. He feared the dark scowl which would come over his father's face upon the slightest opposition. . . . If he had ever entertained thoughts of resistance, he had none now, and the power to oppose was so completely lost for want of exercise that hardly did the wish remain; there was nothing left save dull acquiescence as of an ass crouched between two burdens [pp. 26–7].

A shrewd and not unsympathetic cameo of his father's state of mind. But in Ernest's case, the will to resist was not crushed; and the voice of the other Ernest spoke of a reality flatly opposed to his parents' vision of the world. According to that voice, Ernest was innocent, himself the victim of a power wielded over him and oppressing him. That voice whispered that this power, so far from being legitimate was a monstrous tyranny; and that it was only through a vast conspiracy compounded of fear and pretence and hypocrisy that the truth was prevented from being acknowledged and thus liberating all those who suffered under its sway. All that was necessary was the courage to speak the truth, to let this other voice struggling to find articulation have its say and to brave the consequences. This dumb Ernest struggled to translate these fleeting feelings in the background of consciousness into such words as these:

> You are surrounded on every side by lies which would deceive even the elect, ... the self of which you are conscious, your reasoning and reflecting self, will believe these lies and bid you act in accordance with them. This conscious self of yours, Ernest, is a prig begotten of prigs and trained in priggishness; I will not allow it to shape your actions, though it will doubtless shape your words for many a year to come. Your papa is not here to beat you now ... [p. 114].

But even as he utters this injunction to himself to listen to and obey this voice, the voice of his *true self*, it is followed by imprecations against his father none the less violent for being couched in the theological idiom. In fact, the adult Butler never was able to rid himself of this conflict; and he continued to the end desirous of reaping the fruits of both worlds. Self-centred, craving affection, seething with resentment at the injustice of his non-acknowledgment and isolation, he remained a tormented lonely, unprepossessing figure, at once shy and timid, yet also courageous and capable of venom. Of Theobald's parishioners he writes, in the paradoxical style so dear to him, that 'they would have been equally horrified at hearing the Christian religion doubted, and at seeing it practised' (p. 56). Butler certainly was clear-minded enough and in part at least generous enough to understand and respond to the vision of the crown of thorns; but his own crushed affections led him to protest overmuch his attachment to the thirty pieces of silver.

> How blest the prudent man, the maiden pure,
> Whose income is both ample and secure,
> Arising from consolidated Three
> Per Cent Annuities paid quarterly.

Butler's is a generous nature turned sour in childhood; and the fruits of his conflict found expression in the literary style of satirical paradox. For satire is the weapon of those who resent the world's injustice, feel the need to resist it, but lack the courage to do so openly and directly without equivocation. Mrs R. S. Garnett puts it very well when she observes that Butler was a man of extreme sensibility, but that he was lacking in moral robustness. 'I will not say courage, for if in his whole age there was anyone who stood up more resolutely against vested interests and powers and potentates and the whole weight of the world's opinion, I do not know his name.'[1]

The trouble was that he could not reconcile himself to this fate, and never ceased to repine at the injustice of his fate in not being loved by those whom he assailed. Ridden by a conflict he never resolved, he could never be wholly sure of himself. He was accordingly unduly self-assertive and aggressive in controversy, arrogant and self-righteous in his own turn, and resorting ever and again to the irony that he needed as a protection against a world that he felt had used him hardly. Self-distrusting, timid, desperately· wanting to be strong and independent, he craved applause, admiration, security and profits that he did not get. This left him sore and frustrated, preoccupied generally with himself. Despite all his achievements – and they were of a substantial nature: *The Way of All Flesh* is established as a minor English classic, whose standing is not likely to diminish with the years – in spite of everything, he remained like his American contemporary, Henry Adams, a figure critical, acrid, haunted by feelings of failure and rejection.

This is the conflict which explains Butler's deficiencies as a moralist. He combines a sharp awareness of the nature of the ills which distort human behaviour with a cynicism always ready to jibe at the simple-mindedness of those who quixotically seek to assail those ills. He has suffered at the hands of the strong; but in the last resort he has no doubts as to where he stands. It is with his oppressors. He hates his father, but his hero is Towneley,

---

[1] *Samuel Butler and his family relations*, 1926, p. 130. Butler himself put it quite laconically and accurately in a letter written about three years before his death:

'I never write on any subject, unless I believe the opinion of those who have the ear of the public to be mistaken, and this involves as a necessary consequence that every book I write runs counter to the men who are in possession of the field; hence I am always in hot water.'

rich, respected, insouciant, a snob. He paints his grandfather, the headmaster of Shrewsbury, as a larger-scale scoundrel than his less worldly father; but he concludes his life with a biography of this same grandfather as a paragon of the most solid virtues, and is particularly delighted when Gladstone himself politely commends it. His connection with Miss Savage, which he found invaluable to his self-esteem and creative powers, was based on an affinity of clear-sightedness where the world's foibles and follies were concerned. But after she was dead, lest anyone should read too much into his association with this gifted and generous lady, he was at pains to tell the world that she was lame and short, ugly and lonely, in sonnets at once grotesque, clever and cruel. His writing is marked by the inability to make unqualified, unequivocal exposure of the ills he so effectively describes. Wrongdoing he pillories only to add immediately that that does not mean that he himself is to be numbered among the naïve souls who believe that they should resist it. Many examples could be given. At his worst, this can find expression in such aphorisms as: 'Pleasure, after all, is a safer guide than either right or duty' (p. 74); or: 'who but a prig would set himself high aims, or make high resolves at all?' (p. 313). 'I may seem to be attacking the abuses of the powerful', he seems to be saying, 'but don't misunderstand me, I am really on their side.' And for all his aggressiveness as a controversialist and the effectiveness of his exposure of much cant and pomposity, there is no doubt that basically he was on the side of those he attacked. At one point he writes, 'I grant that some men will find happiness in having what we all feel to be a higher moral standard than others. If they go in for this, however, they must be content with virtue as her own reward ...' (p. 73). 'To go in for' virtue is typical Butler: an uneasy, flippant cynicism always close to the surface. The point which the passage purports to make is that those who aspire should not grumble if the world's rewards do not fall to their lot. They cannot have it both ways. It is quite true that God and Mammon do not admit of a common service. And it is well that there should be those who understand this and take the nobler course. But lest we infer from this that the service of 'God' rather than 'Mammon' is our clear and manifest duty, Butler hastens to add that while it is well that there should be some who 'go in for this sort of thing', it is decidedly not well that most

men should get it into their heads to do likewise. In short, a
little virtue goes a long way. And Butler is anxious lest there be a
danger of too many men acting virtuously. 'It is well there
should be some who think thus, . . . but it is not well that the
majority should leave the "mean" and beaten path. For most
men, and most circumstances, pleasure – tangible, material
prosperity in this world – is the safest test of virtue' (p. 73).
Progress is and ever has been achieved through addiction to
pleasure and not to what he chooses to call 'the extreme sharp
virtues'. As a moralist, Butler is at best flabby and timid,
and at worst he throws in his lot with the forces which inflict the
suffering which he so sharply bewailed when he was himself the
victim. He attacks the concept of the 'gentleman' for its preten-
tiousness, its cant, its dishonesty, but the essential reason which
he is anxious to make explicit is typical. 'Will being a gentleman,'
he said, 'bring me money at the last, and will anything bring
me as much peace at the last as money will?' (p. 319). Butler
can scarcely complain if posterity has seen fit to remember that
his last recorded words before he died were, 'Have you brought
the cheque book, Alfred?' And yet this is less than fair. For
Butler saw much of the truth, and something within him drove
him on to attack the errors of those in possession of the field,
even though he must have been aware that he was thereby
denying himself the possibility of the encomiums of the established and respected which his diffident nature so craved. Again
and again he selects the right target, only to falter and draw
back as soon as his sights are accurately trained upon it. For
example, on the question of moral conviction and the love of
truth, than which there can be no more important subject, he
writes, '. . . very few care two straws about truth, or have any
confidence that it is righter and better to believe what is true
than what is untrue, even though belief in the untruth may seem
at first sight most expedient. Yet it is only these few who can be
said to believe anything at all; the rest are simply unbelievers
in disguise' (p. 246). This is well said and, had it stopped there,
valuable. But of course it does not. Butler's imp, the other
Ernest, is waiting to pounce, to take back with one hand what has
been given with the other. He goes on, 'Perhaps, after all, these
last are right. They have numbers and prosperity on their side.
They have all which the rationalist appeals to as his tests of

right and wrong. Right, according to him, is what seems right
to the majority of sensible, well-to-do people; we know of no
safer criterion than this, . . .' So only a few care for truth. Why?
Because the truth conflicts with expediency. But then perhaps
expediency is truth after all. Why? Because on this side stand
most people, sensible, prosperous people, with whom we all
want to stand well. And yet, like a dog gnawing a bone, Butler
cannot leave it alone. It is the fraud that irritates him. He cannot
abide so many pretentious deceivers sitting in high places. It
outrages every iconoclastic impulse that is sharp within him. And
he proceeds in the next sentence to redress the balance yet again.
What does it all mean, then? 'Simply this, that a conspiracy of
silence about things whose truth would be immediately apparent
to disinterested inquirers is not only tolerable but righteous on
the part of those who profess to be and take money for being
par excellence guardians and teachers of truth.' Never did Butler
more accurately diagnose his own moral tragedy than when he
pictured his father's dilemma as that of 'an ass crouched between
two burdens'. The sins of the fathers are indeed visited upon the
children, but there is nothing of a supernatural or theological
character in this visitation. Its mechanism can be well enough
understood, if we take the trouble to disentangle the separate
emotional elements whereby neurosis is transmitted within the
ties of the family from one generation to the next. To understand
is not necessarily to forgive; but it is an indispensable first step
on the road to emancipation from thraldom to the weaknesses
of those who bore us. Butler thought to get loose by sustaining
his hatred and denouncing the source of his own self-contempt
to the last. And so the more he struggled, the more he remained
held fast.

4   The Divided Self

'MAN', SAID HAZLITT, 'is the only animal who laughs and weeps, for he is the only animal that is struck by the difference between what things are and what they ought to be.'

Much the same thought was in the mind of Nietzsche when he spoke of man as a sick animal – 'ein krankes Tier'. Man is complex because he is a divided creature. He has the appetites of an animal, but he is unable to give rein freely to them, without suffering guilt. He would like to be an animal, but he is handicapped by moral yearnings. Or, expressed conversely, he would like to be good, but he is handicapped by his animal nature. Although struck by the difference between what is and what ought to be, he finds it difficult to take action to make reality conform to the idealized picture present in his imagination. The result is the unhappiness inseparable from the tension of continuing conflict in a divided self. Action to remedy the deficiencies of reality runs counter to the powerful impulses of acquisitiveness and of domination. It also runs counter to the weight of inertia and the common human disposition to let sleeping dogs lie. On the other hand, acquiescence can itself only be purchased at a high price. While the voice of conscience, the sense of injustice may be stifled, it is difficult to extinguish it entirely in a human being.

The obvious way to preserve unity of a personality thus threatened, is to see reality through rose-coloured spectacles and/or reduce the level of moral aspiration. Freud's reverence for empirical truth did not permit him to recommend the former; he accordingly recommended the latter. Many people fall naturally into the habit of adopting both methods, and thus maintain a precarious equilibrium. Precarious, because vulnerable both in its hold on reality and in the rigour of its moral criteria. In childhood the human being's ability to maintain unimpaired his hold on the reality principle is most vulnerable. He has a profound emotional need for the love of both the people who shared the responsibility for giving him life. Yet he is not perhaps very likely to receive his due in this respect. Reality is accordingly experienced as something painful; and the process begins of escaping from that reality by self-deception. This process has been examined in some detail in the childhood of Elizabeth Barrett and of John Stuart Mill. We need now to examine at close quarters the struggle within the divided self of the adult striving to maintain his equilibrium within a culture as hostile in the main to his moral aspirations as his parents were defective in meeting his infant need for selfless love. The conflict is complex in its symptoms for it may take place at different levels of consciousness.

A common instance of conscious conflict occurs when our courage fails us when the time comes to implement a costly decision. The action taken in the event proves contrary to that originally decided upon. But although fear obtains the upper hand at the decisive moment, we may yet have the courage to acknowledge the truth of this to ourselves. Alternatively, we may find this truthful picture of ourselves too painful to our self-esteem to accept. At this point a variety of reasons present themselves to 'justify' the action in fact performed. These reasons appear convincing; and awareness of the moral deficiency in ourselves, namely fear, which gave rise to the reasons, is quickly suppressed and forgotten. In consequence the original conflict is strengthened by the self-deception concerning our own moral condition; and further energies will be called upon to repress this additional painful self-knowledge. With a little thought everyone can recognize signs of this process at work within themselves. Indeed, a person's moral character largely depends upon his ability to observe this tendency at work in himself in order to counter it by strict adherence to the reality principle, however painful the reality be to his self-esteem. The same process in reverse is much rarer in experience, but is of equal interest. I shall give one or two examples of where people find out not that they lack the courage of their convictions but that they lack the conviction of their cowardice or cupidity; and accordingly when the time comes they find themselves unable to act down to their own immoral intent. In other words, conscience proves more troublesome in the event than had been supposed. The case of Balaam provides a good illustration,

Balaam was summoned by Balak to curse the Israelites. In anticipation of the promised reward, Balaam came forward with every intention of fulfilling Balak's command. But in the event, Balaam, although put to the test three times, instead of cursing Balak's enemies, found himself blessing them – to Balak's intense indignation. On each occasion Balaam had genuinely intended to carry out Balak's wish. He not only failed to do so; he did the opposite. When challenged by the outraged Moabite monarch, he replied simply, and with authority, 'Must I not take heed to speak that which the Lord hath put in my mouth?' When put to the test, the voice of conscience proved to be a more powerful obstacle to Balaam's cupidity and desire to stand well with powerful opinion than he himself had been able to foresee. A comparable modern instance that comes to mind is an occasion in May 1864, in the House of Commons. Mr Gladstone was opposing on behalf of the Government a private motion to extend the borough suffrage to £6 householders. He had been strictly enjoined by Palmerston to avoid any statement which might be construed as a promise of reform on behalf of the Cabinet. Although it went against the grain of his own personal belief, Gladstone duly spoke against sudden or sweeping changes in the suffrage qualifications. But then, to the consternation of the Government Front Bench, came the famous pronouncement: 'I call upon the adversary to shew cause, and I venture to say that every man who is not presumably incapacitated by some consideration of personal unfitness or of political danger, is morally entitled to come within the pale of the constitution.' Palmerston had required him to speak against reform; he himself had intended to do so; Disraeli's comment was that he had revived the doctrines of Tom Paine.

In the above instances the conflict must have been very near to the surface to erupt so unmistakably. The emotional block in each case consisted of weighty considerations of worldly interest. Capable of generating a conflict of much greater tension is the emotion of fear, particularly the fear of the psychic power of a dominant personality. The children of both Edward Moulton Barrett and James Mill furnish excellent cases in point. In an adult world not renowned for its sympathetic insight into the child's mind children are weak and vulnerable. They naturally seek to protect themselves as best they can against superior forces they feel to be alien if not actually threatening. The weapons of self-deception, of repression or evasion, although morally debilitating, are often the only recourse available to a child in its weakness. The price paid by constant effort to appease the power of others is a gradual erosion of the ability to formulate and live with a truthful picture of reality. For the most part we are wholly unaware of what we are doing. At the conscious level it becomes second nature to behave and speak in such a way as not to arouse hostile emotions in powerful people. The normal tact of daily intercourse is frequently no more than the practised dissimulation of our real thoughts in order to avoid ruffling the suspected or intuited susceptibilities of others. If this practice is allowed to become habitual, the original thoughts may be rendered unconscious by desuetude and timidity. We begin quite unconsciously to succumb to another's power. Powerful or dominant personalities can thus harm weaker personalities with whom they come into close and habitual contact.

Sometimes an individual may gradually become alive to the nature of his psychic oppression at the hands of another. The forbidden ground, driven into unconsciousness through fear of the other's susceptibilities, begins to emerge to preconsciousness and eventually into the foreground of consciousness. At this point symptoms of acute tension arise in the hitherto apparently stable relationship. X, awakening to the significance of his obeying an unspoken taboo determined by Y's power, modifies his behaviour accordingly. Y then reacts sharply as he experiences the disturbing change in the balance of power, which threatens his existing psychic equilibrium. If it becomes apparent that this power is to be challenged and the conflict brought out into the open, the tension may assume explosive force. The one seeking liberation has to make a stupendous psychic effort to penetrate the barriers of fear. The other, faced with an unlooked-for threat to his power and self-esteem, tries desperately to shore up his psychic defences.

This situation has rarely been better portrayed in fiction than in a short novel that ante-dates Freud's own writings, namely, Henry James's spine-chilling enigma, *The Turn of the Screw*. The subject which is taboo between the governess and her young charge, Miles, is the reason for his dismissal from school. It is the

enigma concealing the clue to the mysterious communications
between the children and the ghosts of the depraved pair,
Peter Quint and Miss Jessel. The governess struggles to overcome
the resistance expressed in the unconscious dissembling of little
Miles. Her purpose is to confront the terror exercised by the
evil Quint and by bringing it into the open to destroy its evil
power. The tension of the conflict mounts unbearably until
the climax is reached when the governess is on the point of
victory, only to find that the shock of the catharsis has proved
lethally traumatic for the boy. James, with rare delicacy of
perception and skill in the evocation of atmosphere, portrays the
subtle effects on a relationship profoundly disturbed by unconscious conflict. The taboo subject is gradually forced into an
exposed position where its overt recognition cannot be long
delayed. At this point the governess uses a particularly striking
metaphor to describe her relations with the children:

> I do mean, on the other hand, that the element of the unnamed
> and untouched became, between us, greater than any other, and
> that so much avoidance could not have been so successfully effected
> without a great deal of tacit arrangement. It was as if, at moments,
> we were perpetually coming into sight of subjects before which
> we must stop short, turning suddenly out of alleys that we perceived
> to be blind, closing with a little bang that made us look at each
> other – for, like all bangs, it was something louder than we had
> intended – the doors we had indiscreetly opened. All roads lead
> to Rome, and there were times when it might have struck us that
> almost every branch of study or subject of conversation skirted
> forbidden ground.

This area of 'forbidden ground' arises out of the clash between
the pressures of the cultural environment on the one hand and
the moral strivings of the individual soul, on the other, as it strives
to maintain its own inner unity and self-respect. 'There is no
private life which has not been determined by a wider public life,'
wrote George Eliot in *Felix Holt, the Radical* (Ch. III). I propose
here to look at this conflict between private aspiration and public
pressure, its sources, symptoms and effects, in four separate
examples drawn from fiction. If the selection is the arbitrary
one of personal taste, the comparison may yet not prove un-
fruitful. The examples are Dickens's Dombey (1848) and Dorrit

from the 1850s, Tolstoy's Ivan Ilych from the 1880s, Sinclair
Lewis's Babbitt from the 1920s, and finally, Arthur Miller's
Willy Loman from the 1940s. These figures embrace Britain,
Russia and the United States; they extend over the last century
of our epoch. In each instance for comparative purposes something of the following aspects will be presented: the author's
critical reflections on his cultural milieu; the degree to which the
central character becomes aware of his milieu in these critical
terms; the resultant conflict in the hero between his critical
conscience and his vested resistances to the new picture of reality;
and finally, the denouement: emancipation or resignation,
victory or defeat for the moral conscience.

In the case of Dickens I have had recourse to two novels.
Dombey is a notable study of the corrosive effects of culture upon
character, but Dombey's eventual awakening is sudden,
mechanical and entirely unconvincing. In the case of Mr Dorrit,
there is no awakening, but the rendering of the internal struggle
with its momentary glimmerings of the truth is done with rare
poignancy. Dombey is Dickens's classic study of a human life
subjugated by pride. The novel has as its background Mr
Dombey's London business house, whose ruling values consist
of the narrow pursuit of commerce and the accumulation of
wealth. Money is the axis on which the life of that even greater
Midas symbol, Mr Merdle in *Little Dorrit*, revolves. But notwithstanding his macabre suicide, Merdle is a passive if not an
innocent figure, in whose ambience others wreak the havoc of
their will to power and acquisition. Dombey is driven by great
energy; he worships actively at the altar of commerce. His
tragedy is his monumental pride which prevents any spontaneity
or warmth from thawing the frozen well-springs of his nature.
He unbends sufficiently for an appearance of humanity in his
relations with his son, Paul, who, he hopes, will perpetuate his
name in the house of Dombey. There is delicate irony in the
famous scene in which Paul petrifies Dombey with his naïve
questions about the nature of money. In the depths of Dombey's
magisterial complacency there exist the faint stirrings of distant
unease. Even a Dombey within some recess of his being has to
acknowledge his kinship with humanity. Paul cannot resist the
inquiry why money, given its almighty power, did not save him
his Mamma. Can it be that money is cruel? Although Mr

Dombey reassures the child in shocked tones that 'a good thing can't be cruel', the child is not convinced. But he does not repeat his question, for he had detected his father's discomfort.

Dombey is a more than life-size caricature of what happens to a man consumed by the *animus dominandi*. Every relation he enters into is used to assert the grandeur of a reigning Dombey. He had so impressed the first Mrs Dombey with awe of his magisterial authority that she had withered and died. 'He had been "Mr Dombey" with her when she first saw him, and he was "Mr Dombey" when she died.' Need more be said? What aroused Dombey's admiration and drew him to the woman he made his second wife was precisely the pride which mirrored his own. By taking unto himself the *hauteur* of Edith he thought to double his own stature, only to find that it produced a head-on collision with a will as implacable as his own. His own pride, thus challenged, retreated into itself, sullen and unyielding.

> Who wears such armour too bears with him ever another heavy retribution. It is of proof against conciliation, love, and confidence! against all gentle sympathy from without, all trust, all tenderness, all soft emotion; but to deep stabs in the self-love, it is as vulnerable as the bare breast to steel.

Immured within the walls of his pride and vanity Dombey is put beyond reach of a genuine relation with another person. His growing isolation festers and turns to hate even the emotions he might be expected to feel for those nearest to him. 'With a dull perception of his alienation from all hearts, and a vague yearning for what he had all his life repelled,' he might have turned to the daughter whose love he had cruelly repelled. But Dombey can only respond to duty and submission, whereas Florence offers him gentleness and affection, the more to remind him of the contrast between her softening influence and his own impenetrability. His guilt inspires self-justification, 'a distorted picture of his rights and wrongs', and a continued estrangement from the living world by his self-inflicted and towering obduracy. For the house of Dombey and the pride of Dombey are sacrificed the love of wife and children, and in their place is reared the social circle of the Toxes, the Bagstocks and the Skewtons. The icy breath of Paul Dombey's frozen christening provides the keynote of the novel, as a symbol of all human relations that come within the Dombey ambience.

How far is Dombey aware of his situation? There are two occasions when Mr Dombey is brought face to face with the truth of his condition and his relations with others. The first arises out of the elephantine tactlessness of Cousin Feenix at Dombey's dinner table. He relates with naïve gusto the story of a loveless marriage undertaken by a girl in order to acquire property. The suggestion that they must have proved an ill-matched couple is met by the retort, '*She* is regularly bought, and you may take your oath *he* is as regularly sold.' 'In his full enjoyment of this culminating point of his story, the shudder which had gone all round the table like an electric spark struck Cousin Feenix, and he stopped.' The universally known but suppressed truth about Dombey, his real nature and his relations with his wife and family, is through social gaucherie forced into momentary exposure. There is a shocked silence. The only one to be outwardly unmoved by the episode was Dombey himself, who remained impervious. His features retained the 'mould of state' into which they had been cast that day; his only comment on the story being the solemnly enunciated 'Very good'.

The second occasion when Mr Dombey's self-deception is punctured is not an accident. It results from a servant's inability to suffer longer the outrage to her sense of justice. Susan Nipper, Florence's faithful attendant, like many of us in the immediate presence of Power, suppresses truth. But because she dearly loves her mistress, she has her point of no return when her indignation at Florence's treatment by her father can no longer be held in check.

> 'There ain't a person in your service, sir,' pursued the black-eyed, 'that has always stood more in awe of you than me and you may think how true it is when I make so bold as say that I have hundreds and hundreds of times thought of speaking to you and never been able to make my mind up to it till last night, but last night decided of me.'

Mr Dombey, sick in bed, is for the moment at the 'black-eyed's' mercy. He is obliged to listen to an honest account of the sufferings of his daughter at his hands. Mr Dombey reacts powerfully but it is the reaction of outraged pride manifested in paroxysms

of anger. Dickens's treatment of Dombey's psychological condition is external and superficial. Only once does he hint at the
depth of hidden conflict that must be present. He comments on
Dombey's relations with Florence:

> It may have been that in all this there were mutterings of an
> awakened feeling in his breast, however selfishly aroused by his
> position of disadvantage, in comparison with what she might have
> made his life. But he silenced the distant thunder with the rolling
> of his sea of pride. He could hear nothing but his pride. And in his
> pride, a heap of inconsistency, and misery, and self-inflicted tor-
> ment, he hated her.

Dickens's development was not yet adequate to portray hidden
conflict between a man's consciousness of his real character
and of his moral inadequacies.

For such an advance in understanding we must look to the
masterpiece of Dickens's maturity, *Little Dorrit*. As pride is
pilloried in *Dombey and Son*, so *Little Dorrit* arraigns the drive for
social status. William Dorrit is cast down into the shabby,
depraved world of the debtors' prison through the money power.
Through that same power he is raised to prestige and position.
But the consuming passion of Mr Dorrit's life is not to enrich
himself so much as to command deference. In the Marshalsea
he achieves this by his ostentatious pretension to gentility, by his
arrogance, and by the abandonment of his self-respect. By his
example he perverts those who through poverty and ignorance
are so accustomed to defer to those who assume the right to
command that they admire in their 'superiors' what is the
reverse of admirable.

> 'Why, perhaps you are not aware,' said Plornish [the plasterer
> of Bleeding Heart Yard], lowering his voice, and speaking with a
> perverse admiration of what he ought to have pitied or despised,
> 'not aware that Miss Dorrit and her sister dursn't let him [Mr
> Dorrit] know that they work for a living.'

William Dorrit may have come down in the world, but he will
not let it be thought that a Dorrit could so demean herself as
actually to work for a living. He is still the proud Father of the
Marshalsea with a position to keep up. Yet for all his false pride,

selfishness and snobbery, he is not entirely blind to the truth of his position. For this reason he is an altogether more complex and convincing creation than Mr Dombey. Dickens describes him mercilessly, the victim of his own vanity with the jail rot upon him. But he is lit by the glow of the author's compassion, and so he comes alive for us in a way that Dombey never does. We are permitted a glimpse of the struggle within, and we feel something of the dimensions of the tragedy of that pathetic wisp of humanity.

In return for the favour he confers by his gracious presence, Mr Dorrit levies what he euphemistically terms 'testimonials'. In the case of honest John Chivery, the son of the turnkey on the lock, the testimonials take the especially welcome form of cigars – a measure of generosity on John's part not entirely unconnected with his unrequited passion for little Dorrit. Meeting one day with unaccustomed shortness of manner on John's part, Mr Dorrit correctly associates it with the visit which in unaccustomed sartorial elegance he had just paid to Amy. Divining the rebuff his daughter must have administered, he tries to drop her a hint tactfully to refrain from being quite so candid with young John, to agree in fact to 'lead him on'. Little Dorrit could not find it in her heart to rebuke him, nor does she need to; she remains silent. The effect on Mr Dorrit was electric, and is portrayed in terms which reveal Dickens's remarkable powers of observation of human character.

> An uneasiness stole over him that was like a touch of shame; and when he spoke, as he presently did, it was in an unconnected and embarrassed manner. . . . While he spoke, he was opening and shutting his hands like valves; so conscious all the time of that touch of shame, that he shrunk before his own knowledge of his meaning.

For a moment the barriers are down, but Mr Dorrit's momentary honesty characteristically takes the form of maudlin self-pity. 'What does it matter whether such a blighted life as mine comes to an end, now, next week, or next year?' Conscious of his self-abasement, he seeks to justify himself before her in an outburst of retrospective self-idealization. Before his incarceration, the man her mother knew was a very different fellow, he tells little Dorrit, 'I was young, I was accomplished, I was good looking, I was independent – by God I was, child! – and people sought me out, and envied me. Envied me!' There follows a bout of euphoria in which he assures her of all those things he would have done for her, had his fortune turned out differently. His wish-fulfilments consist of projects of social aggrandizement. Little Dorrit would have married a gentleman, she would have ridden her own horse at his side, the multitude would have trudged deferentially in the dust beneath, and so forth. His mood fluctuates between despair and aplomb; and through her gentle patience he recovers by degrees his self-esteem. The author's diagnosis, accurate and unsparing, draws our attention to the ravening egoism at the heart of self-pity and self-deception. 'All this time he had never once thought of *her* dress, her shoes, her need of anything. No other person upon earth, save herself, could have been so unmindful of her wants.'

Mr Dorrit's humbug is never seriously threatened because of the social tact which generally accepts at face value people's own evaluation of themselves. Something of a social crisis is necessary to prick the bubble of his self-esteem. A moment occurs when even the long-suffering patience of brother Frederick is tried beyond endurance; and William Dorrit finds himself confronted by the truth of an honest and outraged conscience. The episode is reminiscent of Susan Nipper's confrontation of Mr Dombey. The occasion of Frederick Dorrit's revolt is long after the Dorrits have been released into the great world of Merdles and Barnacles, of Society and Wealth. Suddenly he, who knows full well the family's debt to little Dorrit, finds quite intolerable their patronizing of her in their new-found affluence, She is graciously permitted to visit her old friend Mrs Gowan, when the Gowan connection with the Merdles is revealed. Their ingratitude, snobbery and dishonesty, contrasted with the uncomplaining devotion and loyalty of Amy, suddenly spark even Frederick's crushed spirit into revolt.

> Brother! I protest against it! . . . Brother, I protest against pride. I protest against ingratitude. I protest against any one of us here who have known what we have known, and have seen what we have seen, setting up any pretension that puts Amy at a moment's disadvantage, or to the cost of a moment's pain. We may know that it's a base pretension by its having that effect. It ought to

bring a judgement on us. Brother, I protest against it in the sight of God!

William Dorrit is 'utterly discomfited'.

The pretension and falsity of Mr Dorrit's life are again illustrated in the London hotel scene when Mr Dorrit, fresh from his social triumphs in the City with Merdle himself, finds himself confronted by a ghost from the past in the shape of honest John Chivery. John has called to pay his respects and present Mr Dorrit with a modest gift of cigars for old times' sake. Mr Dorrit's wild outburst of anger, his complete loss of self-control, his brutal repulse of the young man's naïvely affectionate gesture, are followed by inevitable remorse and self-loathing. Mr Dorrit returns to the bosom of his family in Italy full of plans for further conquest including the marital conquest of Mrs General. But from the moment of the Chivery interview he steadily disintegrates. The shame of his position has been gradually and unconsciously gnawing at him. As he weakens, his confusion and moral decay grow more pronounced. The old world of the Marshalsea, so savagely and for so long repressed, forces its way slowly to the surface of the old man's mind, until he is finally no longer able to distinguish the past from the present. In his declining power and increasing irascibility, he projects his own condition on to his scapegoat brother, rebuking him for *his* age, his weakness, his tiredness, his inability to keep awake, his proneness to allow his articulate conversation to deteriorate into drivel. The evocation of the past and its eruption into the present at the great dinner where Mr Dorrit is on the brink of proposing to Mrs General is among the most brilliant achievements in all Dickens. The final collapse occurs when the old man makes his speech under the illusion that he is back in the Marshalsea addressing the collegians. In the course of the meal little Dorrit noticed that

> he all of a sudden looked at her, and looked about him, as if the association were so strong that he needed assurance from his sense of sight that they were not in the old prison room. Both times, he put his hand to his head as if he missed his old black cap – though it had been ignominiously given away in the Marshalsea . . .

At the final dissolution of the banquet he reverts to the prison completely and never recovers consciousness of his present state.

> Quietly, quietly, all the lines of the plan of the great Castle melted, one after another. Quietly, quietly, the ruled and cross-ruled countenance on which they were traced became fair and blank. Quietly, quietly, the reflected marks of the prison bars and of the zig-zag iron on the wall-top, faded away. Quietly, quietly, the face subsided into a far younger likeness of her own than she had ever seen under the grey hair, and sank to rest.

Mr Dorrit's long and unsuccessful struggle with the vanity he had generously assimilated from his culture was at an end. The truth from which he had fled all his life, crushed and battered and ignored for so long, finally forced its outraged way to the surface of Dorrit's decaying faculties, and asserted its ultimately unshakeable ascendancy.

Tolstoy in his *The Death of Ivan Ilych* presents us with the pro-foundest of all moralities for Everyman. Ivan Ilych was a judge, a member of the Court of Justice; the most memorable thing in his life was his dying at the age of forty-five. Ivan Ilych's life was commonplace, characteristic of multitudes; in his life the mirror of our daily lives is held up for inspection – with this difference. Whereas we accept our own routine existences with unreflecting equanimity, the mirror which Ivan Ilych holds up reflects a picture from which we shrink with fear and revulsion. Tolstoy succeeds as no one else has done in convincing us of the truth of his simple and awful thesis, that 'Ivan Ilych's life had been most simple and most ordinary and therefore most terrible'. We are reminded of Bernard Shaw's parallel observation in one of his Prefaces: 'Nothing that is admittedly and unmistakably horrible matters very much, because it frightens people into seeking a remedy: the serious horrors are those which seem entirely respectable and normal to respectable and normal men.'

What form did the ordinariness, conventionality and un-eventfulness of the life of Ivan Ilych take? Neither subservient nor a toady, he was yet not of independent disposition and mind. His duties in life he accepted uncritically from those of superior station. From early youth he 'was by nature attracted to people of high station as a fly is drawn to the light, assimilating their

ways and views of life and establishing friendly relations with
them.' If the fashion indicated a respect for things vain or sensual
or even liberal Ivan Ilych would sedulously conform, 'but always
within limits which his instinct unfailingly indicated to him as
correct'. Sometimes in the early years he did things which
troubled his conscience or even disgusted him, 'but when later
on he saw that such actions were done by people of good position
and that they did not regard them as wrong, he was able not
exactly to regard them as right, but to forget about them
entirely or not be at all troubled at remembering them.' With
such a capacity for comfortable adjustment and elasticity of
conscience, with antennae so delicately and quickly attuned to
sensing the currents of dominant opinion, Ivan Ilych was
admirably equipped to rise in the world and advance his career;
and this Ivan Ilych was most anxious to do.

He becomes an examining magistrate; and this proves an
interesting and attractive job because it gives him considerably
wider scope to enjoy the emotions inherent in wielding power
over others. Not that Ivan Ilych abused his power. On the contrary, he sought to wield it discreetly that it might not appear
harsh or too obvious, 'but the consciousness of it and of the
possibility of softening its effect, supplied the chief interest and
attraction of his office.' Ivan Ilych marries. As might be pre-
dicted, his wife has every virtue; she is pretty, very correct, and
well connected. He married her, of course, because he fell in
love with her but the fact that the marriage was approved by his
social circle was not indifferent to him. The marriage was
entirely successful until it met its first challenge. When his wife
became pregnant, she became irritable and jealous, and friction
developed between them. Ivan Ilych in self-defence retreated
more and more behind the protective wall of his official duties.
So assiduous is he in the pursuit of them that he becomes
Assistant Public Prosecutor and his work becomes even more
attractive. As for his domestic life, it was one of mutual exacer-
bation punctuated by episodic amorousness, 'islets at which they
anchored for a while and then again set out upon that ocean of
veiled hostility which showed itself in their aloofness from one
another'. And this situation he accepted with resignation
because it appeared to him inevitable and therefore normal.
There was always the retreat into professional affairs, made still

more conducive by still further promotion with its parallel increase in power and right to deference.

And then, all unprepared, at the height of his powers there comes to Ivan Ilych the terrible, premature sentence that he must shortly die. The course of his mysterious illness is as short as it is unheralded; and amidst great suffering Ivan Ilych's casual worldly life has to learn to adjust itself to the idea of its imminent dissolution. More than his physical suffering, which is very considerable, is the gnawing inescapable obsession with *It*, the knowledge that pursues him through every distraction and consolation, through every minute of the day and his intermittent sleep, the knowledge that he is doomed. But what torments him and poisons his closing days still more than his obsession with dying is the falsity with which he is surrounded. It is true that this falsity, this deception is no different from what it had always been, from what Ivan Ilych himself had always unconsciously practised. But now for the first time its real significance comes home to him in its full horror, for it succeeds in reducing to triviality not just his life but also his death. The way in which human beings customarily deal with facts that are painful or otherwise unacceptable is to deny them or, if this is not possible, to ignore them. The painful fact to be assimilated and managed in this instance is the forthcoming decease of Ivan Ilych, a fact on no account to be admitted or alluded to. Thus does Ivan Ilych find himself enshrouded in a world of protective falsehood and pretence. Everybody knows he is going to die; he knows he is going to die; they know he knows he is going to die; but the polite fiction must be maintained to the last that he is temporarily sick and in process of being cured. It is this enveloping, stifling aura of unreality and deception that tortures Ivan Ilych more than all else.

> The awful, terrible act of his dying was, he could see, reduced by those about him to the level of a casual, unpleasant, and almost indecorous incident . . . and this was done by that very decorum which he had served all his life long. He saw that no one felt for him, because no one even wished to grasp his position. Only Gerasim [an illiterate servant] recognized it and pitied him.

The hollowness of his daily relations with his own family, with whom he ought to have been most intimate, is a condition which habit had taught him to regard as normal. It now haunts him with the retribution of lonely isolation when the warmth of human emotion is the only thing that can help him. Instead he is surrounded by, and himself called upon to maintain, the stereotype behaviour demanded by the external conventional roles. As he throughout his professional life had assumed the lawyer's functionary pose to his clients, so now the doctor assumes his 'doctor-patient' relationship, and his wife the understanding, tolerantly affectionate marital role. All alike share in the falsity that accompanies the etiquette of middle-class relations. His wife, responding to what is required of her, sends for a specialist; and anticipating objections, silences them by the conventional assertion that she is really doing this for her own sake. Only Tolstoy's dry irony and candid observation could have produced the comment: 'Everything she did for him was entirely for her own sake, and she told him she was doing for herself what she actually was doing for herself, as if that was so incredible that he must understand the opposite.' Even her apparent concern for him masks her essential self-preoccupation. If she once permitted herself really to understand that he was dying, she would be called upon to face up to the full reality of the tragedy. She would have to meet him on the plane of his isolation and suffering, to confront his pathetic need for compassion and love. But, as she has been reared in false social values, these things are no longer within her competence.

At one point only is all the pretence jeopardized. The grim truth, so thinly veiled, thrusts its unwanted presence above the surface of polite discourse, threatening to command attention. His dying almost becomes real. The family have taken a box for Sarah Bernhardt, and they are dutifully spending a little time with the invalid, whose presence inconveniences them, but who cannot decently be altogether ignored. Conversation is of the theatre and appropriately trivial, 'the sort of conversation that is always repeated and is always the same'. They are so mindful of their chatter that at first they do not notice the invalid's growing indignation, but gradually his glittering eye freezes them one by one into uncomfortable but unmistakable silence. 'The silence had to be broken, but for a time no one dared to break it and they all became afraid that the conventional deception would suddenly become obvious and the truth become plain to all.' The conflict between the two planes of reality at this point almost erupts; but the family, sensing danger, recoil quickly before the flashpoint is reached.

But for Ivan Ilych in his extremity there is no recoil available. He, who like them has successfully evaded the reality of his submerged consciousness his life long, can do so no longer. In anguish and fear, alone and helpless, he is finally overcome; the last barriers of his self-pride are broken down; and he allows himself to look straight in the face the fundamental but hitherto tabooed question. Can he after all have been mistaken in the way he has conducted his life? As he passes it in review, the only part that he remembers vividly and with pleasure is his childhood; whereas the nearer he approaches to the present the more dubious and trivial become his pleasures. The inverse ratio between his capacity for worldly advancement and his capacity for joy becomes clear to him. 'It is as if I had been going downhill while I imagined I was going up. And that is really what it was. I was going up in public opinion, but to the same extent life was ebbing away from me.' What he finds most unbearable is the apparent futility, the meaningless absurdity of a life lived without joy and doomed to culminate in horrible agony at its mid-span. The idea not only shocks him; it leaves him incredulous. He simply cannot believe that it could be so. But the only alternative is to acknowledge that his life hitherto must have been governed by a wrong conception of its purpose. But this would imply that he had not lived as he ought to have done. And this was no less absurd, for he had manifestly done everything properly according to assumptions never called in question by any responsible person with whom he had ever come into contact. And so, comments Tolstoy, he 'immediately dismissed from his mind this, the sole solution of all the riddles of life and death, as something quite impossible.' But the conflict continues. Racked by his dilemma, he twists and turns now this way, now the other in increasing mental anguish as death approaches. His sufferings continue because the conviction goes deep that somehow his life might yet be justified. Tolstoy brilliantly evokes the tenacity with which even at the threshold of death the ego continues to resist the truth. Finally, however, Ivan Ilych succeeds in grasping his error.

It occurred to him that his scarcely perceptible attempts to struggle against what was considered good by the most highly placed people, those scarcely noticeable impulses which he had immediately suppressed, might have been the real thing, and all the rest false.

At the end he comes to realize that his life like that of his footman, his wife, his daughter, his doctor had been not real, but a grotesque, daily renewed mask to veil the realities of life and death. He sees them as we ourselves were made to see them when the story began with Ivan Ilych's funeral, when his wife was already mainly concerned about her State pension, when his friend was anxious not to flout the conventional etiquette but also anxious not to miss a rubber of bridge. Ivan Ilych himself came to understand the truth while there was yet time; and because he understood he was able for the first time to forget his own sufferings in the genuine compassion he felt for those around him living their lives on a wrong and artificial basis, and yet unable to free themselves from its thrall any more than Ivan Ilych had been when in full possession of life.

Although Sinclair Lewis's Babbitt is a pathetically comic figure Babbitt's situation is not so very different from that of Ivan Ilych. Babbit flourished in America in the 'twenties, a resident of a fashionable suburb of Zenith. A real-estate man by profession, a Republican in politics, a Presbyterian, a member of the Chamber of Commerce, an Elk, a booster, a family man, virtuous, well-liked, Babbitt epitomizes the good-hearted, un-reflecting go-getting regular guy. He views with pride the rising sky-scrapers of Zenith as temples of the new religion. He shares in the prosperity of the 'better class', the business and professional groups. He reflects accurately the tastes and opinions of his tribe. He advocates, without practising, prohibition; he is hostile to labour and unions, he pays his debts, he contributes to recognized charities; he is conventional in all things, and when he cheats it is strictly within the recognized limits; he is virtuous though not excessively so; his individuality is genuinely his own but indistinguishable from millions of others; he nurtures social aspirations, and accordingly his tastes like his politics and his religion are susceptible to advertising. 'These standard advertised wares . . . were his symbols and proofs of excellence; at first the signs, then the substitutes, for joy and passion and wisdom.' For Babbitt in early middle age, notwithstanding his popularity, his prosperity, his virtue, his domestic bliss, finds life less than satisfying. To say that he was unhappy would be to overstate the case. He is restless, uncomfortably aware that all is not well, yet his feelings are vague, and he cannot analyse the nature of his discontent.

'He who had been a boy very credulous of life was no longer greatly interested in the possible and improbable adventures of each new day.' Sleep has become an escape from reality, from the grind of the real-estate business, from his family who are no more interested in him than he is in them. He feels spasms of guilt about his business practises; and because he dislikes his family, he dislikes himself. His wife is good and kind but dull and sexless, habituated to married life as to a common halter. Babbitt grows increasingly anxious and restless. He worries about business, he worries about smoking and his health, he worries about his culture or suspected lack of it, he is not sure of his social status rating. When the McKelveys consent to come to dinner, the Babbitts, gratified and anxious, are made to feel their place. The invitation is not returned, and they smart. But when the Babbitts are invited out to the Overbrooks, people not quite of Floral Heights ranking, the Babbitts feel little compunction in not returning the invitation. At the office too, things are not exactly what they ought to be. Obliged to dismiss an employee for graft, he hears in return some candid truths concerning a shabby business deal of his own. This he rationalizes as the need 'for the broad-gauged men to get things done; and they got to be rewarded.'

Uneasy and dissatisfied, Babbitt is sustained by his fear of, and yearning to be liked by, his fellow-boosters. Isolated from them by a mild illness, he is beset by self-doubt. In his gloom he is half prepared to admit that perhaps life is empty and sterile. His religion is respectable, remote from humanity, mechanical; his golf, his bridge, his conversation, these too are mechanical; his human relations are almost all on the level of back-slapping jocularity. Perhaps life has to be the way it is, Babbitt muses. Yet he shrinks from the candid avowal of so much futility. Even making money did not bring much pleasure, rearing children to rear others seemed in itself a somewhat pointless activity; while Presbyterian glimpses into the life to come left him either unexcited by the prospect or frankly sceptical. What does he want? Wealth? Social position? Travel? . . . Of course; but these things are within his reach; yet he cannot be numbered among the light of heart. He is on the edge of cynicism or despair, when he meets an old college friend, now a radical politician. Babbitt's self-doubts crystallize in this moment of cathartic release. The gravity of Babbitt's conflict is, however, blurred at this point by the author's inability to curb his comic impulse. Babbitt's charm and appeal lie just in the naïvety that make him a comic as well as pathetic figure. But by portraying Babbitt satirically, Lewis weakens the credibility that Babbitt's inner conflict is a thing of high seriousness. The old college friend reminds Babbit of his own aspirations in youth, how he was a source of inspiration to them all. Babbitt suddenly shy and self-conscious fills with pride:

> I always say a fellow ought to have Vision and Ideals. I guess some of the fellows in my business think I'm pretty visionary, but I just let 'em think what they want to and go right on – same as you do. . . . By golly, this is nice to have a chance to sit and visit and kind of, you might say, brush up on our ideals.

Perhaps after all it is not a case of Lewis being unable to prevent himself giving rein to his comic vein. Is he suggesting that for the Babbitts of the world the moral vision is necessarily blurred and pathetic? that their idea of moral truth is so addled that it can be 'brushed up' periodically? Either way, Lewis's artistic sureness of touch falters here.

Babbitt's moral crisis reaches its climax when a strike occurs in Zenith. Babbitt's attitude is that of all right-thinking men instinctively alive to the subversive potential of agitators or strikers. His instincts are those of the Chamber of Commerce – they erupt in full force when a strike become a serious threat to the business community. Babbitt's initial reaction is 'sound'; and when he sees a drove of shabby men in procession towards the poorer part of town, 'he hated them, because they were poor, because they made him feel insecure.' But then he notices in the procession his old college friend, even the State University History Professor of a distinguished Massachusetts family. What impresses him is that there's 'nothing in it for them'. The cause of Babbitt's 'conversion' is Dr Drew's sermon at the Chatham

Road Presbyterian on 'How the Saviour Would End Strikes', urging workmen to practise more Christian love for the boss. Babbitt decides upon open revolt. He reminds the boosters that strikers too are people, confused by their inability to understand the high mysteries of merchandising and profits, but who fundamentally are 'no more hogs for wages than we are for profits'. Heresy of these dimensions evokes after the first shock of the thing the severest reprisals. Pressure is put on Babbitt through his wife as well as his friends. But Babbitt stands firm. He refuses to be bullied into joining the Good Citizens' League whose true social purpose he well knows. But the pressure is sustained. His friends begin to freeze towards him, the pillars of society cut him publicly, his clients cool off, big business deals no longer come his way, he is increasingly conscious of social ostracism and the puzzled misgivings of his wife. A whispering campaign gathers momentum. Babbitt is isolated and frightened; only his pride prevents him from asking to be allowed to return to the fold. Finally when his wife is ill with an appendicitis, and all his old friends rally round with their wealth and boisterous sympathy, Babbitt is relieved and grateful. Public opinion swings back in Babbitt's favour. His reconciliation is complete. He even joins the Good Citizens' League.

The comic aspect becomes more pronounced in the closing stages; but Lewis never wholly loses sight of his underlying serious purpose. Although Babbitt's catharsis was of the most superficial, his conflict was real enough. Nor is the restored Babbitt wholly unchanged by the crisis of middle-age through which he has passed. If not seared by the flames, the Babbitt soul has felt something of their scorching play. He was disturbed by thoughts such as he had not been aware of since his youth; he knew that he had struggled in vain to escape from a net which had closed over him through his own inadequacy. He is a humbled man. He is anxious to leave his grandchildren an honourable business. At the same time a man must be practical. But he wriggles uncomfortably. His conscience does not return entirely to a state of torpor. And when his son elopes with the girl next door and throws over college for a factory job, Babbitt comes to his rescue.

'Well,' he says shyly, 'those folks in there will try to bully you, and tame you down. Tell 'em to go to the devil! I'll back you. Take your factory job, if you want to. Don't be scared of the family. No, nor of all Zenith. Nor of yourself, the way I've been.'

Among the most psychologically acute studies of this moral and social conflict is Arthur Miller's *Death of a Salesman*. Willy Loman never begins to understand his own spiritual tragedy; but the author's compassionate diagnosis of Willy's hopeless struggle against his environment moves us profoundly. Willy's vice, to which he remains blind, lies in his persistent distortion and falsification of reality at the dictates of his vanity. When his disillusioned son confronts him with the bitter truth at the climax of the drama he seeks the phrase that will wound the most in order to penetrate the barrier of Willy's devouring pride. 'Pop!' shouts Biff, 'I'm a dime a dozen, and so are you!' To be one, no more and no less, of the great human family, a part of the common clay that goes to make up the expression on the human face, represents for Willy Loman the degradation of being 'a dime a dozen'. As such it is fiercely rejected by a consuming vanity and so inevitably he does indeed become 'a dime a dozen'. Willy is no leader of men, as his son finally tells him; but this elementary truth is one that is too big for Willy to live with. Rather than face this, Willy has preferred the deception of self-inflation and hot air. It has corrupted Willy himself, both his sons, and has worn to a tragic wisp the tired figure of Willy's wife, through whose devotion and grip on reality the family largely owes its survival.

Willy is a salesman; such philosophy as he has acquired is the shallow, boisterous vision of the adman. Success is the high goddess of life. Success is equated with riches and the world's esteem. And the way to realize the dream is to sell yourself to the public, to invent match-winning slogans, to boost the product to the consumer, above all to study his ways sufficiently to be well-liked. Ultimately Willy's idealized image of himself is neither money nor power as such, though he believes these are the true goals of the sensible man. The goal he really seeks with persistent pathos, and which is his perennial undoing, is to be well-liked. Willy is not well-liked, of course; he is suffered more or less compassionately. The nearest perhaps he ever got to realizing his ambition was the day at Ebbets Field when Biff really was a star of his school football team. Willy never forgets it. As he relives the golden moment, his euphoria feeds over and over again his starved and stunted ego.

> Like a young god. Hercules – something like that. And the sun, the sun all around him. . . . When that team came out – he was the tallest, remember ? . . . And the cheers when he came out – Loman, Loman, Loman! God Almighty, he'll be great yet. A star like that, magnificent, can never really fade away!

The mood and the idiom recall Mr Dorrit telling Amy of his golden youth.

Judged by the only standards Willy values, Willy himself is a total failure. After a lifetime on the road, he is off salary and entirely dependent on commission. Finding this too great a strain for his failing resources, he asks to be given a head-office job, only to be told that the firm can no longer afford to keep him, that he is in fact fired. The one practical solution to his financial crisis is to accept his friend's generous offer of employment. But his pride cannot permit it. Instead he lives off his friend under the fiction of borrowing. A reality so painful he can only live with by increased recourse to fantasy. To escape from the real world he identifies with his brother Ben who has emigrated and made good; and he projects his own frustrated ambitions on to his favourite son, Biff. But it is precisely in his relations with his son that he is most vulnerable. For Biff is the crippled product of the pressures generated by Willy's neurosis. Carrying the burden of all Willy's hopes, he has been doted upon, boosted and protected from criticism all his life. If he pinches the ball at school, if he is rough with the girls, if he drives without a licence, if he cheats in class, Willy is always in the background, the 'good' fairy hovering to protect and excuse his protegé. The final crisis comes when he fails an important examination prior to college entrance. Evasion is no longer possible; he is faced with a vital test of character. Biff genuinely needs Willy; and at this crucial point they are both found tragically wanting. The traumatic episode where Biff surprises Willy in peculiarly humiliating circumstances with a tart in a Boston hotel bedroom finally shatters the father's authority for a son reared in complete dependence on him. For Willy the occasion is so utterly painful that it is promptly relegated deep within his unconscious; so that he remains genuinely bewildered and infuriated by his son's career. For Biff never looks up again. All thought of college entrance is abandoned. Smarting with self-pity and resentment at his betrayed idol, Biff becomes a shiftless, kleptomaniac bum. The father alternates between longing for his son's return, and towering, intolerable rage at the prodigal's evident failure when he does return.

Willy's unconscious conflict is brilliantly rendered. The tension rises as Willy, at each fresh rebuff, takes flight into his protective fantasy world. When the encounter with the external world lacerates his own raw ego, he summons up brother Ben from Alaskan gold-fields. When his sons' shabby behaviour overwhelms him, he is increasingly haunted by ghosts of past failures. Finally, the self-mortification and strain of the continuous quarrel with his father prove too much for Biff; and the suppurating abscess bursts. Willy is not permitted to evade any longer; he is trapped by a distraught son, unable any longer to bear his father's humbug. He starts by telling his father that they know of his project to gas himself. Willy, with the evidence before his eyes, can scarcely deny it. Biff then passes in review all the facts that have been censored and evaded because they wounded Willy's sensitive ego. 'The man don't know who we are! The man is gonna know! We never told the truth for ten minutes in this house.' And the father learns the facts of his son's wretched career, with attendant explanations. 'And I never got anywhere because you blew me so full of hot air I could never stand taking orders from anybody! That's whose fault it is. . . . I'm not bringing home any prizes any more, and you're going to stop waiting for me to bring them home!' Willy, wrought into intolerable agony, jabs back in the only way he can, 'You vengeful, spiteful mut!' And Biff at the peak of his healing anger, is suddenly beyond all anger, breaks down and sobs. 'Pop, I'm nothing! I'm nothing, Pop. Can't you understand that? There's no spite in it any more. I'm just what I am, that's all.' For the moment Willy too is reconciled by this glimpse of his son's repressed longing for the affection his father has yearned to receive but has not been able to give. But Willy's vision has been enlarged altogether too suddenly at a time when his nervous energies are exhausted. His deepest wounds have been laid bare. None of his customary resistances have been able to stand up to the final exposure. The only avenue of escape that is left him is to abandon for ever a reality which has mastered him. For Willy the truth is not to be borne; and the death of a salesman is a suicide's death.

(1) Dorrit is a man who wants to be a worthy father but who is consumed by a feverish desire to have his station recognized. In pursuit of this end and out of vanity, he behaves ill to those whom he owes most. His guilt finally breaks through his inner resistance; and under the strain of the resultant confusion of identity he dies.

(2) Ivan Ilych is a commonplace man: he puts his petty pleasures and ambitions before the question of the meaning of his life. Consequently, when he faces a terrible crisis, he finds himself bereft of spiritual reserves. There rages a fierce struggle between his customary self and those selfless and generous impulses he has long since suppressed. He understands too late that joy in life had been denied him because of his self-pre-occupation. He inhabits a world of isolated creatures unable to communicate with each other.

(3) Babbitt epitomizes the little man, more good than evil, but fearful of finding himself out of step with all the other Babbitts. He wants to do right; but life is comfortable, and he is weak. With his ideals repressed, life becomes increasingly mechanical and savourless. The good example of others momentarily arouses him from his torpor, and he tries to live according to his principles. The effort is, however, too much for him. Babbitt's need of the community's approval goes deeper than his will to orient himself according to his inner light.

(4) Willy Loman's outstanding trait is his capacity for self-deception. His idea of success is superficial but specific. The unrealistic claims he makes for himself and his son deprive him of his stability. Although his wife loves him, she cannot save him. For Willy has leaned upon and used her, not loved her. Willy has lost the power to communicate; suicide is logically his sole remaining resting-place.

In each case the moral is fundamentally the same. Each man has an inner self which exists, however weakly, and tries to be heard and to influence conduct. Failure occurs because of the external pressures which make it impossible for the individual to act up to the demands of the ideal self without arousing acute fears or putting beyond reach keenly desired pleasures. In the grip of the ensuing conflict, the individual is subjected to powerful temptation to deceive himself as to his real situation and his duties in that situation. To the extent that truth, both empirical and normative, is evaded, the conflict appears on the surface to be resolved in the most comfortable and inexpensive fashion. But the resolution of the conflict is a false one; and therefore unconsciously it continues the more fiercely for being repressed. And the individual becomes increasingly aware of the joylessness, loneliness, and lovelessness of a life doomed to incommunicability with others. Ultimately the individual pays a very high price indeed for his temporizing and his fear and his need to dominate or to be liked.

An important source of their inability, despite their inner promptings, to take the necessary first steps to resolve their difficulties is the example and pressure of the outside world. Dorrit does not listen to his good angel because the world urges him to use his riches to establish himself on a grandiose scale. Ivan Ilych flees the happiness he knew as a child because the world assures him the correct goal of aspiration is professional advancement. Babbitt tries to break free from the obstacles of his social and professional environment but they reassert their outraged hold upon him. Willy Loman is the victim of the high pressure sales values and 'get rich' philosophy of his social milieu. In each case the collective will triumphs over the weakness of the individual.

5 Inequality and Power: Theory and Practice

(i) *Theory*

THE ARGUMENT so far has been conducted in terms of human psychology and individual character. We noticed in purely psychological terms the proneness of human beings to enter into relations of dominance and submission with one another. Confident egos expand their field of effectiveness and weak or diffident ones comply with them. The fact of power even at the personal level is, then, a very pervasive element in the common experience of daily life. When we turn from the individual to look outwards at society, the presence of power as an element in our experience immediately looms much larger. Large numbers of individuals acting in concert begin to generate power on a vastly increased scale. Given the age and ubiquity of inequality and power as factors of social experience, the development of an elaborate metaphysic of justification is to be expected. Indeed, it is a truism that political philosophy has traditionally concerned itself with the search for some kind of moral justification for the power and coercion of governments. The arguments to justify State power have been many and various. It is frequently defended as a necessary evil, although some arguments, generally associated with the Right in politics, aim to defend power as a good in its own right. However reluctant people may be to defend the use of force or power in purely personal relations, they experience no such reluctance in finding rationalizations to justify its regularized use in the community's public life. Perhaps the most forceful and uncompromising statement of the claims of power is to be found in De Maistre.

> There can be no human society without government, no government without sovereignty, no sovereignty without infallibility, and this last privilege is so essential that its existence must be assumed even in temporal sovereignty (where it does not reside in

fact) as an essential condition of the maintenance of society. (*Du Pape*, 1821, Bk. I, ch. xix).

De Maistre is unusual in the candour with which he makes explicit the assumption of infallibility which is latent within the concept of sovereign power. Power is necessitated because of the incorrigible waywardness of man; but since power is wielded by a few people over many, the logic of justification requires the assumption that the few be less wayward than the many. At the outset we find ourselves therefore committed to the principle of inequality and the proposition that power and virtue go hand in hand. The basic assumptions of authoritarianism would seem to contradict the facts of man's moral and religious experience. And this relates significantly to the idiom and manner of much of conservative political writing. Conservative writers themselves have been quick to detect the significance of the querulous assertiveness or stridency of much of the writing of their political opponents. It is only fair to mark that theirs too is a characteristic and not fortuitous style. The general tone is one of scepticism, well-bred to the point of a rather weary worldliness. The accent is one of urbane, secular pessimism, a thinly veiled impatience at the necessity of reminding the public of facts so obvious. Negatively, the style may be expected to betray symptoms of suppressed irritation at the first signs of moral earnestness. To be guilty of this is the surest way to convict oneself of immaturity. The antipathy is not to earnestness as such. The conservative style can be eloquent in earnestness when denouncing the heresies of their opponents. But their deepest distaste is aroused by any form of moral enthusiasm, which will be put down as 'high-minded', 'priggish', 'canting', or 'holier than thou'.

Even a superficial reading of conservative writing will reveal the touchy preoccupation with the phenomenon of 'moral earnestness' which would seem to irritate, trouble or even frighten them. Such people are felt to be dangerous since the established order is felt to depend upon the maintenance of 'a due sense of proportion'. The moral aspirant, 'hotfoot for certainties' is liable to disturb the peace or the slumber of the quiescent conscience. Shaw's Inquisitor expressed the feeling well in describing the social function of the Holy Inquisition in the trial of St Joan. 'A gentle and pious girl, or a young man who has obeyed the command of our Lord by giving all his riches to the poor, and putting on the garb of poverty, the life of austerity, and the rule of humility and charity, may be the founder of a heresy that will wreck both Church and Empire if not ruthlessly stamped out in time.' The Church is right, since it is accommodated to the needs of the great mass of ordinary men, sinners all perhaps, but whose defects and shortcomings the Church understands and charitably tolerates. The point is again vividly illustrated in a German cartoon on the subject of the Synod's Edict of Excommunication against Tolstoy.[1] The cartoon depicts the giant Tolstoy, a rugged heroic figure, struggling under the weight of a cross so immense that it is bursting asunder the roof and portals of the church. Outside the threatened walls stand the outraged pygmy figures of the clerics of the Orthodox Church, expostulating in impotent fury. The caption reads: 'Hinaus mit ihm! Sein Kreuz ist viel zu gross für unsre Kirche!' ('Out with him! His cross is much too big for our Church.') On the conservative view of the matter, it is Tolstoy who is in error, because he cannot cut himself down to life-size and is accordingly unable to understand normal men whose problems he can neither diagnose nor prescribe for.

It is precisely the charge that Dostoevsky's Grand Inquisitor levels against Christ in that most influential of modern parables from *The Brothers Karamazov*. During the Inquisition Christ returns to a Spanish town, is arrested by the Inquisitor, and indicted on the three counts of his answers to the question put to him by Satan on the high mountain. The first temptation was that he should prove his divine power by changing the stones into bread. Christ refused on the grounds that he had come to give men the gift of freedom, whereby they would freely choose to follow him. If he consented to purchase their obedience with bread, he would destroy the very possibility of freedom. Obedience so bought would be morally worthless. Man does not live by bread alone. The Inquisitor does not question the moral force of this argument. He maintains that men cannot normally live according to such a standard. Man may not live by bread alone, but his appetite must be satisfied before he is asked to consider the claims of virtue. And even so, only a very few will

---

[1] It is reproduced from the *Bettmann Archive* in G. Steiner's *Tolstoy or Dostoevsky*, 1960, p. 255.

prove capable of seeking the bread of Heaven. Man craves not freedom but someone to worship. His purpose is far from being the freedom of conscience to choose between good and evil. Most of all he wants peace; he would prefer death to the suffering inherent in the responsibilities of moral choice. Anyone who will relieve him of this burden he will readily worship, and once he has found his god, he will tolerate no dissent. He demands community of worship, and will persecute ferociously those who threaten his security.

The vain offer of power by miracle is followed by the second temptation, that he should consent to rule by mystery. Again, the Inquisitor does not deny Christ's wisdom, acknowledging that had he consented to tempt God by casting himself down, his faith would have dissolved, and he would have been hurled against the rocks. But again, he asks, does Christ not know men and their weaknesses? Without miracle and mystery they cannot live. Or is it, he asks ironically, that Christ has come not, as he professes, for all men, but only for the elect who have strength enough to bear the Cross? In the great crises of life, mystery is indispensable to man. If Christ denies him mystery as well as miracle, then he will have recourse to miracles of his own invention, to witchcraft and sorcery. Ultimately it is power to which men respond. Characteristic of their weakness was their demand that Christ should 'prove' his credentials by stepping down from the Cross. Again Christ refused to meet such a challenge. The only love that he could accept was a love that was freely given. 'Thou didst crave for free love and not the base raptures of the slave . . . But Thou didst think too highly of men therein, for they are slaves, of course, though rebellious by nature.'[1]

Finally, in the third temptation, Christ banishes Satan altogether by rejecting his last offer, the offer of power and dominion for their own sake. For there were shown unto him 'all the kingdoms of the world, and the glory of them'. 'All these things will I give thee, if thou wilt fall down and worship me.' The acceptance of this gift would in itself have bought man's willing and absolute worship. The striving for universal unity, in which all men will live in the harmony characteristic of an ant-heap,

[1] Everyman ed., Vol. I, p. 262

is the third of the abiding urges which dominate men. Even the conquests of the Timours and the Genghis-Khans were an unconscious expression of man's urge to achieve by force the peace of universal unity. By refusing the sword of Caesar, by declining the weapons of authority as well as those of miracle and mystery, Christ turned away from the last opportunity of bringing the hearts of men beneath his sway. His alternative, the gift of freedom, can bring men only to disaster and ruin.

It is an astringent portrait, not untouched by Dostoevsky's own self-hatred. Its force lies in the consistency with which it hews close to the view of man's nature necessary to justify the right of Power to rule, the power in this instance being clothed in the authority of the Church. The balanced and 'mature' view of the human situation is that which sees man as inescapably bound to inhabit a universe where pain and suffering, a measure of injustice, of imperfection, of human fallibility and absurdity are enduring. There is nothing that can be done to alter this basic condition of human life. Therefore it befits a wise man to resign himself in perfect adjustment to his necessarily imperfect mortal life. Inability to do so is a sign of immaturity. Rigorous resistance to evil in all its forms wherever it raises its head, smacks a little of *hubris*, of arrogance and impiety. Since evil is a necessary part of the great scheme of things, its elimination would threaten the whole mysterious balance of the divine cosmos. Without evil, freedom would be impossible for man; and freedom is his highest vocation. 'In this light, evil itself becomes a necessary adjunct of human freedom', writes Professor Steiner. Professor Oakeshott says much the same thing when he echoes F. H. Bradley: 'We live in the best of all possible worlds, and *everything* in it is a necessary evil.'

It is not a novel metaphysic, and has rarely been better expressed than by the ancient Psalmist. The author of the 73rd Psalm, however, only reached this position after a powerful inward struggle to overcome his initially lively sense of injustice. But then who is to know what internal anguish our contemporary pessimists and realists have had to surmount before manfully resigning themselves to the imperfections of the world? The Psalmist's lamentation is occasioned by his bewilderment that the wicked should prosper in the world and the seekers after power inherit the earth.

They are not in trouble as other men; neither are they plagued like other men. Therefore pride compasseth them about as a chain; violence covereth them as a garment. Their eyes stand out with fatness; they have more than heart could wish. They are corrupt, and speak wickedly concerning oppression: they speak loftily.

The ungodly increase in riches, while the Psalmist, conscientiously cleansing his heart, is chastened and plagued for his pains. In his anguish he tries to convince himself that reality is 'really' otherwise. The candour of the original analysis is undermined by self-pity; and the process of self-deception starts. The truth, he acknowledges, is 'too painful for me'. Unable to deny the evidence of his eyes, he calls theology to his aid to redress the balance of a world intolerable to his sense of justice. The apparent triumph of the power-seekers is short-lived and illusory, and ultimately God will ensure that they will be humiliated and brought low. 'Surely thou didst set them in slippery places; thou castedst them down into destruction. How are they brought into desolation, as in a moment! they are utterly consumed with terrors.' Then quickly recovering himself, he recognizes the futility of a wish-fulfilment grounded ultimately in chagrin and envy. 'So foolish was I, and ignorant.' Acknowledging his error, he returns to the problem. And his ultimate solution is one of acquiescence in a reality which, however painful must express the will of Him who is set over all. In revolt lies madness, since God must be his strength at all times. Difficult it may be to understand a wisdom so full of paradox, but we must rest confident in the ultimate goodness of God. 'I have put my trust in the Lord God, that I may declare all thy works.' Reconciling ourselves to the inexorable fact that evil has its place in the world, we must learn not to question the mysterious and inscrutable ways of God. However repugnant to our emotions, they will be seen on reflection not to offend our reason. The idiom today, as befits a more secular age, is not always couched in theological terms, but the accent has not changed much. 'The highest and most easily destroyed of human capacities', Professor Oakeshott tells us, is what Keats termed *negative capability* and defined as that condition 'when a man is capable of being in uncertainties, mysterious doubts, without any irritable reaching after fact and reason.' The nostalgia is unmistakable. It is the longing of the true romantic for an ill-defined, twilight world, a world of intimations, where we are secure in our acceptance of reality, undisturbed by any tetchy, awkward hankering of unsettled and unsettling men.

The emphasis is repeatedly on style and method, on guidance by intimations emanating from unimpaired traditions, on conversation rather than argument, while reliance on general principle is suspect as a symptom of rationalist politics. The intimations are frequently so elusive and phantomlike that it is not easy to come to grips with the content of the argument. For there is an argument; and if the original premises, sometimes made explicit, are examined, they will be seen to derive from a simple metaphysic, the metaphysic of human egoism. Granted that, morally speaking, we ought to be unselfish, the argument runs, a condition of survival is that we are at least sufficiently self-regarding to ensure the continued autonomous activity of our own ego. Unselfishness presupposes and rests upon selfishness, which is thus the predicate on which the entire moral argument and the possibility of moral behaviour is raised. Thus it is inevitable and in the nature of things that the hand of every man should always to some extent be turned against the hand of every other man.

The urge to dominate is, then, inherent in the necessity of the struggle to survive. But security and survival are specific attainable goals within the reach of the determined man. With satiety might not the urge to dominate wither? Unfortunately not, since in the necessity of the original struggle man has learnt to acquire a taste for domination. And this continues, after security has been achieved, to find an outlet in the quest for power, prestige, status, wealth. Since these are appetites which feed upon themselves and are insatiable, we may safely conclude that the urge to dominate others, to manage men in fact, is natural to man in his present circumstances. Nor does the evidence suggest any flexibility or susceptibility to modification of these fundamental human drives. The notion that by greater understanding we may achieve greater powers of control to redirect is pure myth. Accordingly, the first act of realism in politics is to accept without repining these inexorable facts. True, there are other sides to our complex nature; the urge to dominate does not exhaust our attributes. But the other qualities are more precariously based; and wisdom in politics consists of building upon that which is most dependable rather than upon that which is possibly most elevating to the soul. Successful adjustment to the restricting circumstance of any human society will require a thorough understanding and acceptance of the supremacy of the law of human egoism. In Oakeshott's words, 'The enterprise of these politics will be to make use of the *strongest*, and not merely the *highest*, human impulses in a continuous attempt to correct ascertainable mischiefs and to suppress actual malpractices in society. . . .'

Policy, to be viable and practical, must be based on a capacity to observe accurately men as they are. If we do this, we will see that they are most readily stirred to exert themselves on behalf of themselves, their kith and kin, and their friends.

Thus is the moral argument stood on its head, and tailored to everyday use. The idiom is contemporary, but the argument has an ancient lineage. Witness the reasoning of Thrasymachus and Glaucon on the nature of justice in the Platonic Dialogues. 'Men revile injustice, not because they fear to do it, but because they fear to suffer it', states Thrasymachus. And Glaucon drives the point home in the famous parable of Gyges' ring.[1] The moral is plain. Only fear of reprisal stands between every man and the gratification of his lust and appetite for power. Is it seriously suggested, Glaucon asks Socrates, that any man who could steal with impunity, ravish his neighbours' womenfolk, kill or set free his neighbours at will, would refrain from doing so through a love of justice! When men act justly, either they have not been put in the way of temptation, or they do so under compulsion out of fear of the consequences of acting otherwise, never willingly.

Adeimantus then intervenes to anticipate the objection that parents and educators inculcate in their offspring a love of justice and a disposition to eschew injustice. The exception is only apparent. For their actual behaviour and their expectations

---

[1] A shepherd discovers in curious circumstances a golden ring possessed of magic properties. By turning the bezel of the ring to the inside of his hand, he learns that he may become invisible. He is suddenly possessed of the power to choose visibility or invisibility. Thus the question is posed: how will a man, suddenly vested with such formidable power, use it? The question is swiftly resolved. Gyges makes all speed to the centre of power, the palace, where he proceeds to seduce the queen, kill the king, and usurp the crown.

concerning their children's behaviour reveal that they praise not justice but the appearance of justice. To seem to be just, while at the same time behaving quite otherwise, is to get the best of both worlds. 'Their desire is that their children may seem just, and may thus obtain the rewards that reputation brings to the just man – offices of state and advantageous marriages, and all the benefits which Glaucon has been enumerating.'[1] All men will readily agree in singing the praises of virtue and justice in the abstract. These qualities they acknowledge to be beautiful but they are also keenly aware that strait is the way and narrow the gate for those who would live a life of virtue. Injustice gives quicker returns and higher immediate dividends than justice. This at least is the conviction of the vast majority.

> They have no hesitation in pronouncing wicked men happy if they are rich and powerful, or in giving them honours, both public and private; while they dishonour or slight all who are weak and poor, though they acknowledge them to be the better men. . . . They say that the gods have actually given misfortunes and a life of sorrow to many good men, and the opposite to many evil.[2]

Young men hesitating as to what principles they should adopt to guide them in their ascent are bound to take note of these salient facts, and draw the appropriate lesson. To be just will bring no advantage. But to appear to be just while in practice dissembling sufficiently to compete on equal terms will reap the rich rewards of the world. This double life may tax severely the energies of the aspirant, and call for heroic virtues. Those who do not refuse the challenge will adopt as a maxim the following indispensable formula for success: 'The fore-court of my house of life I must adorn with the presentment of virtue, but behind the walls I shall hide the crafty subtle Reynard whom that wise Archilochus loved.'[3]

In more than two thousand years the 'realists' have not found it necessary to undertake any noticeable modification in their portrait of the essential *homo sapiens*. Accordingly, the inference is that the main aims of a genuinely democratic politics ought to be the satisfaction of the wants of such men as these, and the

---

[1] *The Republic*, Everyman ed., pp. 40–1
[2] *ibid.*, p. 42
[3] *ibid.*, p. 43

discovery of the means to induce them to the necessary effort to obtain them. The social rights which ought to command our deepest respect are the right to own private property and the right of voluntary association. These basic rights will enable all men to strive according to their enormously diverse capacities to get what they can by their own efforts. The aims of these men will be to obtain rewards which will be satisfying in proportion as they differentiate them from their fellow-competitors. And since men customarily regard their families as extensions of their own egos, the minimum satisfactions will include the elevation of their families to higher status and remuneration levels, in order that they too shall increase their range of enjoyment and sense of worth. Fundamental too among the rights of these men is the right to seek the job of their own choosing, and having got it, the right to do it in their own way free from arbitrary social interference by planning theoreticians. And again, since it is important that they may be able to make like provision for their families, they must be free to educate their children in their own way according to their own lights.

Freedom, thus defined, is guaranteed to secure all that is most treasured by those individualists who are particularly infuriated by socialist restriction, and who at the same time feel themselves to be endowed with the requisite talents and energies to secure the desired pre-eminence. This does not exhaust the content of freedom. Freedom to express your point of view, freedom of speech as it has traditionally been called, if not an absolute right, is nevertheless a legitimate ambition entitled to compete for recognition with the other more important ambitions of men. The importance of this aspect of freedom has been enormously exaggerated, and represents a quite extraordinary distortion of emphasis. In the real world as distinct from the altogether unrepresentative world of intellectuals the lives of men do not revolve around a felt necessity to express themselves. On the contrary, most men have nothing to say. But 'for most men, to be deprived of the right of voluntary association or of private property would be a far greater and more deeply felt loss of liberty than to be deprived of the right to speak freely.'[1]

These, then, are the characteristic political rights which flow

[1] Oakeshott, 'The Political Economy of Freedom', *op. cit.*, p. 44

from the metaphysics of egoism. The functions of government itself in such a society may be defined in the essentially negative terms used by Macaulay more than a century ago:

> Our rulers will best promote the improvement of the nation by strictly confining themselves to their own legitimate duties, by leaving capital to find its most lucrative course, commodities their fair price, industry and intelligence their natural reward, idleness and folly their natural punishment, by maintaining peace, by defending property . . . and by observing strict economy.
> . . . Let the Government do this: the People will assuredly do the rest.[1]

In the present-day context, this means that Government's role is firstly to maintain by means of a fiscal thermostat an unimpeded arena where men may organize production and distribution for profit; secondly, to maintain unimpaired the 'open' or plural society by preventing any group, including itself, from obtaining any great concentration of monopoly of economic power; thirdly, to ensure through educational channels that talent is efficiently selected and groomed for its role of staffing the existing vacancies in the ranks of the managerial *élite* on whom allegedly the efficiency of productivity ultimately depends; and finally, lest authorities should proliferate and encroach upon men's sense of freedom to advance themselves, Government may release these inhibitions and frustrations by remedying minor restrictive mischiefs. In this way Government may ultimately enhance the total coherence of the existing arrangements.

Expressed in sociological terms, the metaphysic of egoism predicates a society grounded on the impulse to emulation and a reverence for the principle of inequality. Indeed, the predilection for inequality is elevated to the status of a natural sociological law. The much lamented inhumanity of man to man, the proud man's contumely, the scorpions of office, the snobberies of sycophants hotfoot for baubles, badges and ribbons, the power of wealth, the struggle for life, the vast diversity of talent and ability, of strength mental and physical, from the winged eagle in his eyrie to his humblest victim in the plain, all these things bespeak the character of our universe. They are plainly rooted in the order of nature. To seek to reduce their incidence, still less to abolish their sway, is to attempt the vain impiety of

[1] Essay on *Southey's Colloquies on Society*, in *Critical and Historical Essays*, 1880 ed., p. 122

setting one's shoulder to unbalance the harmony of the cosmos. Inequality is endemic in human as in the rest of nature. It is demonstrable, we are told, by uniform evidence drawn from such diverse fields as psychology, biology, genetics as well as history and anthropology. Sex, hunger, the instinct to survive, these may be common to all; but not equality. On the contrary, difference and inequality confront us at every turn where human beings congregate together now as always in the past. What has the Hottentot or Kamchatka coolie, we are asked rhetorically, got in common with a Russell or an Einstein any more than had the slaves of the agora with Aristotle or Alexander?

This psychology is a simple one, the psychology of Machiavelli, familiar to conservatives of every age. Man is a fearful and ambitious creature, fearful of others and accordingly anxious to dominate them. Their environmental conditions are often such that they are obliged to fight from necessity. But even when there is no necessity, the *animus dominandi* becomes a matter of habitual impulse. Thus men are never satisfied. However high they reach, their appetite for further power and control remains insatiable. Desire always runs ahead of the capacity to acquire; and so men are doomed to restlessness and discontent with their lot. This it is which is the source of the endless flux of human affairs and the eternal change of the wheel of fortune. 'For, since some desire to have more, and others are afraid to lose what they have already acquired, enmities and war are begotten; and this brings about the ruin of one province and the exaltation of its rival.'[1]

The picture conjured up as endemic to the human condition is one of endless strife: the war of commerce between individuals and the war for power and position between provinces and nations. Accordingly, the prime concern of the wise statesman is to learn not only to distrust men, but to recognize that a condition of equality among men is both foreign to their nature and incompatible with the essential task of governing them. The key to success for princes studying politics or the art of human governance is first to create an *élite*; secondly, to give them a vested interest in identifying the prince's power and privilege

---

[1] Machiavelli, *Discourses* trans. and ed. Leslie J. Walker (London 1950) 2 vols, vol. I, p. 295, I, xxxvii, 1

with their own; and thirdly, to afford them the necessary coercive means to fasten their yoke on those who need to be so ruled but who may not be expected altogether to relish it. This is the art of politics realistically appraised in the light of our controlling and unchanging human nature.

> . . . where considerable equality prevails, no one who proposes to set up a kingdom or principality, will ever be able to do it unless from that equality he selects many of the more ambitious and restless minds and makes of them gentry in fact as well as in name, by giving them castles and possessions and making of them a privileged class with respect both to property and subjects; so that around him will be those with whose support he may maintain himself in power, and whose ambitions, thanks to him, may be realised. As to the rest they will be compelled to bear a yoke which nothing but force will ever be able to make them endure. Between force and those to whom force is applied a balance will thus be set up, and the standing of every man, each in his own order, will be consolidated.[1]

Here again, Machiavelli reveals that quality of candour which has done much to alienate his fellow-spirits in every generation. In the above passage, the motives for inequality and power are laid bare, and there is no pretence that the whole structure is rendered legitimate or for that matter needs validation through the consent of the subjects to the power of those who have been raised up and put in charge over them. There is no attempt to conceal the nakedness of the struggle for power once the principle of equality is departed from. As for the legitimization of the rule of those who hold the power, this rests in the doctrine of *raison d'état*, one of the most influential political concepts to have flourished in the Western world. For direct illustration of the elements of Machiavelli's theory of power the reader could hardly do better than turn to Bruno Traven's well-known 'Western', *The Treasure of the Sierra Madre*,[2] a grim parable of our times.

---

[1] *Discourses*, I, lv, 9; *op. cit.*, vol. I, p. 336

[2] According to Traven, society is made up of two categories of men: those who have and those who have not. Everyone sees the world through the spectacles of his own interest. That interest is determined by the economic fact which divides those who have something to lose and therefore something to defend from those who have nothing to lose and everything to gain. The novel is an extended sermon on this psychological text.

Three men, to escape poverty, try their luck prospecting for gold in the Mexican mountains. The nature of this community of three is well analysed. The three were brought together not by friendship but by love of gain. Their emotions did

Machiavelli's doctrine of *raison d'état* still requires close analysis, since these ideas largely govern the conditions under which human beings even now live at the collective level. Although the British as a nation have always been loath to countenance Machiavellism as a respectable doctrine (there being no precise Anglicism for *raison d'état*), few have excelled them in the consistency of their adherence to its central principles. In discussing Machiavelli's thesis, his own claims concerning his method must be critically examined. Hostile to metaphysics, little interested in speculation, severely naturalistic and empirical in temper, Machiavelli considered it to be self-evident why men lived in states, and was therefore uninterested in constructing a systematic political theory. He conceived it as his job to describe objectively and dispassionately men's customary behaviour in the world of politics and diplomacy. Insisting that he was content to leave to others the job of telling men how they ought to behave, he applied himself to the more modest task of summarizing the range of their actual practice. In short, Machiavellism had always and everywhere existed; Machiavelli simply committed it to paper in coherent and articulate fashion. The plea disarms by its apparent modesty. If we were to accept it, we should be

---

not extend beyond a common understanding of their temporary mutual dependence. The bonds between them resemble those which draw men together in the comradeship of war. But as their mutual help derives from circumstances arising out of their common greed, jealousy and distrust are never far beneath the surface. Their danger is apparent when the eldest of the three unveils the 'real' relations obtaining between them. To the others' indignation he claims to be the only trustworthy one. Not because he is of greater integrity, but because he is too old to decamp with the plunder undetected. The testing time will come when they have raised twenty kilos of pure gold. The only real obstacle in a man's way is the life of the other man. 'Slay or be slain' is the inescapable logic of the universe.

Finally, their donkey caravan, laden with its cargo of gold dust, starts out on the long trek to Mexico City. Obliged to leave the eldest in an Indian village, the other two continue without him. They are soon overtaken by their mutual suspicions, however. Dobbs, the more unscrupulous, proposes that they rob their absent comrade of his share. Curtin's indignation provokes Dobbs into the accusation that Curtin had silently conceived of the project of getting rid of him, Dobbs, and thus absconding with the lot. Curtin, genuinely horrified at this accusation, is appalled as the realization of his danger floods over him. For the accusation, unfounded though it was, sows the seed of suspicion and fear. His peril, like his dilemma, is immediate and inescapable. Even if he could keep awake one night, Dobbs would get him the next. The only solution was to do to Dobbs what Dobbs clearly intended to do to him. 'Slay or be slain. There is no other law.' But even when by a stratagem he has succeeded in disarming Dobbs, he cannot bring himself to shoot him in cold blood. He thus forfeits his temporary advantage, and when finally exhaustion overtakes him, he is deprived of his weapon as he sleeps, and shot down.

'Dobbs was the stronger and the more unscrupulous. He was the stronger owing to his robuster conscience. The unscrupulous man survives the man who hesitates.'

doing less than justice to the influence of Machiavelli in particular and to the role and influence of art in general on human behaviour. People like Tolstoy and William Morris were right to insist on the profound importance of art as a moral influence on the life and behaviour of all who come into contact with it. However passionately the individual artist may subscribe to an aesthetic of art divorced from morals, to a theory of art for art's sake, the fruit of his labours cannot but contribute positively or negatively to the total moral ambience which shapes our lives for good or ill. Machiavelli was very much more than a mere painter of existing practice. And Meinecke in no way exaggerates when he writes, 'Machiavelli's theory was a sword which was plunged into the flank of the body politic of Western humanity, causing it to shriek and rear up.'[1] Machiavelli's work haunted the vision and conscience of later generations by the ruthlessness with which it penetrated an abiding aspect of human experience. Men had hitherto been disposed to turn away from this spectacle in distaste or sorrow, or by a gloss to pretend that the world of nature was somehow not so far removed as the record might suggest from the world of reason. Behaviour of the kind described by Machiavelli existed in plenty in the annals of the European political world, but when it had been reduced to a systematic doctrine, when the spontaneity and crude vigour of animal life was polished into a coherent work of art, a new situation had been realized. Realism in politics had been permanently modified in content. Human behaviour had been permanently influenced by the moral injection of the concept of *Necessità* into a behavioural world, squalid enough in all conscience, but not hitherto sustained and dignified by a sophisticated metaphysic.

The heart of Machiavellian metaphysic is the insistence that there is a fundamental, unchanging human nature which prescribes the same limits to human behaviour at all places and in all times. Any possibility of genuine progress, of improving the general level of behaviour, is ruled out on this view. Good there is in human nature, but evil there is too; therefore the better part of wisdom lies in recognizing this condition without repining or seeking to alter the unalterable. In this way the condition may be best exploited to advantage or, at any rate, to the minimum of disadvantage.

[1] Meinecke, *Machiavellianism*, English trans., 1957, p. 49

'Reflecting now upon the course of human affairs, I think that, as a whole, the world remains very much in the same condition, and the good in it always balances the evil. . . .'[1] It is a view which is fatalistic so far as the lot of humanity as a whole is concerned, but leaves ample scope for vigorous individual activism where intelligence and ruthlessness are combined in equal measure. And how are the essentials of this common human nature to be understood and regulated by reason? It is a composite picture studded with mordant aphorisms compounded partly of shrewd observation but mainly of cynical generalizations spiced with malice. Examples of the latter are too well known to linger over: 'Men forget more easily the death of their father than the loss of their patrimony'; or:' For it may be said of men in general that they are ungrateful, voluble, dissemblers, anxious to avoid danger, and covetous of gain; as long as you benefit them, they are entirely yours. . . .' The phrases are well turned; but these and kindred remarks are not freshly observed. They carry the smell of the study and are prompted in part by inward emotion. At other times, however, Machiavelli is eminently capable of acute insight. Witness his discussion of the peculiar difficulty of the obstacles which beset the path of those who are disposed to attempt innovation or reform in politics. In addition to the resistance offered by those who do well for themselves out of the existing arrangements, and the timidity of their opponents acutely conscious that the laws are in favour of the powerful, the reformers will have to reckon with the inertia of the general public which arises 'from the incredulity of mankind, who do not truly believe in anything new until they have had actual experience of it.'

As it is, we find ourselves condemned by circumstances to inhabit a world moved by suspicion and fear and governed by force – an internal police force, an external military force. And the central doctrine of *raison d'état* is simply that any act whatsoever will admit of ultimate justification, if it is necessary to the safety of the community. Deception, betrayal, broken faith, torture, murder, arson, rape, axe, bullet, dungeon – no means is intrinsically excluded from justification provided *salus populi* can be pleaded in excuse. Proposals to assassinate one's own servants to promote one's political ends are the extreme

[1] *Discourses*, II, Preface, 5; *op. cit.*, vol. I, p. 354

instance of the Machiavellian or allegedly realistic method in politics. Machiavelli recommended this method if the circumstances were propitious. 'There are many who think therefore that a wise prince ought, when he has the chance, to foment astutely some enmity, so that by suppressing it he will augment his greatness.' So enamoured of the logic of a calculated *raison d'état* is the writer under the stimulus of his own ideas that he seems entirely to overlook the capacity for elemental moral outrage even among the torpid and intimidated. Even Hitler required a 'pretext' before he felt able to devour the Czechs;[1] not because of any moral scruple on his own part, but through fear of public opinion, in particular of the susceptibilities of the British and French – susceptibilities which in the event proved to be less tender than he could reasonably have foreseen. The Führer's favourite plan for manufacturing a suitable pretext was to arrange the assassination of the German Minister in Prague.[2] Machiavelli in his theory no less than Hitler in his practice fatally underestimated the stubbornness of human resistance to those who take advantage of the frailty of our behaviour to insist upon the vanity of our aspirations. It may seem to 'realists' that today as in the past the human capacity for moral response is not such as to inspire a great deal of confidence. But writers who assume that for practical political purposes it may be left out of account altogether do so at their peril. Lord Morley in his Romanes Lecture for 1897 made a palpable hit when he observed that had Machiavelli been present at Calvary two thousand years ago, the only people of any consequence he would have noted would have been Pontius Pilate and the Roman legionaries.

[1] The point is well illustrated by Joel Chandler Harris in one of his inimitable Brer Rabbit stories. Brer Fox calls on Brer Rabbit only to find that ole Brer Rabbit is away 'raidin' on a collard patch' and Miss Rabbit 'wuz tendin' on a quiltin' in de naberhood' with the little rabbits accordingly left playing 'hidin'-switch' unattended. It was clear to Brer Fox that it would be flying in the face of Providence not to make short work of those rabbits. But hungry though Brer Fox was, he wastes valuable time in setting the rabbits seemingly impossible tasks – to break up a large sugar-cane stalk, to fill a 'sifter' with water, to put a huge log on the fire – in order to 'justify' the wrath he is anxious to simulate. The little rabbits are saved by the timely return of Brer Rabbit, the moral presumably being that 'he who hesitates is lost'. Yet it is significant that Brer Fox did hesitate. He could not bring himself to gobble them up in cold blood just like that. The explanation Harris gives is that he was 'skeer'd fer ter gobble um up 'ceppin' he got some skuse'.

[2] Von Papen had similarly been considered as an eligible victim during the plans for the liquidation of Austrian resistance, thus, in J. W. Wheeler-Bennett's phrase, giving added piquancy to the term 'travailler pour le roi de Prusse.' (*Munich: Prologue to Tragedy*, 1948, p. 48.)

The legitimacy of *raison d'état*, we are assured, is strictly pragmatic. It serves as nothing else can to secure the safety of the State. For all his vaunted honesty of analysis, Machiavelli is less than candid here. Whatever part of the historical record we may choose to examine, it should be immediately apparent that such means, whether or not they have secured the State, have certainly not succeeded in ensuring the peace and prosperity of the community. The community has been exposed over and over again to the ravages of war, and its resultant suffering, poverty and death. The real beneficiary of Machiavelli's recipe is far from being *salus populi*; it is the wealth, power and security of the ruling group. His genuine touchstone is the same as that which troubled the Psalmist of old, namely, the fact that the wicked prosper in this world, whereas the valiant, the faithful, the true go down to defeat. The root of Machiavellian thought, indistinguishable in this respect from that of Marx or Trotsky on the Left, is the powerful conviction that the prophet unarmed is impotent because he is liable to destruction. The career of Savonarola made an indelible impression on Machiavelli's political imagination; but it was the manner of his dying rather than his manner of life from which the moral was drawn. Strength of character, nobility of soul are to be respected, but only if they are consistent with the acquisition and retention of power. Of what use are they if they take the possessor to the scaffold? And if such doctrine is found to be morally less than satisfying, Machiavelli's advice is to consult not what men say about such things but what they do. The standards of one's time are determined by majority behaviour; and if we live as the world lives, we can scarcely be thought guilty of any grave immorality. On the contrary, to act otherwise would be to be guilty of pretension, to set ourselves up as righteous critics of the common run of mankind. It is the Machiavellians who not only are the realists but who retain also the common touch and are free from priggishness. The argument is a familiar one.

Machiavelli's permanent influence can perhaps be summarized under two heads: (a) his effect on Western man's conception of the nature of morality, and (b) his fragmentation of the medieval world outlook by the 'liberation' of an autonomous political realm. So far as the moral issue itself is concerned, the doctrine of *Necessità* was not the invention of Machiavelli. As

Professor Powicke has shown, as far back as Gregory VII the practice of overriding the positive law on grounds of necessity was not unknown; and under certain extreme circumstances such behaviour is countenanced by Aquinas himself. But it is one thing to assert that necessity knows no law, that a natural emergency may on occasion drive men to do that which they generally regard as 'sinful'. It is quite another to identify this alleged necessity with the normal requirements of political men acting on behalf of the community. A necessity justifying bad faith and violence and deriving from such political values as the defence of natural frontiers, obedience to the logic of history, or the simple assertion of economic or military power – a *Necessità* so conceived substantially modified the traditional morality of Christendom. Lucifer, whose power had been readily acknowledged within his own dominions, had hitherto been excluded from Paradise. He was now permitted to cross the threshold of the kingdom of morality. It was Machiavelli's dreadful 'accomplishment' to have succeeded in winning an honoured and respected place for immorality in statesmanship.

Machiavelli's other significant 'achievement' was to clear the road for the emancipation of politics as an autonomous discipline from the tutelage of theology. The omnipotence of the Renaissance prince heralded the arrival of the nation State, which was to shape the main contours of its behaviour according to a logic of its own. *Le nouveau Messie est le roi.* Even Sir Thomas More did not question his allegiance to the secular sovereign. But when he discovered that the requirements of this allegiance conflicted with his loyalties to the Catholic Christendom in which he had been nurtured, he responded to the challenge with the sacrifice of his life. The dilemma was resolved, but only at the cost of intense anguish. 'I die the King's good servant, but God's first.' More's martyrdom symbolizes the conflict which must have racked the souls of thousands of anonymous men who experienced the clash of forces out of which the modern world was born. It is difficult for a modern even to imagine a world in which in 1532 a group of Spanish businessmen in Antwerp wrote to the Sorbonne for a ruling as to whether their commercial ventures were ethically justified. The right was asserted on behalf of one human activity after another to an autonomous existence according to the logic of its own needs and tradition indepen-

dently of the ruling theology of Christendom. The unity of the
medieval synthesis was defied by art, science, economics and
finally politics, as each in turn vindicated its claim to independence in a plural universe. Machiavelli's *Prince* was a master-
stroke of the polemical publicist in this campaign so far as it
concerned the political realm. It was an important contribution
to a general cultural development that was to generate immense,
new productive energies. The medieval world was crumbling;
and it was replaced by the organized administration of the
industrial and military machines of the modern nation States.
These new leviathans equipped themselves to harness human
energy to their scientific and commercial purposes on an unprecedented scale. The material gains were undeniable. But the
price paid for this freedom from the felt restrictions of the
medieval theological and moral canon was destined eventually
to grow into a direct threat to the sources of human life itself.

The relativism of the Renaissance separates as a great
watershed the dualism of the modern period from the absolut-
ism of medieval value. Much of the spirit of modern relativism
may be traced back to the radical influence of the doctrine of
raison d'état. But the time has come when we are compelled
to ask whether *raison d'état* has not now established itself as a
new sovereign absolute in its own right, one, that is, to which
every other human interest and value must give way. Boccalini
of Loreto in his *La Bilancia Politica* (published posthumously in
1678), speaks directly to the most urgent preoccupation of the
1960s:

> The interest of the State is exactly like a hound of Actaeon, it
> tears out the entrails of its own master.... The man of politics gets
> firmly into his head the principle that everything else must give
> way before the absolute necessity of asserting and maintaining
> oneself in the State; he sets his foot on the neck of every other value
> in heaven and earth. The desire to govern is a daemon which even
> holy water will not drive out.[1]

Boccalini's account of the significance of power for the
politician is today paralleled by the role of the doctrine of *raison
d'état* in the minds of contemporary students of international
diplomacy and strategy. The belief in the inevitability of *raison*

---

[1] quoted by Meinecke, *op. cit.*, p. 76

d'état with its reliance on violence and the threat of violence as the controlling force in human affairs is uncritically accepted. State power relations expressed in a dynamic equilibrium of terror have come to assume an independent life of their own.

The logic of the armaments race, of the war of all against all, and its source in human greed and fear, has never been more succinctly expressed than in Treitschke's enunciation of the two essential tenets of Machiavellism.

They merit quotation in full, since they will be seen to go to the root of the matter.

> 1. Your neighbour, even though [*es sei denn*] he may look upon you as his natural ally against another power which is feared by you both, is always ready, at the first opportunity, as soon as it can be done with safety, to better himself at your expense. He is forced to do it, if he is wise; and could not hold back, even if he were your brother.
>
> 2. It is altogether insufficient for you to defend your own territory; on the contrary, you must keep your gaze fixed dispassionately on everything which could influence your situation, and you must in no way tolerate that anything inside these boundaries of your influence should be altered to your detriment, and never hesitate a moment, if you can alter something there to your advantage. For you can rest assured that the other will do the same, whenever he can; and if you delay in doing it now on your side, then you will get behind him. Whoever fails to increase his power, must decrease it, if others increase theirs.[1]

It could scarcely be more pithily expressed. If men live by love for their neighbour, statesmen live by the opposite law. Never has the principle of the national interest, here enshrined, been more devoutly worshipped than today. That its pursuit has manifestly brought the entire globe and its inhabitants to the brink of annihilation seems in no wise to deter its enthusiasts, theoretical or practical. Confident, aggressive, exhilarated with their new triumphs, our new Machiavellians have gone over to the offensive. The trouble, they assert, is the confusion of false antitheses that has hitherto dogged and bedevilled well-meaning but confused minds, occupying positions of power. This is particularly the case, it is alleged, in the United States, where statesmen have been inhibited in the international sphere by the mistaken supposition that the politics of the national interest

---

1 quoted by Meinecke, *op. cit.*, p. 371

are antithetical to the claims of morality. The genuine and relevant antithesis, according to them, is that which obtains between a morality divorced from political reality and one that is founded upon it. It is true, they freely admit, that without being able to rely upon altruism and self-sacrifice for the common weal, the State could not continue to exist. Internally, therefore, statesmen must continue to foster such traditional morality. But he who attempts to pursue such aims in the international sphere can only do so to the detriment of the national interest. And the national interest is the only legitimate aim and standard of value in the international sphere; for outside the confines of the nation State no community exists. He who ignores this rule threatens the security, the lives and property of his fellow-citizens and is thus a great danger to them. In this way they triumphantly conclude the argument by standing morality on its head; and accuse their opponents,who naïvely advocate that men should love one another, of being moral perverts.

> The moralistic detractors of the national interest are guilty of both intellectual error and moral perversion.[1]

If our logic protests at such a tortuous dialectic whereby white is made to appear black, goodness is indicted as the main source of evil, and people are shown to be threatened by their own altruistic strivings to love and serve their fellow-men, we are assured that truth is more complex and mysterious than we in our simplicity had supposed. Our disappointment, we are told, our moral bewilderment arises from our false expectations that we might inhabit a logical universe in which truth is unitary, simple and exempt from self-contradiction. No doubt it would be simpler if we did inhabit such a universe. The longing that it were so is no doubt understandable, even to be sympathized with; but those who are old in the wisdom of the world know better. And if we would be wise, we will seek to emulate them and learn to accept that which is unalterable. Some will generously concede that man's moral aspirations should be recognized unequivocally for what they are, and even valued as such; but the conclusion they arrive at, sorrowfully perhaps but inexorably, is still the same. Friedrich Meinecke expressed this attitude very plainly, when he wrote, 'Nevertheless the message

[1] Hans J. Morgenthau, *American Foreign Policy*, 1952, p. 33

of pure Christian idealism, which recognizes no compromise between mind and nature, is always certain to be listened to with seriousness and respect, and a sense of sorrow that the world cannot be altered by it.'[1] This is an honest statement by an honest man. It is therefore of some significance to recall that Meinecke lived to experience the reversion to barbarism under Nazism; and that he had the courage and candour to revise his judgement that it must be accepted that Christian 'idealism' is impotent to change the world.

(ii) *Practice*

Sociological theories of inequality and power are powerfully buttressed by Hegelian metaphysic, viz. that 'the real is the rational'. That which *is*, which already exists, carries with it an undeniable status when measured against that which possesses only potentiality, the status that 'it might be'. Human beings are frequently 'doubting Thomases', profoundly incredulous about that which is not habitually experienced. Human behaviour as we know it is extremely cautious in its willingness to attempt to manoeuvre in any context other than the one it knows. The State, or the politics of living within the context of a power struggle, is real enough in that it is a part of universal historical experience. The shape of the State, its dimensions, its omnivorousness, its scale of activities have varied according to the period; what has not varied is that man has lived in groups governed by power. Such groups we call 'States'; those wielding power we call 'rulers', those subject to power we call 'subjects'; and those engaged in the struggle for power engage in what we call 'politics'. These are self-evident truths, so deeply embedded in our historical and daily experience that to call them in question at the factual level would cast doubts upon our sanity.

But to affirm that 'the real is the rational' is to go a step further than the recognition of the realities of power in the world. It is to assert that the existence of the State, the sheer ubiquity of power, the ineluctability of political struggle, give them a claim to our support. We should recognize that something so enduring and pervasive, so inseparable from all existing experience, must have a claim upon our reason. It exists; therefore it must be rational.

[1] Meinecke, *op. cit.*, p. 425

If he who denies the facts of political power is insane, so is he who denies their normative status. To deny the 'ought' in a case where the existential quality is so obvious is as irrational as to deny the 'is'. To deny that men ought to live in States, subjecting themselves to others' power or engaging in power politics, is of the same order of rationality as to deny the law of gravity. To live in States is natural in the same sense that it is natural to breathe, to eat and drink and procreate. Indeed, the one follows from the other. Man lives in the State because, as Hobbes reasoned, he is driven by a need to secure his survival, and the State is merely the natural institutional embodiment of this need. Therefore, to challenge the rationality of the State is indistinguishable from challenging its necessity. It is as impossible to do either as it is to challenge the fact that we are human beings. The statement that human beings live in States is tautological. Part of the definition of a human being is that he is a creature whose natural impulses compel him to live in States.

Politics is ineradicable because the *animus dominandi* is ineradicable from the human heart; so long as some men are driven by this force, others weaker than they will consent to be coerced by them. Power is inevitable in social relations because men hate the idea of 'equality' more than they are attracted by the idea of their own 'welfare'. Men have always lived under the coercion of the State and will always so live because it is the only means of securing them against their principal fear – anarchy or the breakdown of law and order on which civilization depends. The first mark of a sober, responsible judgement is to understand at least this. This is the substance of the argument that 'the real is the rational', translated into social and political terms. The argument at first sight would seem compelling indeed. But this is only one side of man's life, the external side. It is necessary to look also at the familiar but insufficiently emphasized accompaniment of our social and political experience.

The other aspect of experience, equally familiar, universal and constant, is war. Men who live in States make war against each other. They have always done so; they still do so. War between States has the same status of ineluctable fact as the facts of politics, of power, of the State. It may be a fearful price to pay, but it has always been argued that the price of war was

a lesser evil than the price of anarchy. If men have to choose
between anarchy and the periodic relapse into a condition of
war, they will choose the latter. Better the evil that we know,
from which recovery is possible, than the perpetual endurance
of the war of all against all where life is 'nasty, solitary, poor,
brutish and short'. Thus the phenomenon of war is real. And if
the argument in favour of the rationality of power, of politics,
of the State was valid, then war too by like logic is no less rational.
And yet there is a noticeable reluctance to accept this logic. A
few try to do so with a certain bravado, but it is a false bravado.
The majority evince definite symptoms of unease at this point.
The reactions are confused, ranging from resignation, religious
invocation, even anger. The outright moral rejection of its
'rationality' is a minority reaction because the 'political' side
of the argument is so deeply ingrained. The voice of a Barbusse
even in 1965 is rare; the voices of the many are not markedly
different from 1916.

> 'There are those who say, "How fine they are!" '
> 'And those who say, "The nations hate each other!" '
> 'And those who say, "I get fat on war, and my belly matures on
> it!" '
> 'And those who say, "There has always been war, so there
> always will be!" '
> 'There are those who say, "I can't see farther than the end of
> my nose, and I forbid others to see farther!" '
> 'There are those who say, "Babies come into the world with
> either red or blue breeches on!" '
> 'There are those,' growled a hoarse voice, 'who say, "Bow your
> head and trust in God!" '[1]

What is this but the common man's version of the scholar's
political analysis? Meinecke, writing in 1924, put it thus: '*Raison
d'état*, power politics, Machiavellism and war can never be
banished from the world, because they are inseparably bound up
with the natural aspect of State life.'[2] This was doubtless the fruit
of much reflection, the work of a skilled craftsman at labour in the
quietude of his study. To judge from their writings, many present-
day scholars still hold Meinecke's view. They suggest that war
is something which we all know and live with, but which we

---

[1] Henri Barbusse, *Under Fire*, 1916, Everyman, p. 339
[2] Meinecke, *op. cit.*, p. 429

should not regard with undue morbidity. Yet there are people for whom such an attitude is impossible: these people respond emotionally as well as intellectually to the living reality of what Meinecke then treated as simply a 'fact of life'. War is a word which describes laconically that which is 'necessitated' by the conditions of man's life. It divides like the seasons those intervals of peace from those intervals of war. But war·can be defined in different terms, which scholars have generally been disposed to reject as not part of their academic business.

They are not soldiers, they are men. They are not adventurers, or warriors, or made for human slaughter, neither butchers nor cattle. They are labourers and artisans whom one recognises in their uniforms. They are civilians uprooted, and they are ready. They await the signal for death or murder; but you may see, looking at their faces between the vertical gleams of their bayonets, that they are simply men.

Each one knows that he is going to take his head, his chest, his belly, his whole body, and all naked, up to the rifles pointed forward, to the shells, to the bombs piled and ready, and above all to the methodical and almost infallible machine-guns – to all that is waiting for him yonder and is now so frightfully silent – before he reaches the other soldiers that he must kill. They are not careless of their lives, like brigands, nor blinded by passion like savages. In spite of the doctrines with which they have been cultivated they are not inflamed. They are above instinctive excesses. They are not drunk, either physically or morally. It is in full consciousness, as in full health and full strength, that they are massed there to hurl themselves once more into that sort of madman's part imposed on all men by the madness of the human race.[1]

Or again:

All sorts of groans, sighs, death-rattles, now and then interrupted by shrill screams, filled the whole room. . . .

'Iván Bogáev, Private, Company Three, S— Regiment, *fractura femuris complicata*!' shouted another doctor from the end of the room, examining a shattered leg. 'Turn him over.'

'Oh, oh, fathers! Oh, you're our fathers!' screamed the soldier, beseeching them not to touch him.

'*Perforatio capitis!*'

[1] Barbusse, *Under Fire*, pp. 241–2

'Simon Neferdov, Lieutenant-Colonel of the N— Infantry Regiment. Have a little patience, Colonel, or it is quite impossible: I shall give it up!' said a third doctor, poking about with some kind of hook in the unfortunate Colonel's skull.

'Oh, don't! Oh, for God's sake be quick! Be quick! Ah —!'

'*Perforatio pectoris* . . . Sebastian Seredá, Private . . . what regiment? But you need not write that: *moritur*. Carry him away,' said the doctor, . . .[1]

Or again:

Of a hundred and fifty doctors in the city, sixty-five were already dead and most of the rest were wounded. Of 1,780 nurses, 1,654 were dead or too badly hurt to work. . . . There were so many [casualties] that he began to pass up the lightly wounded; he decided that all he could hope to do was to stop people from bleeding to death. Before long, patients lay and crouched on the floors of the wards and the laboratories and all the other rooms, and in the corridors, and on the stairs, and in the front hall, and under the *porte-cochère*, and on the stone front steps, and in the driveway and courtyard, and for blocks each way in the streets outside. Wounded people supported maimed people; disfigured families leaned together. Many people were vomiting. A tremendous number of schoolgirls . . . crept into the hospital. In a city of two hundred and forty-five thousand, nearly a hundred thousand people had been killed or doomed at one blow; a hundred thousand more were hurt.[2]

Over everything – up through the wreckage of the city, in gutters, along the river banks, tangled among tiles and tin roofing, climbing on charred tree trunks – was a blanket of fresh, vivid, lush, optimistic green; the verdancy rose even from the foundations of ruined houses. Weeds already hid the ashes, and wild flowers were in bloom among the city's bones. The bomb had not only left the underground organs of plants intact; it had stimulated them. Everywhere were bluets and Spanish bayonets, goosefoot, morning glories and day lilies, the hairy-fruited bean, purslane and clotbur and sesame and panic grass and feverfew. Especially in a circle at the centre, sickle senna grew in extraordinary regeneration, not only standing among the charred remnants of the same plant but

[1] Tolstoy, 'Sevastopol in May 1855' in *Tales of Army Life*, trans. Maude, World's Classics ed., 1958, p. 128

[2] John Hersey, *Hiroshima*, Penguin 1958 ed., pp. 43–5

pushing up in new places, among bricks and through cracks in the asphalt.[1]

Need we apologize for such lengthy quotation to make the platitude that war is horrible? Everyone knows this; but there are different levels of knowing. If everyone knew this as an imaginative understanding of mind and heart, international relations experts, diplomatic correspondents, defence strategists and the entire posse of newspaper leader-writers would no longer find it possible to conduct their daily discussions on premises so humanly obscene. It is necessary to keep steadily before the imagination something of the feelings aroused by a realistic picture of war.

The period of post-Renaissance man has been pre-eminently a period characterized by the triumph of the doctrine of *raison d'état*. This has had incalculably tragic consequences for the possibility of human moral and spiritual development, upon which alone humanity has always depended for its chance of a good and worthy life, and upon which humanity now depends for the chance even to survive. Meinecke in his authoritative survey of the changing circumstances in which *raison d'état* has found expression in modern war, distinguishes three periods, to which we, living after 6 August 1945, must now add a fourth (the following labels are not actually used by Meinecke):

(a) the feudal agrarian – mercenary stage; (b) the mercantilist – standing army stage; (c) the capitalist – national conscription stage; and (d) the continental cartel – nuclear megacorpse stage. Viewed thus from the centre of interest of death and destruction, modern European history will be seen to divide on the great watersheds of the Westphalia Treaty in 1648, the Revolution in 1789, and the annihilation of Hiroshima in 1945.

The stability of the late-Renaissance monarchies and principalities was generally precariously balanced because of the still active threat from the great feudatories with their licensed retainers and their *condottieri*. Wars were wars of mercenaries, sporadic and protracted, part-time so to speak, a transitory accompaniment of normal peace-time commercial and civil life. Peace and war were no sharply etched antitheses but part of a large kaleidoscope of the totality of social life, the one shading

[1] Hersey, *op. cit.*, p. 100

into the other, and neither clearly distinguishable from the other. Conspiracy and diplomacy were continuous activities which from time to time required the application of violence made available by hired mercenaries, and at other times seemed to demand a truce, an agreed pause in the murderous joust, as the more appropriate response to the commercial and power needs of the warring State. War was no doubt far from being relished by those unfortunate enough to be resident in the area where the skirmish was being waged at any given time; but for the most part the majority of the people were not seriously inconvenienced thereby. Life went on; men were habituated to war as a regular and not too impossible condition of civilized life. The one thing that emerges clearly from such fascinating contemporary records as the Paston Letters or the Stonor Papers was that the yeoman or small businessman in the provinces was able to prosper without serious setback even though living in areas where the struggle of the 'bastard' feudatories was fought out in the Wars of the Roses.

As the power of the new States was consolidated with the suppression of the centrifugal and anarchical forces of the feudatories, the new monarchies grew in administrative control, command of economic resources and military power. With the opening up of new colonial possessions in the Americas and Asia, the importation of precious metals wherewith to finance the expanding arteries of commerce, the emergence of the mercantilist economies of the seventeenth and eighteenth centuries, the central administrative and military power was able to command new and growing sources of taxation. These were sufficient to afford the new luxury of maintaining a standing army in time of peace in readiness for war. War was no longer the monopoly of hired professionals, but no more was it a total national effort. Peace and war became much more sharply differentiated social conditions, however. War could now be waged with larger resources in terms both of men and treasure. But wars were not wars of annihilation fought *à outrance*; rather were they wars of attrition, waged by disciplined armies, controlled and curbed by military and diplomatic skill so as not to exhaust the relatively restricted resources available to the warring monarchies.

The French Revolution created an entirely new situation, a

change quantitatively so far-reaching as to rank as qualitative. It saw the birth of the invention of compulsory military service. The overthrow of the caste structure of the *ancien régime* meant the removal of the social barrier to the creation of a citizen army. Napoleon was quick to perceive the possibilities inherent in the civic military fervour and spontaneous rush to arms to defend the Revolution against the powers of the First and Second Coalitions. The national army, spawned by the Revolution in defence of *liberté* and *égalité*, could be directed into more traditional channels of national aggression. In consequence the whole of Europe was plunged for more than a decade into convulsions of unprecedented slaughter, reaching a climax in the terrible carnage of the Borodino. Thereafter it was only a matter of time before French power was broken, and the old state system temporarily restored. Yet, despite the immense significance of universal conscription as an instrument of national power, a full century elapsed after Waterloo before the full logical consequences were developed. Why this was so, was not a question which it occurred to contemporaries to ask. To them the age was noteworthy as the age of progress and optimism akin to the days which saw the collapse of the *ancien régime*, when 'bliss was it in that dawn to be alive'. Wars there were in the nineteenth century, but they were short and severely contained. They never looked like erupting into continent-wide conflagrations of the Napoleonic order, although 1870 sounded the tocsin's warning. After the squalid Crimean struggle, symptoms of a moral revulsion against war itself began to make themselves felt. Institutions of international law took a greater leap forward than at any time since Grotius first made his proposals. International agreements were negotiated, designed to set limits to the barbarism of war by such means as covenants prescribing the rights of prisoners of war. While wars themselves were perhaps felt to be never entirely avoidable, the feeling grew that it would prove possible to mitigate their most evil consequences. It was necessary to ensure that war should be waged within limits set by the common interest of preserving the continuance of Western civilization with its commercial prosperity and cultural values.

That the nineteenth century dwelt in the shelter of a fools' paradise, is now plain to all. But what were the conditions which enabled the illusion to survive for a century? Men did, no doubt, learn something from the experience of the Napoleonic wars. *Raison d'état* was unleashed by Napoleon without qualification, such as might have given even Machiavelli occasion to pause. Men felt the ground quake beneath them and in fear drew back. The feeling was reinforced by the normal reaction after the exhaustion of war. With the passage of time national rulers found their energies increasingly absorbed in containing the class struggle within their own borders. Moreover, the principalities of central Europe and the Italian peninsula were absorbed in the struggle for national self-determination. In central Europe the convulsions generated by Germany's struggle for national hegemony might well have endangered the peace of Europe. Fortunately, the climate of German opinion was not sufficiently inflamed to permit Bismarck to apply the method of *raison d'état* with Napoleonic ruthlessness.

The possibility always existed that European man could have turned his steps away from the path to destruction. Man's one hope was to assert his moral strength and affirm his humanity. The alternative was that a pitiless national *raison d'état* should succeed in mobilizing the forces of militarism and capitalist productive power. In retrospect it seems that man's humanity was doomed to be vanquished by *Thanatos* or the will to destruction. But it was not seen in that light by contemporaries. While this too could be dismissed as a characteristic piece of human self-deception, there was some evidence to support late-nineteenth-century hopes that man's future would lie along paths other than those of the twentieth-century cataclysms. A growing volume of opinion was coming to understand the true nature of war stripped of its wicked romanticism. The creation of the international Red Cross and the signing of the prisoner-of-war conventions testify to the emergence of the humanitarian conscience. Even Bismarck found his military freedom of action effectively circumscribed by the power of Prussian public opinion.[1] The human capacity of man for concern for his fellow-man is also capable of generating its own momentum, given the requisite courage and determination of the few.

---

[1] In 1871 the Prussian siege of Paris was protracted throughout the winter; Bismarck wished to force the issue by shelling the besieged capital. He was prevented from doing so by the shocked reaction of Prussian public opinion to the barbarous proposal to make war upon helpless women and children by shelling an open city.

The contemporary 'lunatic fringe', the despised 'cranks' and 'woolly idealists' were also at work striving to alert the populations to the appalling dangers that confronted them while there was yet time. Indeed, the logic of their diagnosis and their eloquence have never been bettered. Tolstoy's imperishable indictment and agonized plea to his contemporaries to stop the preparations for the holocaust he so accurately foretold are known to all. Less well known is the work of the Swiss novelist Edouard Rod. In *Le Sens de la Vie* (1889) he tried to give warning of the storm that was brewing:

Every day we weigh the chances of war for the morrow. And every day that eventuality becomes more unavoidable. Imagination refuses to believe in the possibility of the catastrophe which is coming at the end of our century as the result of all the progress of our era, and yet we must become accustomed to facing it. For twenty years past all the resources of science have been exhausted in the invention of engines of destruction, and soon a few cannon shots will suffice to destroy a whole army. It is not as formerly when a few thousands of poor fellows were armed for whose blood money had to be paid; now whole nations are armed to the last man, preparing to cut one another's throats. . . . To prepare them for the butchery their hatred is inflamed by assuring them that they are hated. And kindly men of good will are caught by that trap, and then in obedience to a senseless command crowds of peaceful citizens fling themselves on one another with the ferocity of wild beasts. . . . And they will go like sheep to the slaughter not knowing where they are going, . . . And they will go unprotestingly, submissively and resignedly, not knowing and not understanding that the strength is theirs, and that the power would be in their hands if only they wished it so, . . . We know that the best of us will be mown down, and our works destroyed in the germ. We know this, and tremble with rage, but we can do nothing. . . . We are enslaved by the laws we have made for our own protection and which now oppress us. . . . And it would be well if the matter concerned only one generation. But it is much more than that . . . these ambitious statesmen . . . have so inflamed national hatred that on tomorrow's war the fate of the whole race will be staked. The vanquished will have to disappear, and a new Europe will be formed on bases so unjust, so brutal, so bloody and dishonoured by such crimes, that it cannot but be worse than that of today – more iniquitous, barbarous, and more violent. One feels that a

terrible hopelessness hangs over each of us. We rush about in a
blind alley with guns pointing at us from all sides. We work like
sailors on a sinking ship. Our pleasures are those of a man condemned to death who is allowed to choose his favourite dish a
quarter of an hour before his execution. Terror paralyses our
thoughts and the highest exercise of our intelligence is to calculate,
by studying the obscure speeches of ministers and the words of
monarchs, and by ruminating on the utterances of diplomatists
with which the newspapers are filled, when we shall be killed –
this year or next. A time can hardly be found in history when life
was more insecure and more crushed by oppressive horror.[1]

Unless we assume that man is an animal foredoomed to
destruction by his own irrationality, the very clarity and force
of the above analysis made in 1889 demands from us an explanation of the forces which prevailed over the voice of sanity.
Opinions only differ when it comes to the question of emphasis:
whether to lay the primary responsibility at the door of an
irrational economy, namely capitalism, or on the ambitions of
nationalism unprepared to measure the cost, or on militarism.
In practice they are all interwoven with each other. Ultimately
what happens in the affairs of men is determined by the moral
stature of men. Economic, political and legal institutions, social
customs and the content of communication media all react
upon each other and influence the moral climate. History is
the aggregate product of human behaviour, itself the expression
of men's beliefs about their world, their wants and duties in it.
The case would seem a strong one that the primary factor in
determining the disastrous outcome to the nineteenth century
was the factor of militarism. The efforts of the Tolstoys, the
Rollands, the Rods and countless anonymous ones were frustrated in the last resort by the omnipresent and irresistibly
pervasive influence of the institution of universal military
service to which the entire civil populace had become habituated.[2] It is idle to teach men their solemn duty to obey the
ancient injunction 'Thou shalt not kill' when the State, with
all the 'moral' authority which the sovereign law exerts over
men's minds, prevails upon every available adult male to under-

---

[1] *Le Sens de la Vie*, 1889, 17th ed., 1904, pp. 209–13, an earlier edition of which
is quoted by Tolstoy in *The Kingdom of God is Within You.*

[2] England free from conscription until 1916 was also the country which saw most
resistance to World War I, although the resistance was very weak.

go training in the skills and techniques of killing. The moral and educational influence of such an institution as military conscription is incalculable. Its physical power in the hands of the practitioners of *raison d'état* is self-evident. Its moral power is even greater. Conscription, originally adopted as a strictly defensive measure, became eventually at least as important a factor in threatening the peace of Europe as the technological advances in the weapons themselves.

War now came to draw upon much more dangerous emotions. As States became national 'democratic' States, entire peoples were taught to identify their own interests with those of the State. Wars were no longer confined to professional soldiers; they were waged by the mobilization of entire populations not for limited ends but for survival as a 'Great Power'. In the eighteenth and nineteenth centuries, wars were in truth efforts to attain the goals of diplomacy by other means. Thus when adequate force had been applied at a given pressure point, there was a reasonable expectation that a peace treaty might be negotiated. Some territory might have to be yielded; but a State's capacity to remain in the game was unimpaired, life was long, and at the next trial of fortunes the tables might well be reversed. By the twentieth century nations could with growing plausibility see everything at stake in titanic struggles in which all manpower, even woman power, was mobilized for war. Moreover, rapidly developing technologies were expanding at an unprecedented rate the power of the war machines. By concentrating enormous numbers of men in limited areas, by feeding, supplying, equipping and reinforcing the fighting areas over immense communication lines, Capitalism enabled the contending sides to survive the attrition of prolonged trench warfare. All previous ritual slaughters were dwarfed in comparison.

Before turning to the final period of European *raison d'état* militarism, there are two lessons to be drawn from the experience of the first half of the twentieth century. The first relates to the ancient doctrine, beloved of military strategists and diplomatic historians, of the balance of power, the modern version of the still older myth of the Chancellories, *Si vis pacem, para bellum.* According to this theory all organized groups are always engaged in the quest for power. Thus a most dangerous situation exists whenever a power vacuum invites exploitation of its possibilities by rival power groups. The doctrine is analogous to the doctrine of the separation of powers in the law of the constitution. The best safeguard against the danger of a monopoly of political power is to establish a number of concentric circles of authority checking the latent ambitions of each. In international relations, the parallel notion is that the best deterrent against the peace-breaker is the presence of a stable and equal power confronting him. In short, the struggle for power is the only goal to which able and energetic men in any community will consent to devote their lives; and accordingly the best way of minimizing explosions between competing groups is to ensure that the separate pinnacles remain at the same level, so that none feel threatened by nor tempted to subjugate the others. The events of August 1914 were a tragic but decisive comment on this theory. The statesmen of Europe had devoted immense energies and diplomatic skill to negotiating interlocking treaties to ensure a most delicate balance of power. The cataclysm began to erupt at the point of most perfect balance. The fallacy lies in the supposition that men trained and psychically geared to the struggle for power will ever be capable of abandoning it through conviction of the futility or irrationality of its further pursuit.

The second point touches upon the behaviour of the Powers in the years preceding the Second World War. The accepted view is that resistance by violence, that is the wholesale slaughter of men, women and children, was morally the only correct response to the aggressive acts of Hitlerite Germany; that reluctance to understand this moral imperative and act upon it was directly responsible for the appeasement of Hitler which in its turn made the Second World War inevitable. Some even confuse non-violent resistance with 'Munich' appeasement or even outright Pétainist collaboration. The immediate causes of the Second World War may be classified under two heads: those events which made possible the Hitlerite ascendancy inside Germany; and those events which permitted the eruption and expansion of the Hitlerite forces beyond the German frontier. In each case the answer is not to be found in the moral deficiencies of the German people alone, although their share of responsibility is obviously very large. This is not the place to analyse the causes of the Nazis' rise to power nor to attribute responsibility for those causes. It is sufficient to point out that the punitive elements in the Treaty of Versailles, the vindictive continuation of the Allied Blockade of Germany after the armistice, the occupation of the Ruhr, the deflation of German currency, the restriction of American immigration quotas from Central Europe, the economic blizzard and mass unemployment, were all vitally relevant factors in the growth of Nazism. They were all factors within the power of nations other than the Germans to influence, modify or actually prevent. In short, they reflected the moral deficiencies of Britons, Frenchmen and Americans as well as Germans. Moreover, the single most important factor in creating the conditions and climate out of which Nazism emerged was the First World War itself. This conditioned men to the 'legitimacy' of mass slaughter and inhuman cruelties, and left a legacy of hatred and resentment in frustrated and authoritarian groups among the vanquished.

Having themselves contributed generously to the pathological conditions out of which Nazism in Germany arose, the Western Powers proceeded either to condone or neglect all necessary non-violent action whereby the Nazi power could have been prevented from embarking upon external aggression. Economic sanctions were rejected when they were proposed by the League against Japan for her invasion of Manchuria in 1931, and again against Italy for her invasion of Abyssinia in 1935. By the hypocrisy of the one-sided Eden doctrine of Non-Intervention, the Spanish Republicans were sacrificed to the invading Fascist and Nazi troops in support of the Falangist insurrection. Confronted with the illegal and aggressive acts committed by Hitler against international law and against the physical existence of Austria and Czechoslovakia, the Western Powers deliberately refused to concert counter-measures of a collective non-violent character while there was still time with the U.S.S.R. and the Powers of Eastern Europe. Western ruling circles feared the Bolsheviks, who then threatened nobody outside their own frontiers, so deeply that at first they welcomed the growth of Nazism in central Europe as a barrier against the 'Bolshevik threat'. They also hoped that Nazi power might be induced to turn eastwards and destroy the Bolsheviks on their behalf. Even when the reality of the Nazi threat had been correctly appreciated, hostility to Russia continued to inhibit the necessary initiative or response to Russian initiative until it was too late,

By the summer of 1939 when the Hitler-Stalin Pact was suddenly announced, the legacy of accumulated error was such that any course of action whatever by the Western Powers would have led to immense suffering and loss of life. Given the existing limits to the moral understanding and courage of Western man, it was at that point inevitable that resistance to Hitler would be by time-honoured military means. It was the only kind of resistance which was understood; and even violent resistance is less morally debilitating than cowardly appeasement. It does not follow, however, that that was the right course of action to take. To say that it was then inevitable does not mean that it was morally right. To make this distinction is important in order to clarify our minds as to the nature of right action now and in the future.

Hitler almost certainly could have been prevented from achieving power in Germany by wise and unselfish economic action on the part of other Europeans, acting in concert with democratic and peaceful groups in Germany. Even after Hitler had come to power, it is possible to argue that he could have been prevented from successful aggression by determined economic and non-violent concerted action against international acts of aggression through the League of Nations. After this failure, too, non-violent resistance to Hitler in the days following 2 September 1939 would have resulted inevitably in terrible violence, suffering and death by most of the European peoples. The price of moral obloquy must in the end be paid. The eternal balance is kept. Obedience to the moral law brings its own reward; neglect of it brings its tribulation and sorrow.

> If you love and serve men, you cannot by any hiding or stratagem escape the remuneration. Secret retributions are always restoring the level, when disturbed, of the divine justice. It is impossible to tilt the beam. All the tyrants and proprietors and monopolists of the world in vain set their shoulders to heave the bar. Settles for evermore the ponderous equator to its line, and man and mote, and star and sun, must range to it, or be pulverized by the recoil.[1]

What would have been the eventual outcome we cannot know. Mankind would have seen something of the force of moral example and heroism of non-violent resistance on a larger scale than in the modest examples in Norway and Denmark. Even

[1] Emerson, *Lectures and Biographical Sketches*, 1868, p. 186

in that darkest hour it cannot be assumed that faith in humanity and the capacity to respond to moral example must necessarily have perished.

The ultimate outcome, had we resisted the Nazis non-violently in 1939, is scarcely within the realm of speculation. The result of violent resistance we do know. It is a matter of history. As the fears and hatreds generated by the world conflict grew, the Nazi leadership made up of increasingly desperate and hate-filled men stepped up the original cruel persecution of the Jews into the mass tortures and genocide in the death camps of Auschwitz, Buchenwald, Maideneck, Belsen and elsewhere. On the Western side where men had been dragged reluctantly into war in defence of civilized values, the moral conscience was rapidly eroded with the gravest of consequences. The initial shock at the razing of a small town like Guernica by aerial bombardment or the blitzing of Coventry was soon followed by condonation of our own saturation bombing. This was deliberately aimed at breaking civilian morale by fire curtains transforming cities like Hamburg, Dresden and Berlin into raging infernos, consuming indiscriminately vast numbers of human beings. And finally, the Japanese, who had already sued for peace, suffered the atomic bombing of Hiroshima – a crime unique in the annals of men. For this everyone of us who supported World War II on either side, whatever our motives, must unavoidably bear some responsibility.

The fourth and latest age of European power politics had opened. For a brief moment it seemed possible that mankind might have been stayed in its headlong plunge to destruction by the shock of Hiroshima's martyrdom. But guilt led those responsible to suppress the truth and it was long before the full facts began to be known. In any event they were soon apparently forgotten by those in power. Whatever the capacity of Governments to assess the moral significance of the dropping of atomic bombs on Japanese people, there was no doubt about their assessment of the military implications. Reactions at top policy level in the camps of the mammoth military Powers that met along the Elbe and over the ruins of Hitler's Reich Chancellory in Berlin were rapid indeed. No sooner had the dust settled on the charred and twisted skeleton of Hiroshima than a new arms race, more deadly, more swiftly dynamic than any in history was under way. Today, after less than two decades, the whole of mankind stands in imminent and grievous peril. It is no longer possible to be reasonably confident of the survival of human and animal life. Under the shadow of the mushroom cloud we all of us, the very young as well as the very old, are compelled to lead what we still politely choose to call our lives. The arms race itself still continues in the desperate struggle of each to subjugate the other to his will or in the current euphemism 'to negotiate from strength'. A struggle to reach and thus secure strategic primacy of control of the moon and even the more distant planets has by no means been ruled out. While below millions of men dwell permanently on the verge of starvation in a world of privilege, affluence and luxury.

In this horrifying situation, one gleam of hope may permit a belief in the possibility of keeping this death struggle under control until such time as enough people on both sides are able to awake from their deluded torpor and assert themselves. There is the strength and stabilizing influence of the neutral nations. If the two sides were ever to succeed in carving up the entire globe into cold war reservoirs, humanity's final hopes would almost certainly be extinguished. Seen in this light, one is compelled to marvel at the shortsightedness with which the West Europeans have permitted their ruling classes to establish American economic and military hegemony over the continent. Britain has not yet been fully integrated into the economy of the Atlantic community, although admission to the Common Market would complete the plans for common capitalist planning from Scotland to the toe of Italy. The conditions for capital investment and expansion, originally created by the economic blood transfusions of Marshall Aid and subsequent defence loans, were given fresh momentum by the steady inflow after 1958 of private entrepreneur capital from the United States into Europe. In addition, integration of the great international trusts inside Europe continues to gather pace as merger follows merger. Price maintenance or market sharing agreements are entered into by European firms on an international plane; while an increasing trend to establish corporate agreements on a trans-atlantic scale is already well entrenched. Chrysler, Westinghouse, Smith Corona, Goodrich and Du Pont enter into agreements with Simca, Le Creusot et Joument, Haaman, AKU, and

Englebert respectively.[1] While the lobbies are at work to ensure Britain's absorption in the common economic-military effort, far-sighted planners are already mooting the next step of creating a free trade area out of the entire Atlantic bloc. In such a mammoth economic-military unit, sovereign power will doubtless reside in Washington, but the struggle for control over the localized nerve centres of the American strategic deterrent is likely to grow more bitter.

In conclusion, it is necessary to summarize the nature of the 'realist' fallacy. Realism consists in accepting as fact the view that man is moved more by fear and acquisitiveness than by reason. He clings tenaciously to the belief that security lies in armed might. The slightest familiarity with the experience of this method practised again and again through countless ages is sufficient to show how illusory it is. But to act in accord with fear is always easier; when fears are uppermost, the voice of experience is silenced by a built-in incredulity concerning one's own fallibility. Although the law is universally valid, somehow we ourselves will constitute the exception. In like manner everyone knows that man is mortal, but it is exceedingly difficult to accept the idea of one's own death. Death essentially is something that always happens to other people. Yet, however strong the evidence that man will not listen to reason, there is no hopeful alternative other than to continue unceasingly to spell out the rational course of action. As Freud put it, 'The voice of the intellect is a soft one, but it does not rest till it has gained a hearing. Finally, after a countless succession of rebuffs, it succeeds.'[2]

The quest for security through armed violence is self-defeating for a very simple reason. Such efforts generate similar efforts on the part of the opponent; and in the dynamics of the ensuing competition still larger quantities of fear and hate are mutually generated. Every act of violence, every threat of violence, directed at men similarly immature, incites a ready emulation. Violence comes only too easily to men. Given the natural predisposition to unleash aggression in this way, powerful inhibitions are necessary to restrain such tendencies. The threat of violence

---

[1] See M. Barratt Brown, *After Imperialism*, 1963, chaps. 9 and 10; Anderson and Hall, 'Politics of the Common Market', *New Left Review*, July-August 1961; and J. H. Dunning, 'United States Overseas Investment and European Economic Integration', *National Provincial Bank Review*, May 1960

[2] *The Future of an Illusion*, 1962 ed., p. 49

finds a ready and eager response. Violence evokes violence, which in its turn 'justifies' further violence. To suppose that victory by violence will somehow advance human welfare is entirely illusory. On the contrary, humanity's most dangerous instincts will receive further confirmation at the 'realistic' level. The emotions of resentment and desire for vengeance left smouldering in the defeated party must also be included in the reckoning. Violence begets violence; the threat begets the threat just as an elastic rubber ball flung at a hard surface bounces back at similar velocity. The illusion is as old as man; its hold does not appear to have slackened even today when the price of the illusion may be the life of the species itself. The illusion is that man lives by *raison d'état*; or, expressed most simply, that man lives by care for himself. He does not; and by persisting in this illusion he does and can only succeed in destroying himself. For the law of life is the law of love. We do not make this law; but it is nevertheless binding upon all men. And defiance of the law brings in its wake the inescapable penalty.

It is a truism that mankind's security and wellbeing are dependent upon the level of moral development attained, and equally that man is endangered by the blunting of his moral sensibilities. Yet this is exactly what happens whenever violence is practised and accepted as 'right' or 'just' or 'necessary'. Mankind can with terrifying swiftness be habituated to ever-growing patterns of violence. In 1871 Bismarck was prevented by public opinion from shelling an open city. Today after rapid acclimatization through a succession of events such as Guernica, Coventry, Lidice, Dresden, Auschwitz, and finally Hiroshima and Nagasaki, we have daily to listen to politicians, soldiers, editorialists, defence correspondents, discussing contingent plans for the possible destruction of tens or hundreds of millions of human beings. The competition set in motion by war speeds up technical developments in the means of destruction. The technology of terror, the engines of destruction themselves greatly add to the existing quantum of terror, and make it increasingly difficult to establish an atmosphere in which rationality might prevail. But much the most serious outcome of the cycle of war is the deterioration of moral standards. We are secure in so far as men shrink with revulsion from doing cruel things to men; we are in peril in so far as men learn to talk glibly of cruelty or when they react casually to the persecution of others. It is this moral fact, not the existence of nuclear weapons as such, which constitutes the gravity of our present peril.

Already the apologists of 'realism' are busy exhorting us to accept the realities of life in the atomic age, and learn to live with the Bomb. According to these theorists – and they are to be found high in the councils of Church and State – we have never been so secure as we are today under the umbrella of the Bomb. The terror inspired by the equilibrium of fear is such that we can rely on the Bomb as an effective deterrent, a super-policeman guaranteeing the peace of mankind. In other words, the peace which man has been unable to gain through two millennia of the advocacy of brotherly love will now be secured through fear. What we failed to win under the symbol of the star of Bethlehem, we shall gain under the symbol of the mushroom cloud. Men will not act rationally from love, but they will learn to do so from fear. In fact, the atomic age has at last 'proved' what so many men have always wanted to believe in their hearts: that the doctrine of the carpenter of Nazareth is a monumental irrelevance; that his sacrifice on Calvary was pathetic, noble perhaps, but futile and pointless. For this is the logic of the doctrine of the maintenance of peace through the deterrent. And it is curious to hear such doctrines on the lips of Bishops and Churchmen.

If it were possible to secure the true welfare of mankind through an increase in reliance upon fear, it would mean the reversal of our entire legacy of moral values. The people best equipped to live in such a culture would be precisely those with the most blunted sensibilities. Those with a genuine love of their fellow-men, possessed of a true capacity for outrage at cruelty and oppression and the threat of such, would finally be proved to be the cranks and neurotics the majority have always claimed them to be. Moral insensibility would be the first qualification of personality stability under such conditions. Nor is this any fanciful hypothesis. It is beginning to happen as more and more citizens capitulate in order to do the work required by the industries of death. This fundamental truth has been well stated by Robert Bolt in his *A Man for All Seasons*. Henry VIII in a final attempt to break More's will to resist, sends to the prisoner in the Tower his beloved daughter Meg, under promise that she will try to persuade her father to consent to the Oath of Supremacy. Fearful for the life of her father, as Henry had calculated, against her own true judgement she is moved to plead to make the worse appear the better cause. More is himself sorely vulnerable, weak from long imprisonment, moved by the love he bore his daughter. Margaret in her desperation seeks to turn More's own oft-repeated arguments against him in order to gain his life. No one was more keenly alive than More to the psychological dangers of martyrdom, or more suspicious of those who might use a good cause to advance their own ambitions for celebrity or glory. He had often warned against heroes themselves, as well as against hero-worship. But even in the Tower, faced by his daughter for the last time, he could not be prevailed upon to carry his suspicions of 'heroism' to the length of denying that there are limits beyond which a man may not go without sacrificing his integrity. More agrees with Margaret that the State is three quarters bad, and that the responsibility for this cannot be laid at his door. Seizing her opportunity, she pleads, 'Then if you elect to suffer for it, you elect yourself a hero.'

And More replies:

That's very neat. But look now . . . If we lived in a State where virtue was profitable, common sense would make us good, and greed would make us saintly. And we'd live like animals or angels in the happy land that *needs* no heroes. But since in fact we see that avarice, anger, envy, pride, sloth, lust and stupidity commonly profit far beyond humility, chastity, fortitude, justice and thought, and have to choose, to be human at all . . . why then perhaps we *must* stand fast a little – even at the risk of being heroes.[1]

---

[1] Bolt, *A Man for All Seasons*, Heinemann (Drama Library edition), 1960

6 Reason and Emotion in the Logic of Equality

SOME POLITICAL philosophers, notably Plato and Rousseau, have attempted to lay down the principles which would govern a rational or 'ideal' society. But traditional political thought has been mainly concerned with the attempts to find a justification for State power in order that it may be legitimized. This has meant that the violence on which all States ultimately rest has received at least tacitly the moral absolution of the philosophers. The consequences of this for the moral judgement have been far-reaching. An unquestioned belief in the morality of State power operates as an effective inhibition against detached investigation of the nature of power and its effects in human behaviour. More-over, once the State, with its ancillary military and industrial agencies, is acknowledged as morally legitimate, the problem is inescapable of how this morality can be reconciled with the morality of the world's religions, which emphasize the ethical paramountcy of gentleness, renunciation, poverty. Under pressure we may be tempted to emasculate the teaching of Jesus Christ, for example, by labelling his ethical demands 'ideals', which can then safely be relegated to a plane of unpracticality. Or it may be acknowledged that these are imperatives for those who aspire to holiness, and are appropriate for the *réligieux* in the cloister. A dual standard of values is permitted to make its appearance. The familiar arguments then commence as to the nature of the secular good, relative to the circumstances, needs or understanding of the time.

The belief that moral values are unitary, not plural, to be applied under all circumstances is rightly seen by those attached to our existing way of life as revolutionary in purpose. Such a radical attempt to bridge the gap between the 'is' and the 'ought' rests on an appeal to universal rational principle transcending all parochial or national particularism. Since particular group loyalties still determine a large part of the behaviour of men, it is to be expected that a belief in a unitary moral universe will evoke strong resistance at the level of theory of knowledge. Many theoretical arguments have in fact been accumulated to rationalize the compromises arising out of the dual plane of values inherent in our existing society. Most fundamental is the denial of the existence of 'Truth', viz. a single unitary system of moral values known to man. The contemporary liberal pragmatist or positivist echoes Pilate's scepticism. At first glance he might appear to occupy strong ground. The grounds for the view that truth and falsity are logical categories inapplicable to moral values are not difficult to understand. In one obvious respect, the world of the physical sciences contrasts sharply with the world of human studies. In the former, rules and procedure exist to achieve agreement as to what the truth obliges us to believe. In the humanities, however, such means do not appear to be available. Diversification of opinion, extensive within a single society, is as nothing to what confronts us when we attempt to establish a single realm of discourse between different geographical cultures or historical epochs. The view is immediately plausible which asserts the relativity of moral judgements and denies the possibility of universal objective moral principles. If the alleged truths are rationally accessible, why do they appear in such conflicting guise to eminently reasonable men? *Quot homines, tot sententiae.*

This view is reinforced by strong emotions. The lesson of religious intolerance and its painful consequences took a long time to learn, but it has been learnt. The Roman Catholic claim, for example, to be the one true faith is resented by Protestants because they cannot agree, but more especially because to them it smacks of intolerance. The situation is analogous with the liberal empiricist's reaction to those who claim to have access to absolute moral standards. Such a claim, it is alleged, betrays a lack of humility and an unwarranted confidence in human reason applied to matters beyond its competence. It represents a failure to respect the intelligence and integrity of all those cultured and civilized men who unequivocally reject this view. Nothing is calculated to give greater provocation than the appearance of an assumption of infallibility or the claim to have direct access to truth denied by one's opponents. Simply to believe in 'the truth' is itself widely held to be a sinister mark of an authoritarian or 'totalitarian' character.[1]

If we assert that truth in morals is unitary, not plural nor relative, and that objective grounds exist for giving a specific content to moral obligation, it will certainly be suggested that we are claiming to be the only ones in the regiment in step. In one sense this may be true enough, and we must have the courage to admit it. What cannot be admitted is that this view logically entails intolerance. The discussion is about theory of knowledge. To hold any view in such a way as to suggest that we have no saving sense of our own fallibility, that there may be no error in our premises or our logic, that 'in the bowels of Christ we *may* be mistaken', is to be intolerant. But to argue that a moral rule can itself be right or wrong because it can be tested by reference to a superior rule is not intolerant. Nor is the opposing view that asserts that no superior rule exists, and that moral rules are accordingly contingent to a particular culture.

The critical assumption underlying this book is that a universal moral rule is accessible to the human mind, and that it is the principle of human equality. It is not suggested that the adoption of the principle of equality is itself necessarily productive of goodness, nor that it is an infallible guide as to what ought to be done in every possible circumstance. Simply that the concept is central to the discussion of any moral problem. This is far from being generally agreed. The question of referents whereby the

---

[1] *See* J. A. C. Brown, *Techniques of Persuasion*, 1963.

George Orwell's definition of authoritarianism is cited: the assumption 'that an opponent cannot be both honest and intelligent. Each of them tacitly claims that "the truth" has already been revealed, and that the heretic, if he is not simply a fool, is secretly aware of "the truth" and merely resists it out of selfish motives.' Dr Brown continues, 'From this it follows that the heretic is either a criminal or mad, and the appropriate treatment is prison, death, or (on the assumption that he is suffering from a sort of moral imbecility) some form of "corrective training" directed at removing "criminal thoughts" and instilling a new code of morals' (p. 35).

A man who believes in 'the truth' is held to be intolerant. A tolerant man is one mature enough to be uncertain as a result of his appreciation of the complexity of moral problems.

'Thus totalitarianism, whether in religion or in politics, appeals to this type because it leaves no question or problem open but provides certainty. Although outwardly compliant, the authoritarian is strongly ambivalent towards his parents and parent-figures, whereas the humanist, who has been brought up without fear of his fundamental impulses, expresses whatever hostility he may feel openly and does not mind uncertainty. He is mentally more flexible and seldom takes the view that "there is only one right way of doing anything"; for him there are various shades of grey, not simply black or white' (pp. 56–7).

moral rules are themselves to be settled is among the most hotly disputed. This is why the conclusion is tempting that moral disputes spring from fundamental differences of value, which cannot be bridged by rational means, since there is no agreement about the general guiding rule.[1] It is proposed, therefore, to examine the logic of the arguments which purport to establish that moral values can only be criticized within the framework of rules governing that particular moral system. This view rests on the belief that right and wrong are relative concepts, that fact and value are quite separate modes of experience, and that attempts to show that differing value systems are themselves subject to a universal value test are doomed to failure. The second stage of the argument will need to examine in some detail why it is that there is no disposition among men to agree about the nature of this moral referent, if, as is suggested, it is rationally discernible and governs the conflicting value systems by which men in practice appear to govern their lives. And finally, as the argument about equality is particularly prone to resort to the *argumentum ad hominem* with the suggestion that certain arguments may be discredited as being 'emotional', I shall attempt to say something on the connection between reason and emotion in the formation of moral judgements.

(i) *Are Moral Values Rationally Neutral?*

Political philosophers have for centuries concerned themselves with the problem of the legitimacy of law and the State. Some have rested on an appeal to some form of Authority, ranging from Divine Right to Dialectical Materialism; others have relied on the binding nature of contract, others on the principle of consent, yet others on the wisdom of utility. Nor have there been wanting those who have argued that no law that rests on force can be morally legitimate. The argument that has for so long raged between the contending views is today itself discredited. The belief that arguing about the logical foundations of the nature of political obligation was a rational enterprise has itself been singled out as the great illusion. The notion that categories

---

[1] It is frequently suggested that the concept of 'equality' is too vague or 'vacuous' to be of practical value. A short discussion of what is meant by 'equality' will be found in the concluding chapter.

of truth and falsity were applicable to such discussions was a symptom of confused thinking. The prevailing view seems to be that political philosophy in the past has consisted of a series of institutional and behavioural definitions and axioms, recommended on logical grounds falsely supposed to be important as certificates of rational validity. The definition and axioms, if adopted, might well entail important practical consequences, and may therefore be of considerable historical interest. They may even warrant study for the light they may still throw on our present problems. But the logical grounds on which the definitions and axioms were recommended, the source of protracted discussion, are rejected as worthless. When we speak of moral principles, we can rationally mean nothing more than that certain rules of conduct are observed with a greater or lesser degree of statistical uniformity at a given time and place. To suppose that there are universal moral principles binding upon men as such is illusion. Nineteenth-century positivism had finally pushed the logic of its reasoning to its ultimate conclusion.[1]

The role of the philosopher is as a result now largely confined to that of a professional logician who chooses to apply his expertise to linguistic usage in the field of his choice. The political philosopher, for example, may subject political theories to critical analysis to eliminate confusion arising out of logical error or ambiguity of terminology. He will scrutinize the way in which people use their political vocabulary, make recommendations to secure greater precision of usage, expose internal inconsistencies in argument, and bring into the open concealed or suppressed premises. The one thing that is definitely outside the competence of the logician of language are questions of truth or falsity in the sense of the ultimate appropriateness of any specific political theory. If it is necessary to know whether a proposed course of action is prudent or judicious, the recommended pro-

---

[1]There is no doubt what the reaction of the nineteenth-century positivist would have been if it had been possible to confront him with the arguments of twentieth-century logical positivism. George Eliot herself offers a good example. F. W. H. Myers, recalling a conversation with her in 1873, wrote, 'I remember how, at Cambridge, I walked with her once in the Fellows' Garden of Trinity, on an evening of rainy May; and she, stirred somewhat beyond her wont, and taking as her text the three words which have been used so often as the inspiring trumpet-calls of men, – the words *God*, *Immortality*, *Duty*, – pronounced, with terrible earnestness, how inconceivable was the *first*, how unbelievable the *second*, and yet how peremptory and absolute the *third*. Never, perhaps, have sterner accents affirmed the sovereignty of impersonal and unrecompensing law.' *Essays – Modern* (1883), pp. 268–9.

cedure is to inquire what the balance of opinion is among the people whose working lives are spent in investigating and handling the affairs in question.

Thus the curtain is pulled down on the entire metaphysical debate, since arguments about foundations are logically worthless. It would be difficult to exaggerate how momentous a break with the past this represents. It is partly to be explained by the degree of internal cultural homogeneity that has been reached in our society. Its plausibility as a view is clearly dependent on the absence of fundamental divisions of an ideological character within a given culture.[1] Perhaps the principal influence at work has been the reaction against the nineteenth-century ascendancy of theology as 'the queen of the sciences'. A century ago, the kind of issues raised in books like *Essays and Reviews* or *Lux Mundi* constituted focal points of educated discussion. As long ago as 1861, however, we find Goldwin Smith, Regius Professor at Oxford, observing caustically that while twenty years ago geological issues had been 'settled by reference to 'the double nature of a sacrament', nowadays moral and spiritual questions were settled by the methods of physics. By the end of the century the role filled by men of the stamp of Newman, Wilberforce, Jowett, Colenso, Mansel and Maurice as instigators of ideas and debate had passed into quite different hands. Secular physicists or sociologists now made the running: Frazer, Freud, Rutherford, Einstein. Unless a discipline could manifest the hall-marks of professionalism with some claim to scientific status, its prestige seemed strangely diminished. Detachment,

---

[1]This is perhaps best illustrated by a brief glance at a culture experiencing the conflicts of transition. The following tragic episode from Renaissance Florence makes the point. In 1513, the year which saw the overthrow of Soderini's Republic and the return of the Medicis to Florence, two young men, Boscoli and Capponi, were arrested and summarily executed for suspected conspiracy to restore the Republic. Boscoli, when informed of his imminent execution, showed signs of great agitation, and requested that a friar be summoned to confess him. His agitation rose not from fear but from concern over the rightness of his metaphysical 'foundations'. He was torn between the assumptions of pagan stoicism and those of Christianity. Guided by a love of republican liberty, inspired by the example of Brutus, he had learnt from the Stoics how to govern his fears by his reason. His personal courage never wavered. But he was beset by metaphysical conflict. Might not the Christian metaphysic be correct? Was it permissible to conspire even against a tyrant? Hence the urgent summons to the friar, Della Robbia. Would the confessor answer his questions? Did St Thomas unequivocally condemn conspiracy? And when Della Robbia sought to calm him, Boscoli impatiently chided him: 'Father, do not lose time in teaching me what I already know from the philosophers. Help me to learn to die for the love of Christ.'

austerity, purity, neutrality, severe rationality became increasingly the academic virtues most keenly prized. Professor Ryle in his Introduction to *The Revolution in Philosophy* (1956), expressed it thus: 'Philosophers had now to be philosophers' philosophers; and in their colloquia there was as little room for party politics as there is in courts of law.'

The essentials of the problem thus defined are clear. If philosophy was to enjoy scientific status, it had to be put beyond the reach of controversy of the kind associated with politics. Philosophy, like science, like law, must be neutral. To this end it is necessary to establish the view that premises, which are a source of endless controversy without ever appearing to be finally resolved, are logically worthless. Philosophy, thus purified, gets on with the high-status task of 'neutral' linguistic analysis. The claim to moral and political neutrality seems plausible because people can agree in describing events which, because of divergent political opinions, they would regard as controversial as soon as an attempt was made to evaluate them. Factual agreement at the level of the reporter can reasonably be expected, since all that is required is accuracy of observation and professional integrity. But as soon as interpretation of facts begins, trouble may well arise of a kind that is not to be remedied either by more painstaking investigation or by heightened integrity. The issue is irresoluble because each party holds a different set of assumptions, neither of which is susceptible of falsification or disproof. Such is the familiar reasoning, neatly summed up in the well-known aphorism of C. P. Scott of *The Manchester Guardian*: 'comment is free but facts are sacred.' It is a convenient dichotomy, likely to commend itself to liberals in particular as sound common sense.

The superficiality of this view begins to emerge as soon as we attempt to use the formula in cases where two observers are separated from one another by a moral gulf. Differences of the most intransigent kind may well make their appearance – differences that arise at the strictly descriptive and pre-evaluative level. These differences are due to different selections of *significant* fact. In order to form a coherent picture at the descriptive level, it is necessary to choose the facts that are relevant, to make decisions of inclusion and exclusion. Merry and Serge Bromberger's *Secrets of Suez* provides a good example. The following statement concerning Sir Anthony Eden's mode of conducting the Suez war is strictly descriptive. 'On the other hand, the chivalrous component in the Eden make-up prevented him from making use of really psychological bombing – the rocketing of Nasser's GHQ, for example; the paralysing of the vital centres of Cairo and Alexandria; and the spreading of panic' (p. 17). A writer sufficiently morally developed to understand the depravity of indiscriminate killing for political ends would consider as relevant those facts which would explain how it was possible for Eden to order the attack on Suez. Messrs Bromberger, however, moved only, it would appear, by a passion to realize certain political or military ends, select the facts which inhibited Eden from taking the steps necessary to that end, regardless of the cost. Different observers, confining themselves to accurately descriptive statements about the same events, may still seriously conflict with each other. It is not that they disagree about what they are observing. They do not observe the same things, since they are not looking for the same things. Consequently, they do not conduct a conversation or discussion; they talk past one another. People within our common culture can yet inhabit different moral universes. Where this is the case, even when language is confined to description, differences of evaluation may produce descriptive pictures of the same events which cannot be made mutually acceptable. People who acknowledge in politics only the claims of *raison d'état* will *observe* differently from people bound by moral principle, since their standards of significance and relevance are very different.

But the positivist has gone further than insisting that the analytic function in the language of morals and politics is neutral in that it is compatible with *any* values, or that agreement can in principle be guaranteed when we confine ourselves to the weighing of factual evidence. The claim is made that the metaphysical 'foundations' or appraisal techniques themselves add nothing of significance to the picture which has been agreed on a strictly evidential basis. Whatever is to be said of this view, it cannot be claimed to be a politically neutral view. It is itself an intervention in the political debate. For while such a view is compatible with the liberal or pragmatic political stance, it is not compatible with the stand of Christians, Marxists or humanists. In these instances, the metaphysical framework requires every belief to be certified as valid in the sense of being grounded in objective reality. A position that denies metaphysics is itself a metaphysic. A verification principle that defines evidence in such a way as to make it coterminous with sense data, stands itself in need of verification. To say that this principle is 'recommended' as a definition is to evade the issue. At this point in the argument, the appeal is tacitly to Authority, the most discredited of all forms of argument. Why should the *ex cathedra* recommendations of others be accepted?

Probably the most thoroughgoing attempt to establish this view of the status of politics is *The Vocabulary of Politics* by T. D. Weldon. The author attacks the logical status of 'foundations' and deflates the status of political *principles* to the level of convenient saws. Yet he concludes by giving his own 'tests' of appropriateness or rightness of political actions or proposals. These tests, he acknowledges, are not very dissimilar from the kind of liberal utilitarianism espoused by John Stuart Mill, shorn of Mill's 'delusion' that these tests had any objective status. Weldon modestly adopts them as his own personal means of arriving at sensible political judgements much as a wine-taster might discriminate on the basis of a wide experience between different vintages. In short, if we cannot have 'principles', we need not be alarmed since we are left with all we have ever in fact had, and all that is necessary, namely, 'reasons' or pragmatic 'tests'.

It is not difficult to understand why this view should have commended itself to someone in Weldon's position. He was a member of a homogeneous, tolerant, essentially satisfied social class. The ascendancy of the class was marked by prestige, power and prosperity, and it could afford to be and is liberal, civilized, urbane. Essentially three facets of experience sharply impressed him: 1. the freedom of discussion and the comparative ease with which the sources of differences of opinion could be disentangled among people within his culture; 2. the corresponding magnitude of the difficulty of arriving at common conclusions with people from a different but powerful culture in the Communist world; 3. the irreconcilability of this conflict suggesting the advisability of an agreement to disagree with mutual avoidance of proselytism.

This goal is most likely to be brought within reach, if men will deflate their absolute principles. They need to recognize them for what they are, reasons with relative validity. That is, they succeed in persuading those who have been brought up in and conditioned by the culture in question. The motives prompting the adoption of this view may be most creditable and induce us to consider it favourably; but the validation of the view cannot be thus established.

When Weldon gives his reasons for considering a course of action wise, and Weldon's opposite number in the Communist world gives his reasons for concluding the contrary, it is frustrating to be told that the question as to whose reasons are good reasons is not a significant question. For Weldon it is enough that each set of reasons will carry equal conviction to people inhabiting the respective cultures. Communication along rational lines across the cultural frontiers then ceases to be possible. It is doubtful whether Weldon himself was able to stifle all doubts as to the truth of this position. Although he makes a radical attempt to maintain the thesis that there is 'nothing behind or beyond actual political institutions', significant concessions are made in the effort to give convincing analyses of key concepts. A concept inviting rigorous and close scrutiny is expressed in the word 'important'. This cannot be dispensed with, nor does Weldon try to dispense with it. Candour requires him to attempt an analysis of the logical behaviour of this term.

What are the criteria of importance? How do we arrive at them? The analysis indicates that 'context' is a necessary element to be considered in discriminating between degrees of importance. Are we not, then, bound to raise the question whether 'context' is in fact peculiar or unique to a culture? May there not be a considerable overlap between the moral contexts of the capitalist and communist worlds? Why indeed should we take seriously the claims of either to represent the essential truth regarding the nature of a democratic society? Both are in fact cultural derivatives of the European Enlightenment, although each has developed with different emphases elements of the parent tree. On this view the ideological division of the world is not so much one between men wedded to organic and mechanistic theories of the State respectively, but between confirmed collectivists and individualists, totalitarians and libertarians. Rather are there two cultures which share in common subjection to very powerful ruling groups, the difference between them arising out of differing assessments of the *facts* of the matter, namely, on what is happening in the world and why, what are the basic trends and contradictions in communist and capitalist societies, and which are most likely to survive.

It is the cultural overlap between East and West which makes possible a meaningful discourse within a common framework. This was lacking in the case of the Nazis, since they explicitly repudiated the basic premises of all human morality. But even the Nazis were obliged to resort to traditional linguistic usage to express or conceal their diabolic activities. It is only necessary to attempt to reconstruct language on the basis of approbatory terms for evil behaviour and pejorative terms for good behaviour to see the futility of such a linguistic instrument. Even brigands must employ language based on elemental moral truth so far at least as concerns communication within the circles of brigandage. The question might also be raised as to whether there is in common usage in any language a word with pejorative overtones to express an action springing from selflessness or love.[1]

A word must also be said on the social significance of the philosophic attack on the status of metaphysics. Many, particularly among those to whom philosophy seems remote from 'real' problems, may be inclined to wonder what all the pother has been about. If philosophers nowadays must be philosophers' philosophers, if the whole enterprise is an esoteric affair reflecting the peculiar interests of a tiny group, why should the rest of us care one way or the other? Let them get on with it. It is no concern of ours. A popular attitude of sceptical indifference may reinforce the professional pride of a few, themselves indifferent

[1] The only example which occurs to the present writer is the word 'uxorious'. The Oxford English Dictionary gives the following definitions:

1. Of persons: Dotingly or submissively fond of a wife; devotedly attached to a wife.

2. Of actions, etc: Marked or characterized by excessive affection for one's wife. This might appear to be a genuine exception. 'Uxorious' is definitely a pejorative term, and its meaning is to be guilty of an 'excessive affection' for one's wife. Closer examination reveals, however, that in part the word is not an exception, and in part it is the exception that proves the rule.

   (a) To be submissively fond is to be dominated by another. To subject oneself to domination is immoral, and invites a pejorative term.

   (b) The fact that pejorative usage can be associated with 'devoted attachment' to one's wife, indicates the extent to which our culture is historically a masculine one. It is not surprising if the assumptions of masculine arrogance, for so long unchallenged, find uneasy reflection in linguistic usage.

to popular opinion. This is a mistaken attitude. The role of the philosopher in society is always important. His influence, though intangible, permeates society and helps to shape the ideas of people entirely innocent of the original issues. The revolution in modern philosophy has had at least two important consequences.

It has almost certainly had a subtle effect on the respective influence of intellectuals and men of affairs. A theory of knowledge, validating moral judgements only in the limited sense of attributing to them intelligibility and coherence relative to their culture, is essentially pragmatic. Tests of value are pragmatic judgements governed by the facts. The facts are determined by the existing order of society: the judgements by the theoretical framework underpinning the existing social order. To question that framework involves an alternative metaphysic. But since this debate has been discredited as logically bogus, the terms of political debate are restricted to the assumptions of the existing order. These have 'reality' status and constitute the essence of the pragmatic appeal. Men of action generally, when confronted by theories repugnant to them, are very ready in the absence of alternative argument to dismiss theory that is critical of their assumptions as *mere theory* as contrasted with something they call *experience*. In this sense, businessmen together with their military, political and ecclesiastical ancillaries create a conservative climate of opinion in which the theorizing of the intellectual is at a discount. The world of getting and spending is inevitably fashioned in the image of those who get and spend. It can only be effectively criticized in the light of theory deriving from something other than the *ad hoc* experience of the commercial world. Intellectual theorizing is liable to be regarded with distrust as something alien, threatening established power or acquisitive instincts. Theory as such may be condemned in advance as unpractical or the product of the armchair critic. If the countervailing influence of the theorizers is withdrawn, even if they do not throw in their lot with the men of power, an important change in the sociological balance of influence within the society must take place. Such a 'treason of the intellectuals' must ultimately have far-reaching effects.

The other implication of this revolution is a moral one. Earlier critics of logical positivism seemed sometimes to suggest that the morals of positivists themselves must be dubious. This contro-

versy has fortunately long been laid to rest. Nevertheless, the
matter cannot be dismissed altogether. No person's moral culture
is exclusively shaped by his own independent thought. The
legacy of our moral tradition is also important. The full effects of
any significant cultural modification will not be experienced by
the generation directly concerned. This phenomenon is familiar
to sociologists as 'the cultural lag'. Positivists claim that they
are not making a contribution to the *content* of morals, but are
concerned exclusively with the status of value judgements. But
they do claim revolutionary status for the attack on the significance of 'foundations'. People have hitherto commonly supposed
that their justifications aspired to universal rational significance.
It cannot be lightly assumed that a change of this importance in
the assumptions of a society will not ultimately affect moral
behaviour. Given the culture lag, eventual changes in behaviour
are predictable.

Moral decisions are commonly not easy to fulfil. The claims
of others upon us frequently conflict with our own wants. This
being the case, the will stands in constant need of fortification.
Metaphysical belief has certainly been a potent contributory
factor in the psychology of strength of determination of the will.[1]
Nor is it simply a question of wondering about the adequacy of
moral checks unsupported by doctrine, where the temptations
are those of egoism or lust. Intellectual curiosity is among the
finest qualities. But in ambitious and morally confused men, it
can be productive of disastrous consequences, as the ancient
Faustian myth testifies.

> Where
> The soul, that could conceive, and plan,
> Yes, and create its world; whose pride
> The bounds which limit Man defied,
> Heaved with high sense of inborn powers,
> Nor feared to mete its strength with ours.

[1] See *The Law* by Roger Vailland. Marietta, a young peasant girl of Calabria,
suffers a violent but abortive attempt upon her chastity by the village boss, Matteo
Brigante. She finds refuge and solace in an orchard shed with her friend, Pippo.
Vailland comments:

'As soon as they began to embrace, the law of the South, the habits of the South
and everything which, more or less clearly, the two of them had thought till now
about love and the business of love was totally forgotten. Religion having never
been more to them than a superstition shared by others, it did not occur to them

The case of the atomic physicists who by their genius devised the construction of nuclear 'weapons' is instructive here; particularly since the logic of scientific empiricism is identical with that of positivism in morals and politics. The reasoning which led the natural scientists to affirm that their task was strictly empirical, independent of any value judgement, was the same which guided the logical positivists, themselves influenced by the prestige of the natural sciences. The positivists had first sought to assimilate philosophy to the status of science by re-defining its task; and then to emancipate it from the low-status enterprise of metaphysical speculation and the unprofessional, unscientific enterprise of politics. Morals being outside the jurisdiction of scientists or philosophers, and politics being discreditable, what is a scientist to do when confronted in his professional work by political and military pressures? Tragically revealing is the following candid statement by the Göttingen physicist, Professor James Franck, to the Emergency Committee of Atomic Scientists in 1947:

> We scientists seem to be unable to apply these principles [of scientific empiricism] to the immensely complex problems of the political world and its social order. In general we are cautious and therefore tolerant and disinclined to accept total solutions. Our very objectivity prevents us from taking a strong stand in political differences, in which the right is never on one side. So we took the easiest way out and hid in our ivory tower. We felt that neither the good nor the evil applications were our responsibility.[1]

The scientists' tragedy is here spelled out: bewilderment in the presence of morals and politics; dismay on discovering that pragmatism does not produce the right answer in this strange, unaccustomed medium; the unfamiliar feeling of impotence finding expression in 'a plague on both their houses'; and finally the admission that responsibility was shabbily shrugged off by the declaration that good and evil were none of their business.

---

that they were committing a sin; *a morality which has no doctrinal basis collapses in a moment.* They suddenly found themselves exactly like the herdsmen on the hills behind the prosperous city of Uria' (pp. 188–9, my italics).

[1] Quoted by Robert Jungk, *Brighter Than A Thousand Suns*, Penguin Special 1960, p. 41

'Don't bother me with your conscientious scruples. The thing is superb physics' is a remark attributed to one nuclear physicist. The moral degradation of human life under conditions of nuclear terror is not due to any evil in science or to its bedevilment by false methods. It is because of a change in the sense of moral responsibility in natural scientists as well as in political and military leaders. It is not possible to demonstrate that men of the stamp of Copernicus, Galileo, Kepler, Newton could never have been persuaded to work on nuclear 'weapons'. But it is difficult to believe otherwise. The metaphysics of the Renaissance scientists provided their moral convictions with a firm anchorage. The pursuit by science of goals incompatible with those beliefs would almost certainly have done such violence to their natures as to have rendered the conflict intolerable. Be that as it may, it is clear that the very men who exerted such an influence upon the logical positivists are themselves frequently left rudderless and morally bewildered in matters of the profoundest import to their fellow-men. The consequences for mankind have already been tragic.

(ii) *Reason and Emotion of Inequality*

If reason is not an insulated, morally neutral attribute of the mind, the question must be raised as to why there is no general agreement about the nature of our moral referents. Is it not clear that there are unbridgeable gulfs between people, arising out of fundamental differences of value and intractable to rational resolution? The instance generally uppermost in people's minds today is the contrast between the Communist and Capitalist cultures. Yet even here, if we consider only what each has to say about the moral shortcomings of the other and his own alleged virtues, it is not at all clear that the moral referents are significantly different. The other is guilty of tyranny, suppression of freedom, exploitation of the weak. The self is engaged in maximizing the area of freedom, prosperity and justice to all for present and future generations.

Nevertheless, it has to be admitted that the principle of equality is not by any means universally accepted as morally binding. Nor are those who dissent self-evidently less intelligent or less sincere than those who differ from them. To the moral relativist this presents no problem. But the non-relativist, at the risk of appearing arrogant, is logically bound to account for the fact. To do what is right may not always be within my strength; but should it not be possible always to will what is right? But this too is very difficult. Where moral duty is sharply opposed to desire, and is accordingly painful, the mind has a fatal facility for self-deception. It can easily manufacture 'reasons' which 'convince', thereby protecting the psyche from truth that is painful, thus enabling it to believe what it wishes to believe. Freud expressed it as follows:

> Our intelligence, they teach us, can function reliably only when it is removed from the influences of strong emotional impulses; otherwise it behaves merely as an instrument of the will and delivers the inference which the will requires. Thus, in their view, logical arguments are impotent against affective interests, and that is why reasons, which in Falstaff's phrase are 'as plenty as blackberries', produce so few victories in the conflict with interests.[1]

The phenomenon of resistance to truth is familiar enough even where the truth in question is of the physical world. The bitter resistance with which the natural sciences had to contend is common knowledge. Copernicus did not dare publish his heliocentric theory until the year of his death; Giordano Bruno was burnt at the stake; Galileo was compelled to retract the Copernican hypothesis. If our time has seen the growth of a more tolerant climate, the scurrilous vituperation that greeted the discoveries of Darwin and Freud belong only to yesterday. When the subject of investigation is the human being himself, resistance may be expected to be even more virulent than in the case of the physical world. 'It is easy', wrote Tolstoy in *The Kreutzer Sonata*, 'to learn whether there is much iron in the sun, and what other

---

[1] *Thoughts for the Times on War and Death*, 1915, Coll. Papers, Vol. IV, p. 303.

Freud suggests that although logic can produce no end of 'reasons' to order, so to speak, logic is impotent against the affective interests. This would not be surprising. If reasons are 'as plenty as blackberries', what reason is there to suppose that they are true and should command our allegiance? The wealth of reasons are surely produced on the side of and in response to the affective interests, and prevail over the single true reason of the logic of equality, naturally feared by the affective interests. We might do better with a more laconic illustration from elsewhere in Freud: 'Its [the ego's] position midway between the id and reality tempts it only too often to become sycophantic, opportunist and false, like a politician who sees the truth but wants to keep his place in popular favour' (*The Ego and the Id*, 1927, p. 83).

metals there are in the sun and the stars; but it is hard, yes, frightfully hard, to discover that which convicts us of immorality.' But even more elemental and pervasive than the emotional resistance to truth deriving from the need to feel moral is the need not to appear different. The psychic pressure towards uniformity – what used to be referred to as the 'herd instinct' – stems from basic emotions of insecurity. Contemporary sociological investigations have provided very strong empirical confirmation of the thesis so vividly embodied by Hans Andersen in his story, *The Emperor's Clothes*. Frighteningly large numbers of people will apparently deny even the elementary evidence of their senses rather than risk appearing to take a lone or unpopular stand. Even in the scientific world, persistence in advocacy of a hypothesis rejected by a majority of professional colleagues requires courage. But the difficulty goes deeper than that. The pressure exercised by a uniform, received opinion may be so overwhelming that no individual may be capable of emancipating himself sufficiently from a common delusion to bring his critical faculties to bear. The idea with which to challenge existing assumptions is prevented by unconscious resistance or defect of imagination from even arising in the mind. Large numbers of people, for example, recognize the validity of the principle of equality within their own group, but are incapable of grasping its relevance to people outside their group. The extent to which people's capacity to reason consistently is conditioned by traditional and convenient assumptions is strikingly illustrated by H. G. Wells in his fable, *The Country of the Blind*.[1] Experience shows that there is scarcely any limit to the credulity of men, where views are sustained by the unanimity of an uncritical and conservative community. If Wells's

---

[1] Bogota, mountaineering in the Andes, accidentally stumbles on a long-lost tribe of blind people. In this 'country of the blind' he falls in love, only to find his suit unacceptable on account of his peculiarity of being able to see. The bride's father inquires if remedial measures cannot be taken; and Bogota consents to a medical consultation. The doctor diagnoses: 'Those queer things that are called the eyes, and which exist to make an agreeable soft depression in the face, are diseased, in the case of Bogota, in such a way as to affect his brain. They are greatly distended, he has eyelashes, and his eyelids move, and consequently his brain is in a state of constant irritation and destruction.' The prescription is a surgical operation to 'remove these irritant bodies' in order to restore him to perfect sanity. Granted the premise, the logic is flawless. And if we inhabited the kingdom of the blind, it would no doubt be virtually impossible to question the premise that the function of the eyes is 'to make an agreeable soft depression in the face'.

ironic parable seems altogether too fanciful, the example below[1] from life would seem to provide a reasonably close analogy with the Wellsian fable.

Freud himself furnishes us from his own experience with a remarkable illustration of the way in which emotionally un-acceptable knowledge can be unconsciously rejected by the most distinguished minds, even in the presence of evidence that cannot be ignored. He recollects the process of his crucial discovery that the aetiology of every case of neurosis must include feelings of guilt arising out of unconsciously repressed libidinal impulses. He recalls the three occasions on which Breuer, Charcot and Chrobak respectively in conversation with him let fall remarks which clearly indicated that they were aware of the relevance of the patient's sexual history in diagnosing cases of nervous illness.[2] After Freud had published his new and startling discoveries, which fully exploited the insight he owed his teachers, he thought it due to them that he should acknow-ledge his debt. He accordingly raised the matter with Breuer and Chrobak, only to find that each of them denied Freud's recollection of the episode in question. Freud is confident that, had he been able to see Charcot, his response would have been much the same. Freud was not, of course, imputing dishonesty to his distinguished mentors. It was simply that the new truth upon which they had stumbled was so repugnant and would have aroused such antagonism that it was unconsciously rejected until eventually amnesia was complete.

But the simplest and strongest of all forces prompting people

---

[1] The article on *Neuropathology* in the *Encyclopaedia Britannica* (11th ed. 1911) is by F. W. Mott, Fullerian Professor of Physiology, Royal Institution. Ten photo-graphs illustrate different pathological conditions of the brain. (Vol. XIX, facing p. 430, Plate 1) In nine of them evidence of the pathological condition is clearly visible. The caption to figure 1 reads: 'Left hemisphere, case of delusional insanity; this in all respects *might pass for* a normal brain' (my italics). The evidence showed the brain to be normal, but the person, whose brain it was, showed symptoms of acute mental disorder. So the difficulty is 'solved' by recourse to the linguistic 'explana-tion' that this 'might pass for a normal brain'. The idea that mental disturbance including delusional symptoms might be compatible with the possession of a normal brain so radically challenged existing prejudices about the nature of the mind-body relationship that it could not arise.

[2] Breuer had told him that at the heart of these cases were always to be found 'secrets d'alcôve'. Charcot observed: 'Dans les cas pareils, c'est toujours la chose génitale – toujours, toujours, toujours.' Chrobak had advised him that the cause of a particular patient's malady was her husband's impotence; and that the only possible remedy – 'Penis normalis, dosim: repetatur!' – was therefore impossible to prescribe. (Freud, Collected Papers, 1956 ed., Vol. I, pp. 294–296)

to produce rationalizations with which they successfully deceive themselves is that it is easier to succumb to egocentric impulses than to strive to overcome them. In addition, sheer weight of numbers of those who also succumb to their own wants, may give plausibility to the argument that what is done by so many cannot on that account alone be altogether wrong. It is very difficult to believe the truth of that which would 'convict us of immorality'. The truth is not complex or difficult to know or relative but very simple. It has been well summarized in the idiom of the Christian culture by the rationalist, Stuart Mill, in his essay *On Liberty*.

> All Christians believe that the blessed are the poor and humble, and those who are ill-used by the world; that it is easier for a camel to pass through the eye of a needle than for a rich man to enter the kingdom of heaven; that they should judge not, lest they be judged; that they should swear not at all; that they should love their neighbour as themselves; that if one take their cloak, they should give him their coat also; that they should take no thought for the morrow; that if they would be perfect they should sell all that they have and give it to the poor.

But the truth when stated so lucidly and unequivocally is felt to make impossible demands upon us. Therefore the need is great to deny that this can be truth. Mill puts it in these terms:

> The doctrines in their integrity are serviceable to pelt adversaries with; and it is understood that they are to be put forward (when possible) as the reasons for whatever people do that they think laudable. But any one who reminded them that the maxims require an infinity of things which they never even think of doing, would gain nothing but to be classed among those very unpopular characters who affect to be better than other people.[1]

People in fact waver between asserting these things to be true in a mechanical verbalistic fashion without any underlying conviction and affirming that because they cut across the grain of 'human nature', that is, what they themselves want to do, they cannot be true. This inner conflict is perceived much more

---

[1] Everyman ed., p. 101

clearly by Tolstoy than by Stuart Mill.[1] Compare Stuart Mill's
analysis with the reflections of Pierre Bezukhov in *War and Peace*
on the quality of his life in Moscow.

> 'We all profess the Christian law of forgiveness of injuries and love
> of our neighbours, the law in honour of which we have built in
> Moscow forty times forty churches – but yesterday a deserter was
> knouted to death and a minister of that same law of love and
> forgiveness, a priest, gave the soldier a cross to kiss before his
> execution.' So thought Pierre, and the whole of this general
> deception which every one accepts, accustomed as he was to it,
> astonished him each time as if it were something new. 'I understand
> the deception and confusion,' he thought, 'but how am I to tell
> them all that I see? I have tried, and have always found that they
> too in the depths of their souls understand it as I do, and only try
> not to see it. So it appears that it must be so!' (Vol. II, p. 168)

Where Mill speaks of the need for debate to transform into
conviction that learned by rote, Tolstoy draws our attention to
the central difficulty, which is the inner conflict between the
cognitive and conative elements of the mind. This unconscious
conflict is expressed consciously in the feeling that what should
be done is known, but it is nullified by a need to 'try not to see it'.
The root of the matter can be stated quite simply. The difficulty
in perceiving moral truth lies not in the weakness of the intellect
or its incapacity in the field of value, nor in the alleged plurality
of the moral universe. The difficulty lies in large part in the
immense power wielded by received opinion over the individual's emotions. This in turn relates to the comparatively
precarious sense of self-identity in an age where traditional values
have shifted from their moorings, where nothing is settled,
where ordinary people feel increasingly bemused and bewildered. Fear of public opinion may be largely unconscious. Even
those who try to look their fears in the face find this particular

---

[1] Mill holds that the reason why Christian belief has had little appreciable effect
upon behaviour is because these beliefs are only praised and revered, and never
discussed. Beliefs which command universal assent and are never challenged or
criticized, cease to be held as living beliefs. The impulse which had moved the
early Christians, obliged to struggle and suffer persecution for their beliefs, had
been exchanged for the dried husk of respectable and received opinion. The point
is valid, but does not take us very far. There was, for example, no lack of controversy
and debate in matters of penology, but this did not prevent Stuart Mill from being
a vigorous advocate of capital punishment.

fear unusually powerful. 'Men fear thought only less than they fear death' (Russell). To think differently from those among whom we live is so unsettling that our private censors use up great energy in keeping the disturbing ideas at bay. Fear breeds fear, so that self-distrust grows. The integrity and intellectual power of an Aristotle or Marcus Aurelius is not in doubt; but even their thought was vitiated by self-distrust. Aristotle honestly believed the institution of slavery to be in accord with the laws of nature; Aurelius thought it his duty to attempt the extirpation of Christianity.

Unless an individual's sense of identity and purpose are securely located in a metaphysic which transcends the claims of particularist groups, he will be very prone to derive his sense of significance from the values of the group or groups with which he identifies himself. Accordingly any threat to those groups will be experienced as a threat to the stability of the individual ego identifying with them. In Freud's view, the direct threat to ego stability finds expression in the guilt engendered by the conflict between the incestuous id and a hostile super-ego. The dynamics of inner conflict are essentially those of the sexual conflict arising out of the Oedipean parental ties. But as we follow Freud through the mass of evidence accumulated in his interpretation of dreams, we notice the important role played again and again in latent dream thoughts by status anxieties and ambitions arising out of membership of professional or social class groups. Freud generally accepts 'realistically', if not altogether uncritically, conventional standards of class differentiae. These are the social conditions out of which the patient has come and to which he must return. Freud did not interest himself in political attempts to challenge such social assumptions. But such hierarchical class values, resting on the principle of inequality, themselves invite rigorous analytic examination. After all, the defence mechanisms of resistance and repression might well operate in the sphere of class relations as in the sexual sphere, even if the taboos have less force. And might this not provide us with the key to explain why so many rationalizations appear to protect the ego from feelings of guilt engendered by the conflict between impulses of acquisitiveness and aggrandizement and a hostile super-ego? This would explain why so many different moral 'opinions' are to be found, and why moral emancipation is achieved only very slowly and at the cost of great inward struggle.

Ability to look reality in the face is directly proportionate to the strength and invulnerability of the sense of self-identity. Conversely, the weaker the sense of identity, the greater the fear of people who do not belong to the group with which the weak self has for the purposes of security identified. Where fear is present, there is hostility. Where there is hostility there is a need to preserve a stereotype picture of the feared group, which will 'justify' the fear and hatred. This can be most easily achieved by not coming into contact with members of other groups in conditions where they would have to be observed accurately. For example, many white people have either had no experience of living at close quarters with Negroes in their midst, or have only observed their behaviour within the conditions of a master-servant relationship. Where social avoidance is not possible, internal needs to preserve emotional security may well succeed in falsifying the picture of reality to the required extent. There is a direct relationship between clarity of the conception of the self and ability to record and communicate experience of reality with objective accuracy and honesty. The evidence suggests that symptoms of racial prejudice and antagonism are commoner among people who have undergone a sharp change of social status than among those whose position is comparatively stable. When the change has been for the worse, there is a need to find a scapegoat for one's misfortunes. But people whose sudden social mobility has been upwards and not downwards are also more liable to evince symptoms of prejudice than those of a stabler group. This suggests that any sudden change in a person's position in society is liable to arouse anxieties concerning his identity. As a consequence he may then begin to project his own weaknesses and vices on to members of feared outgroups. There are many ways in which the psyche of such persons may deal with evidence and argument incompatible with the picture of reality built up and sustained by their fears. The simplest way is to avoid people likely to present a case that will disturb, and similarly to avoid their meetings and publications. Where this stratagem fails, and reality has to be met, simple logical fallacies in reasoning offer a wide range of opportunities for avoiding painful conclusions. Language too is rich in opportunities for masking and mistranslating reality according to inner psychic needs. It would not be difficult to compile a thesaurus of contrasting terms in common use: the one set to describe qualities of people belonging to one's own group, the other set to describe the same attributes when possessed by members of the group that is feared or hated: e.g. thrifty, stingy; generous, spendthrift; eager, grasping; determined, fanatical; brave, foolhardy; leisurely, idle; smart, flashy; statesman, political manoeuvrer.

If this process is carried far enough, if, that is, the pejorative adjectives are given sufficiently repeated and widespread currency, a dangerous atmosphere might well arise. The mere mention of an offensive label, e.g. Negro, Jew, Catholic, or Communist, Capitalist, Imperialist, is calculated to arouse such tense emotion as seriously to impair an entire community's ability to appraise accurately its experience of reality. Probably the crudest examples of impaired ability to report reality objectively are to be found in the sphere of power politics. Take, for example, the poisoning of the atmosphere by governmental testing of atomic weapons to the danger of the health of mankind. This process is given two separate descriptive labels according to the region in which the event occurs. It may be either 'a test reluctantly undertaken to fulfil our heavy responsibilities to secure and defend our freedom', or it may be 'a crime against humanity inspiring deep disgust and cold anger'. The former is 'correct' usage when referring to the group with which the self is identified; the latter is 'correct' usage when referring to the outgroup. Extreme cases of failure of ability to relate to reality can be illustrated without difficulty from speeches of well-known political figures. For example, at the time of the Suez dispute, one British politician was reported as saying that he would not permit his Government to surrender part of the territory of the United Kingdom, viz. the Suez Canal. When President Eisenhower dispatched federal troops to Little Rock to uphold the federal law set aside by the Arkansas State Governor, another Southern State Governor likened the operation to the suppression of the Hungarian uprising by the Soviet military forces in Budapest. A striking and pathetic example of the fearful individual's capacity to mistranslate seemingly unmistakable aspects of reality in the light of subjective needs is quoted by

Marie Jahoda in a valuable UNESCO pamphlet, *Race Relations and Mental Health*, 1960 (p. 39):

> For example, in public transportation a poster was used showing a group of gay white children playing together with a sad-looking little Negro boy standing unhappily alone. The inscription read: 'Prejudice hurts innocent children.' One prejudiced person, invited to comment on this poster, thought it meant that Negro children prefer to play with other Negro children, and the little boy was sad because somebody wanted him to play with white children.

In examples such as these, what purports to be a descriptive account of experience of the world external to the beholder is merely a report of the strains and stresses of his own internal psychological condition.

In any society there is a strong natural tendency for power to exercise a gravitational force over opinion. Those who devote their energies to the single-minded pursuit of power are more likely to obtain it than those who do not. In the extreme instance such a person's moral concern may be to discern the standards to which it is necessary to conform in order to persuade the appropriate people to entrust him with power. Tolstoy's Boris Drubetskoy in *War and Peace* is a good example of the type. This minority, unrepresentative though they are, appear in the short run to exert considerable influence. The majority, if not themselves interested in power, respect it and take their cue from it. Diffident and easily swayed, they are anxious to stand well with their fellows, fear their ridicule and crave their approval. Many accordingly become adept in developing hypersensitive antennae to prevailing opinion in those circles which enjoy prestige and ascendancy. Like Bunyan's By-Ends in the *Pilgrim's Progress*, they 'somewhat differ from those of the stricter sort, yet but in two small points: first, we never strive against wind and tide; secondly, we are always most zealous when religion goes in his silver slippers; we love much to walk with him in the street, if the sun shines, and the people applaud him' (p. 150). Even among those whom Bunyan refers to as 'of the stricter sort' fear can rarely be altogether excluded as an element in distorting judgement. The fear here is one of total alienation, of finding oneself so far out of touch with prevailing assumptions and practice as to fear for one's ability to maintain communication. In order to carry on a conversation there must be some common ground to which appeal can be made. The moralist tends to be inordinately sensitive to the charge of utopian crankiness. He is tempted to persuade himself either that reality is not as morally intolerable as he supposed it to be, and/or that the moral standards demanded by his moral culture or conscience are not quite as rigid as he thought. If he should engage in politics or otherwise participate in the governance of men, he will have no choice about compromising with the demands of his conscience, if he is still susceptible to its voice. For successful politics, as Bagehot pointed out, is the problem of learning 'to know the highest truth which the people will bear and to inculcate and preach that'.

In this way it is possible to define a person's capacity to discern moral truth as the resultant of twin forces, external and internal; the external force of prevalent opinion with its shifting pressures, and the internal, the degree of psychic stability and moral independence. Given the strength of the reality principle, viz. the desire to keep within range of prevailing moral practice, a person's capacity to discern moral truth will depend upon his own inner status security. A strong 'inner directed' man may withstand a powerfully immoral cultural climate. Even at the height of the Nazi success in Germany men of the stature of Pastor Niemöller and Hans Litten, to cite two eminent examples, survived with their integrity if not always their lives intact. And conversely, individuals relatively unstable, insecure in status, ridden by unconscious inner conflict, may yet retain a fair measure of moral insight, if the surrounding culture of their social class or even nation is comparatively healthy and strong.

It might serve to make the issue clearer if we give a concrete example of the way in which moral truth which is 'inexpensive' or easy to discern for one person is 'expensive' or difficult to discern for another. Speaking very roughly, it is a common assumption among pragmatic liberals that 'knowledge' is that which is generally agreed, in contrast to mere 'opinion', having reference to that which is the subject of controversy. This is a convenient view since it corresponds to the realities of the immediate situation. But it is not valid. Where opinion differs in matters of moral value, it ought as a matter of principle to be possible to test the truth of the competing opinions. For example, in the Union of South Africa, the rightness or wrongness of Apartheid as a political prescription is a matter of acutest controversy. On the empirical view of the matter, we are therefore here in the presence of a competing moral opinion. Knowledge is not in question. It is impossible to say where right finally lies. In our view, which presupposes the egalitarian axiom, it is perfectly possible to say where right lies. Apartheid is morally wrong. This view of the matter also coincides with a virtually unanimous world opinion on this subject, outside the territory of South Africa – outside, that is to say, the geographical region where men have a direct vested interest in the outcome of the current power struggle.

Whereas the moral truth concerning Apartheid is 'expensive' or difficult of access to the majority of Afrikaners, this truth is 'inexpensive' to an Anglican priest such as Father Trevor Huddleston, steeped in a Christian culture and educated in an English public school. (Of course, the courage which Huddleston demonstrated in acting upon that truth in the presence of a hostile body of opinion was very far from 'inexpensive'.) On the other hand, truth which might be comparatively 'inexpensive' for an Afrikaner might prove most 'expensive' for the Englishman; for example, the question of the morality of class privilege in education. It is only necessary to compare the candour and direct simplicity of Huddleston's rejection of Apartheid for the evil thing it is with the embarrassment and evasiveness of his reply to the following question put to him by a press reporter:

'Well, egalitarianism is at the very centre of the teaching of Christ, isn't it? If you are against *apartheid*, as a Christian, do you think you might conceivably be expected to be against the exclusivity of public schools?' 'No, I do not. If the people who go to public schools go there with the idea, conscious or unconscious, of using the experience of being at a public school to obtain an advantage over their fellow-men, these people would be un-Christian. If the society in which the public school flourishes breeds the public-school product to occupy positions which deliberately give one man an advantage over another, that society is un-Christian (in that respect, I mean). But what is un-Christian here is the individual in the first place, and society in the second. Not the public school.'[1]

---

[1] *The Observer*, 25 September 1960, p. 19

(iii) *Reason and Emotion in Equality*

In the last section, an attempt was made to explain the apparent plurality of moral values by uncovering some of the unconscious emotional sources of what purport to be objective moral judgements of an inegalitarian character. What of egalitarian judgements? Are they any less immune from the influence of unconscious emotional sources? Is sauce for the goose not also sauce for the gander? Indeed, it is not the inegalitarian defender of the *status quo* whose judgements are considered to be liable to emotional distortion, but the egalitarian rebel, whose judgements and behaviour are widely held to be explicable in terms of unconscious neurotic conflict. One of the commonest methods of disposing of or preventing a serious hearing of arguments to which one is opposed is to categorize them as 'emotional' or perhaps 'sentimental'. This charge has been levelled over and over again against humanitarians in countless struggles, against advocates of the abolition of slavery, of torture, of child labour, of female disfranchisement, of capital punishment, of racial segregation, of war, of animal slaughter and so on. By describing their views as 'emotional' or 'sentimental' it is meant to imply either that their judgement does more credit to their hearts than to their heads, or that their sense of the public interest has been distorted by the force of their pity, compassion or love of justice. This tactic often secures the dismissal of an argument without further examination. It is an effective pejorative label because there is widespread confusion and inability to disentangle the roles of reason and emotion in the formation of moral judgements. It is also effective because it is undeniable that some moral judgements are in fact vitiated by discreditable or neurotic emotions. The advocate of capital punishment may only too probably be inspired by emotions of fear or revenge. While on the other side it is true that egalitarian and humane moral judgements may in some individuals conceal emotions of self-pity or compulsive rebelliousness.

A moral judgement may be described as 'emotional' when it is wished to imply that it is 'neurotic' or vitiated by unconscious emotional conflict. Or the suggestion may be that a view is 'extreme', 'unbalanced', or 'lacking in judgement' in that a sense of proportion is lacking as a result of excessive ardour, self-committal or misplaced idealism.[1] When the critique is a moral one that cuts near to the bone, it may well be difficult to find a reply to the argument. In such circumstances, the temptation is likely to be very powerful to reach for the *argumentum ad hominem*, to find the maggot which one has a need to feel must exist in every rose. '. . . those are most desirous of honour or glory who cry out the loudest of its abuse and the vanity of the world,' wrote Spinoza (*Ethics*, Everyman ed., 1910, p. 208). This might serve as a model blanket defence against every moralist who disturbs our peace of mind. The purpose of this type of argument is not to demonstrate the fallacy of the argument to be met, but to undermine the rational status of the propounder. While the *argumentum ad hominem* can never of itself be conclusive, it can be very damaging to the standing of the disputant in his claim to objectivity. The weapon was first deployed effectively on the grand scale by Marx against the bourgeoisie as a whole. Marx, refusing to take the manifest content of their arguments seriously, interpreted them as rationalizations for the pursuit of their economic interests. It is not therefore surprising to find that Freud has been freely pillaged by the 'bourgeoisie' in an attempt to make this tactic boomerang upon their opponents. Freudian reductionist arguments have been widely used to undermine the rational status of revolutionaries in terms of their unconscious motives.

The technique itself is not entirely novel. Much may still be learnt both of the psychological problems liable to afflict those beset by and resentful of the injustice of the powerful, and of the technique of reducing rational argument against injustice to the status of displaced neurotic conflict from a study of Dickens's Mr Gridley and the diagnosis of his case by Mr Skimpole in *Bleak House*. Dickens's own sympathies are clearly enlisted on the side of 'the man from Shropshire', but Mr Gridley's emotional condition is such as to provide Mr Skimpole with an easy target for his 'reductionist' technique in argument.

Mr Gridley's grievance concerns the law's delays. Heir to his parent's farm and stock, he finds himself driven to Chancery

---

[1] For example, it was suggested (with little evidence) by the *Guardian* reviewer of *Out of Apathy* (1960), a symposium produced by the New Left in Britain, that the body of opinion represented was largely neurotically inspired in that the judgements allegedly bore the imprint of the unsuccessful, the frustrated, the ambitious whose qualifications had not brought them the rewards they felt they had a right to expect.

as a result of a contested suit regarding a minor bequest to a relative. After many years the suit is still undecided; the entire estate has been swallowed up in costs; and the man from Shropshire has seen his very livelihood sucked away into Chancery. In short, Mr Gridley's grievance is substantial and objectively uncontestable; and Mr Gridley is articulate, even prone to excitability, on the subject. Aggressive where the injury done him is concerned, he is yet on the defensive concerning the state of mind induced in him by his injuries. Less than polite to Mr Jarndyce, his guilt finds expression in an angry acknowledgement, 'I am of a quarrelsome temper. I am irascible. I am not polite!', followed by an account of his sorry history as an apologia. His bitterness is attributable at least in part to his ironic awareness of the world's indifference to his plight. 'Go into the Court of Chancery yonder, and ask what is one of the standing jokes that brighten up their business sometimes, and they will tell you that the best joke they have is the man from Shropshire.' But again he feels the need to justify himself. It is as though he is more than half aware that in reacting so passionately against the evil done him he has assimilated some of it unto himself. His moral unease arises from the contrast between his own anger and the composure of Mr Jarndyce under similar provocation on a much larger scale at the hands of Chancery. At the same time he is imbued with a feeling that gives him no rest that it would in some obscure way be wrong to resent injustice one whit less passionately than he does. If he were not to do so, it would do violence to his elementary sense of the fitness of things and so imperil his mental equilibrium.

> ... if I took my wrongs in any other way, I should be driven mad! It is only by resenting them, and by revenging them in my mind, and by angrily demanding the justice I never get, that I am able to keep my wits together. It is only that! ... You may tell me that I over-excite myself. I answer that it's in my nature to do it, under wrong, and I must do it. There's nothing between doing it and sinking into the smiling state of the poor little mad woman that haunts the Court. If I was once to sit down under it, I should become imbecile.

Mr Jarndyce's reference to the 'monstrous system' incites Gridley to further impassioned denunciation; and the white heat of his anger burns itself out on a note of implacable determination to fight and shame them until the day comes when they shall ultimately have to carry him feet foremost from their Court of Chancery. Altogether a perfect cameo portrait of a frame of mind Dickens knew intimately and portrayed with immense verve in the writing. No less psychologically perceptive is the comment on Gridley's performance which Dickens puts into the mouth of Mr Skimpole. The very real injustice which made such a sharp impression upon Mr Gridley disappears entirely from view in the mind of Mr Skimpole. He sees only an energetic and strong-willed man – an 'inharmonious blacksmith' is his metaphor – driven by a powerful need to discharge his excessive psychic aggression, and finding in the Court of Chancery a perfect outlet.

> . . . he could easily imagine that there Gridley was, years ago, wandering about in life for something to expend his superfluous combativeness upon . . . when the Court of Chancery came in his way, and accommodated him with the exact things he wanted. There they were, matched, ever afterwards! Otherwise he might have been a great general, blowing up all sorts of towns, or he might have been a great politician, dealing in all sorts of parliamentary rhetoric; but, as it was, he and the Court of Chancery had fallen upon each other in the pleasantest way, and nobody was much the worse, and Gridley was, so to speak, from that hour provided for.

The skilful translation of moral and political conflict into subjective psychic neurosis, implicit in Skimpole's diagnosis of the man from Shropshire, carries with it more than a hint of Freudian technique, although Freud's own diagnosis would have been marked by sensitivity to and sympathy for Gridley's objection to injustice.

The question at issue can be stated simply. Is Gridley's state of mind the product of his experience at the hands of society, or are his experiences the product of his own original unbalanced and inflamed personality, predisposed to resentment, needing channels through which aggression can be discharged? Is the test of rationality a stubborn adherence to universal moral principle or is it acceptance of empirical behaviour sanctioned and institutionalized by society? The Skimpole view of the matter, the one with which we have been made familiar by the cruder versions of a debased Freudianism, has rarely been stated more naïvely and forcefully than by William James in an unusually candid passage. He is attempting to define what is meant by the term 'crankiness', a quality which is not necessarily, he tells us, a mark of superior intellect. It is the attribute of the psychopath temperament, recognizable by its excitability, ardour, and general emotional susceptibility.

[The crank] is liable to fixed ideas and obsessions. His conceptions tend to pass immediately into belief and action; and when he gets a new idea, he has no rest till he proclaims it, or in some way 'works it off'. 'What shall I think of it?' a common person says to himself about a vexed question; but in a 'cranky' mind 'What must I do about it?' is the form the question tends to take. In the autobiography of that high-souled woman, Mrs Annie Besant, I read the following passage: 'Plenty of people wish well to any good cause, but very few care to exert themselves to help it, and still fewer will risk anything in its support. "Some one ought to do it, but why should I?" is the ever re-echoed phrase of weak-kneed amiability. "Some one ought to do it, so why not I?" is the cry of some earnest servant of man, eagerly forward springing to face some perilous duty. Between these two sentences lie whole centuries of moral evolution.' True enough! and between these two sentences lie also the different destinies of the ordinary sluggard and the psychopathic man.[1]

The inner contradiction at the core of the 'conventional wisdom' here comes to the surface. It must have required the utmost exertion on the part of James's defence mechanisms at this point to have kept intact his own loyalty to conventional myth. The analysis is naturally probed no further, but it had reached an undeniably interesting stage.

Pejorative usage: crank
= psychopath, emotional, unstable, excitable
= person who actively engages himself on behalf of a good cause.

Approbatory usage: a common person
= immune to obsessions and fixed ideas, stable, amiable, reasonable, prudent, capable of mediating soberly between belief and action
= a person unwilling actively to promote a deserving cause.

[1] *The Varieties of Religious Experience*, 1909 ed., p. 23

Perhaps the first point to make is the peculiarity of the wide-spread tendency to be suspicious of intensity of emotion as such. This is especially true in England where phlegmatic qualities are as uncritically appreciated as 'emotionalism' is distrusted in the discussion of any social problem. Uncontrolled passion is only too likely to distort objectivity of judgement, and is liable to stem from discreditable sources. Men are notoriously vulnerable to such powerful emotions as fear, jealousy and hatred. On the other hand some of the most widely esteemed virtues are based on powerful emotion. Unless the emotion is intense it fails to win our admiration. A mother's love of her child is expected to be passionate, as is a scientist's devotion to truth, if they are to command respect. A love of justice is the more noteworthy if it is 'passionate'; while the attribute of wisdom is felt to require almost as a condition a high degree of emotional 'serenity'. In short, it is not the intensity of the emotion that should arouse our distrust but the nature of the emotion, that is to say, its rationality or irrationality.

It will be objected that emotions of a positive, natural and necessary kind may yet be far from conducive to rationality of judgement. All the world may love a lover, but that does not dispose them to place especial faith in the rationality of the judgement of one in the grip of romantic love. Quite the contrary! In other words, a virtue such as love with the closely related virtues of sympathy, loyalty and compassion, may seem to be independent of or even contrary to reason, because of a strong feeling that these virtues flow from involuntary emotions, excluding the element of choice or veto. It is difficult to rid ourselves of the feeling that emotions which are spontaneous and restricted to a specific context, which are not the outcome of deliberate decision, must therefore be immune from rational control. Love, we shall be told, is blind. He who is detached is more likely to observe truly than he whose judgement is clouded by intensely concentrated personal love. This may be the case in a particular instance, where the capacity for judgement is normally weakly developed or where appetite is mistaken for love; but it is not necessarily the case. It may also be that the lover knows that which is concealed from the rest of the world; that it is *they* who are blind to qualities only discernible by an intensely motivated and thus peculiarly acute perception, focused exclusively on the self at the heart of the beloved. The world looks upon the lover benevolently and affectionately, it is true, but also as upon one a little mad. Yet love is felt to be a great virtue; and a countenance irradiated by love has a unique power to move our deepest emotions. This paradox at the core of the world's view of romantic love as something profoundly beautiful and admirable and yet essentially irrational is sharply challenged by Tolstoy in his description of Pierre Bezukhov's state of mind during his courtship of Natasha Rostova.

> Often in after-life Pierre recalled this period of blissful insanity. All the views he formed of men and circumstances at this time remained true for him always. He not only did not renounce them subsequently, but when he was in doubt or inwardly at variance, he appealed to the views he had held at this time of his madness, and they always proved correct.
>
> 'I may have appeared strange and queer then,' he thought, 'but I was not so mad as I seemed. On the contrary, I was then wiser and had more insight than at any other time, and understood all that is worth understanding in life, because . . . because I was happy.'
>
> Pierre's insanity consisted in not waiting, as he used to do, to discover personal attributes, which he termed 'good qualities', in people before loving them; his heart was now overflowing with love, and by loving people without cause he discovered indubitable causes for loving them.[1]

The mistake that is commonly made is to contrast reason and emotion as mutually exclusive conditions of the psyche. In fact the relations between the two are extremely complex. It is difficult in practice to discern precisely where the one begins and the other leaves off. Certainly the popular image of reason as a cerebral process and emotion as a non-cerebral activity, occupying a position of inferior status on that account, will not survive close examination. As both Spinoza and Freud observed, attitudes are frequently subject to modification or transformation as a result of insight or an advance in understanding or power of discrimination. In other words, it is not true that we are doomed to seek in vain a universe of unitary truth values, since men differ about the nature of their duties as a result of intractable

---

[1] Tolstoy, *War and Peace*, Vol. III, p. 414

differences in their purely emotional, non-cognitive natures. In the modern epoch we have been subjected to a vast barrage of argument designed to persuade us that a sharp wedge exists between the two entirely separate realms of the reason and the emotions. What is inseparably joined in nature is probed by remorseless analysis to demonstrate the totally disparate functions. Facts, we are reminded, are notoriously compatible with conflicting emotional comments as between different persons and even between the comments of the same person at different times and moods. Accordingly we are obliged to infer, so the argument goes, that 'there is no rationally deducible connection between any outer fact and the sentiments it may happen to provoke.'[1] If we doubt this, James urges us to try to imagine the world of the senses which we inhabit, *as it exists*, denuded of our own emotional comment, favourable or unfavourable. The world would then be seen to be one of unrelieved negativity and deadness, stripped of all importance or significance, destitute of the character with which our capricious human emotions alone supply it. The fallacy lies in asking us to do that which is in fact impossible. If our faculties were stripped bare of emotional capacity, it is not the case that the 'reason' would then perceive something negative and dead, reality '*as it exists*, purely by itself'. We have no means of knowing whether in such a contingency anything whatever could then be said to exist, since our knowledge of what does 'exist' depends entirely upon the existing faculties of man, compounded as they are of an indissoluble union of reason and emotion. If it be insisted that James's logical hypothesis might have a possible empirical fulfilment, we can only reply that it might, but that it is beside the point. And if we are asked, 'what guile recommends the world?', what is it that 'condones the world incorrigibly'? we can only reply that we do not know; we only know that it is so. We may wonder in humility and awe, but we may do no more.

> But what, in fact, is this vaporous charm?
> We're softened by a nice conglomeration
> Of the earth's uneven surface, refraction of light,
> Obstruction of light, condensation, distance,

---

[1] William James, *The Varieties of Religious Experience*, p. 150

And the sappy upshot of self-centred vegetabilism
The trees of the garden. How is it we come
To see this as a heaven in the eye?
Why should we hawk and spit our ecstasy,
As though we were nightingales to call these quite
Casual degrees and differences
Beauty? What guile recommends the world
And gives our eyes the special sense to be
Deluded, above all animals?
(Christopher Fry, *The Lady's not for Burning*)

Another reason why men today can be easily persuaded that
a sharp gulf exists between their cognitive and emotional
faculties, lies in the development of physical means of psychotherapy. As a result of purely physical intervention, viz. the
application of drugs or of electric shock treatment, apparent
changes in the patient's attitudes beneficial to his psychic health
may take place without any apparent parallel change or advance
in the patient's knowledge. Or conversely, a seemingly healthy
person may suddenly become a drug addict or a compulsive
alcoholic without any apparent change in the state of his knowledge. In the latter instance, in fact, something new has been
learned, namely the euphoric or consolatory function of certain
drugs or stimulants. But in the former instance, it is not at once
apparent that, in the successful therapeutic application of e.c.t.[1]
or insulin, improved behaviour is the result of an advance in
the patient's knowledge. On the surface it would seem that
the process of change is purely affective, entirely non-cognitive.
But closer analysis suggests that the patient has been suffering
from an inability to *learn* what is necessary to his efficient
functioning; and that it is this disability that is cured by
the removal of the emotional 'block' obstructing the learning
process. Such emotional blocks, or symptoms of unconscious
conflict, are apparently sometimes amenable, at any rate temporarily, to physical modes of treatment as well as to the slower
methods of sympathy, analysis, comfort, example and so on.
That the patient himself may not appear to be aware that his
improved behaviour is a consequence of his having learned
something, of his having made a cognitive advance, may indicate

[1] electro-convulsive therapy

no more than that he is not of a reflective nature or sufficiently trained in articulation to express himself accurately. It is true that a person may learn something incompatible with his existing behaviour without changing his behaviour. But this is readily explicable by the well-known phenomenon of the 'emotional lag'. For instance, a person may well advance his moral understanding of the implications of destroying life solely for the delectation of his palate without immediately becoming a vegetarian. It is one thing to learn to accept something as intellectually correct; it is another to bring the emotions into line with the intellectual conviction to the point where action in the shape of an alteration of behaviour must ensue.

Some influential writers (e.g. C. L. Stevenson) attach considerable importance to the *logical* possibility that there may exist between human beings ineradicable conflicts of attitude which would prove beyond the power of rational analysis to dissolve under any circumstances. In other words, it is conceivable that two people sharing identical beliefs, in possession of all the relevant evidence, each immune from errors of logic or induction, might yet have conflicting attitudes as a consequence of 'innate' temperamental differences. The logical possibility must be conceded; but its empirical occurrence would not seem to be very likely. What needs to be said is that such an assumption, driving such a sharp wedge between reason and emotion, emotion being denied any cognitive component, is impossible of proof and severely pessimistic in its implications. Whereas the opposite assumption, supported though not conclusively demonstrated by modern learning theory, has socially optimistic implications. In the former case, we may be tempted to give up the task of seeking to reduce conflict by rational methods; whereas in the latter case, we have every incentive to seek to expand the areas in which conflict may be resolved by reason and to refuse to acquiesce in the intransigence of caprice, greed, hatred, intolerance, fear. Where men abandon faith in reason, where they are encouraged to acquiesce in the 'naturalness' of unreason, all historical experience suggests that sooner or later the tensions and animosities generated by irrationality will be temporarily dispelled by the resort to violence.

Finally, one further point must be made in reply to those who maintain a sharp distinction between reason and emotion. The conclusions of a rational judgement require implementation. It is difficult to see how a rational faculty immunized against all 'distracting' emotional considerations would then be able to harness the emotional energy to implement the rational policies. Our tragedy is that with the collapse of traditional religious values it has not yet proved possible to harness our emotional energies to the rational goals suggested by scientific inquiry, itself inspired by truly human emotions. A gulf exists between our irrational emotional attachments or prejudices and the sociological behaviour prescribed by methods sanctioned by scientific inquiry. Even where people's irrational prejudices have been weakened by reiteration of arguments demonstrating the irrationality of racial discrimination or capital punishment or reliance on nuclear deterrence, the innermost self refuses to be enmeshed or involved in the struggle to implement the judgement in question because of the gap between the cognitive and affective sides of his nature. The gear lever wherewith to synchronize the two is missing. For ideas to be effective in behaviour, they must move from the periphery of consciousness to the core of the man's self, to what William James called, 'the hot place' in a man's consciousness where his emotional energies can be tapped. If reason is reduced to a purely ratiocinative exercise, the statement 'it is wrong to eat people' is labelled as an 'emotive' statement. The effect of this ascription cannot but be to downgrade its strictly rational status as a moral recommendation; and since reason is the chief weapon of the moral reformer as distinct from the political or military man of action, it is not surprising if the moral reformer finds his weapons blunted. It is a nice point of speculation whether cannibalism would ever have been abolished by people convinced of the sharpness of the dichotomy between reason and emotion. Certainly it is difficult to envisage someone willing to undergo strenuous personal hardship or suffering in defence of a moral conviction, the status of which in his own eyes is that of an 'emotive statement.'

The latter-day liberal would no doubt be unmoved by this argument. Steadfast conviction is precisely what he is in revolt against. Steadfast conviction and willingness to suffer is quite likely to be 'emotively' labelled as extremism, fanaticism, utopianism or even totalitarianism; and the reasons are familiar.

In our time, men of undoubted conviction have wrought havoc.
For a time it would appear as if conviction itself or rather intensity of conviction has become suspect, instead of the content of a
particular conviction. In a world so dominated by fear and hatred
as our own, those who remain loyal to the concepts of human
brotherhood and equality and non-violence will assuredly
need to call on profound emotions if they are to remain steadfast
against such immense odds. For we inhabit a world in which
increasingly large numbers of people are coming to regard as
normal a structure of world power which is rationally and
morally intolerable. It is precisely the 'civilized' tolerance of the
liberal, humane cultured members of this acquiescent society
which is the main stumbling block. The term 'Christianity' has
come to mean many things, but if identified with the moral
force of love and self-sacrifice, it is suggested that the following
passage from Kierkegaard is immediately relevant to our
situation.

> It is the tolerance of the orthodox which best shows how com-
> pletely Christianity is lost. Their solution is: if only we may keep
> our faith for ourselves, the world can take care of itself. Merciful
> God, and that is supposed to be Christianity. That is the power
> which once broke upon the world and through readiness to suffer
> forced Christianity on the world, compelled it more forcefully
> than any tyrant.
>
> The orthodox do not even suspect that this, their tolerance,
> is the effect of sheer worldliness, because they have not really
> either understanding, respect or courage for martyrdom or a
> true belief in eternity, but really desire to have a good time in
> this world. . . .
>
> How low has Christianity sunk, how powerless and miserable
> it has become! It is reason that has conquered: reason that has
> tyrannized enthusiasm and the like, making it ridiculous. That
> is why people dare not be enthusiastic, . . . they are afraid of
> being laughed at instead of put to death.[1]

We inhabit a climate of opinion in which moral aspiration
itself is on the defensive, unsure of its sources in reason and
suspicious of the emotions without which it has no meaning. The

---

[1] *The Journals of Søren Kierkegaard* (1849), 1938 ed., p. 341

diffident are without difficulty persuaded that a cautious pragmatism most befits a reasonable and prudent man. To be pragmatic within the existing society involves evaluation of the likely
consequences of taking 'the next step' within an institutional
framework which now rests on values as grotesque as those of
'nuclear deterrence'. The contemporary dichotomy *par excellence*
is the suggestion that an absolute rejection of values resting on the
threat of nuclear retaliation is 'emotionally' right, but rationally
quite unacceptable.[1] Without the energy, self-sacrifice and
authority of the unimpeded moral vision, the attempt to 'ban
the bomb' would doubtless be unrealistic and 'emotional'. It
would be 'emotional' in the sense that the requirements of power
politics do not permit it. Pragmatically, unilateral renunciation
of nuclear weapons would disturb the extremely precarious
balance of power, and would thus allegedly add to the admittedly
grave dangers already existing. The suggestion is that any
re-alignment would risk producing the very explosion that is
feared, either through encouraging 'the enemy' to take advantage of his temporary gain or through 'our side' panicking
through the blow to its morale. Thus reason in contrast to our
'emotions' indicates that it is right to require men actively to
sustain where they do not themselves perform work which at
some level they cannot but know to be evil. Such is the contradiction of values by which men live. At one level it is impossible
to deny that right is right and wrong is wrong. But in order to
live successfully in the world and to manipulate institutions
sanctioned by generations of political men, it is 'necessary' to
subscribe to a set of pragmatic values that run directly counter
to every moral value.

The choice is plain: to choose as the world chooses, knowing
that the choice is morally indefensible and must lead to evil
consequences, but to be compensated by the approbation and

---

[1] At least one national newspaper of repute has run leading articles on these lines.
One is reminded of Aylmer Maude's dilemma. He tells how as a young man he
consulted about his state of health his physician, Sir Henry Thompson. Sir Henry's
professional advice was that Maude should arrange to have weekly intercourse
with a woman. Maude, eighteen at the time, was somewhat disconcerted at the
prescription, and objected that the proposed course might be morally dubious.
'Oh', replied Sir Henry, 'I thought you consulted me as a doctor about your health!
If you want advice about morality, go to a clergyman!' (Maude, *Life of Tolstoy*,
Vol. II, p. 277). But, Maude ruefully reflected, what was he to do if the priest gave
him contradictory advice?

support of all 'right thinking citizens': *or* to choose what is known to be right, and thus to appear to condemn oneself to impotence and sterility of judgement in a world of political reality far removed from the world of morality. It is true that in the latter eventuality one's recommendations will often appear unpractical and impossible of fulfilment by anyone in a position of 'responsibility' and power. But that would convict one of irresponsibility only if those in power had no other choice. They have always another choice. No man is obliged to be a member of a government. And by refusing to compromise in theory one is maintaining intact the knowledge by the light of which alone humanity is preserved from suffering and destruction. Does it therefore follow that the man who seeks to live his life by the light of moral truth is precluded from participation in political life? It depends on what is meant by participation in political life. If it is meant that we should advocate and accept responsibility for 'necessary political compromise' incompatible with morality, the answer must clearly be 'No'. To accept such responsibility is to compromise truth. But if political activity be limited to giving support to a political movement that is striving against opposition to make headway in the right direction and is not itself seeking political power, it would be perverse to withhold such support on the grounds that the political group in question does not go as far as morally it ought. To withhold support from the Campaign for Nuclear Disarmament[1] on the grounds that it is not in the immediate political context demanding unilateral total disarmament would be to make oneself responsible for weakening a political force striving to take the society a step nearer the goal of non-violence.

The political problem for 'the good man' is twofold: firstly, to do all in his power to close the gap between morals and politics by maintaining undimmed the light of moral truth with its total demands upon all men; and secondly, to lend his support to those groups whose aims approximate most nearly to the moral goal. The truth is that the realities of politics are made up of a myriad separate individual decisions concerning the limits of moral permissibility so far as responsibility for his

---

[1] The issue is complicated in practice by suspicions that CND's own 'power structure' has unofficial links with the Labour Party in particular.

own individual behaviour goes. No man has it within his power to control the limits of practicality or feasibility for the group of which he is a member or for any individual within the group. But he does have it absolutely within his power to determine those limits for himself. Or rather his power is limited only by his own courage and capacity to resist, even at the cost of physical or mental anguish, in order to maintain intact his integrity and self-respect.

7 Conclusion: Equality and Power

No sensible person would seek to underestimate the enormous force of the social will to power throughout human history. Its sheer brute pervasiveness is undeniable. What I have tried to do is not to belittle the facts, but to make plain the consequences that flow from them; and to challenge the widespread pessimism that seems resigned to their inevitability. There are two variants of the argument which have to be met: (a) The kingdom of this world is the kingdom of power; human nature is what it is; the world cannot be changed. Evil is necessarily inherent in the scheme of things; to accept this and recognize it as a due part of life is a necessary part of wisdom. (b) To reject this, to war without compromise upon everything that may appear as irrational or evil in the strict light of universal reason is to be guilty of arrogance, to unbalance the judgement, to risk fanaticism in the pursuit of merely one-sided and therefore fallacious truths, to be like Oedipus 'self-blinded at Colonus'.

Those who seek the classless society, we are told, are seeking the impossible as though they were striving to create a sexless society or a society of men without appetite. To be deceived by a mirage is not simply their private misfortune. The deluded are also a principal source of evil to others. For it turns out that there is some gratuitous and dispensable evil after all – the evil caused by those disturbers of the existing harmonies, the chiliastic, perfectibilist, radical utopians. It is the peculiar offence of these men, a continuing minority with a frightening tenacity of purpose, that they wish to establish the Kingdom of God upon earth, in face of all the evidence of the real world in which equality is decisively rejected. Supremely confident in the truth of their own inner light, fanatically determined to establish the millennium, Jerusalem, the Kingdom of the Saints, Utopia, the Republic, these men do not count the cost. Their characteristic imagery when they conjure up the struggle that lies before them is martial and bloody. The sword will not rest in their hand;

224

they will march through seas of blood. Metaphorical, no doubt, but indicative of the unconscious urge to appease their frustrated, embittered lives by smiting their opponents. Impatient men, hot for certainties, self-righteous men, obsessed and haunted by visions of evil, often of their own making, their names rise before us in an endless host stretching down the generations with a ferocious, awful poetry of their own: Pelagians, Adamites, Taborites, Arians, Albigenses, Ranters, Fifth Monarchy men, Saints, Levellers, Agitators, Quakers, Anabaptists, Thuringian flagellants, Jacobins, anarchists, apocalyptics, Saint-Simonians, Marxists, Bolshevists, expounders of the true faith all; and there are some who do not scruple to add for good measure National Socialists and Fascists. They are all believers, all absolutists, all fanatics, all tarred with the same brush. Thus is the spectre of the army of the avenging horsemen of the apocalypse conjured up for the horrified imagination of the tolerant, temperate, liberal, professional, academic empiricist, relaxed and at home in the 'open' and of course imperfect society. For if there were no imperfections, there would be no opportunity to demonstrate his essential tolerant temper. He is sceptical by nature and conditioning; he believes nothing or at any rate nothing too much. Evidence of committal or conviction arouses his suspicions at once. His nostrils twitch with fear, as he scents the first breath of that alien host of enthusiasts, the horsemen of the apocalypse, the chiliasts, the Fifth Monarchy men taking the trail. The centuries-old legend of St George slaying the dragon is repudiated as romantic infantilism. In his place there rides enthroned the twentieth-century vision of Halifax the Trimmer.

Conservatives are then offered a ready-made psychology of morbid egalitarianism.[1] This is frequently reinforced by a theology to explain the sickness of those who hunger and thirst after righteousness and equality. The reason why radicals and social revolutionaries are unable to reconcile themselves to the

---

[1] cf. Norman Cohn, *The Pursuit of the Millennium* (1957); Communists and Nazis, according to Professor Cohn, are victims of paranoia, whose symptoms are an impairment of their awareness of reality. Nazi symptoms were seen in their destruction of the Jews at the height of their own struggle for survival. The comparable Communist symptoms are an inability to understand that the poor in Capitalist societies are no longer getting poorer. On this evidence, Nazis and Communists are bracketed together as kindred examples of pathology, whose insecurities 'reactivate the infantile complex' and cause them to project their infantile rage upon their particular scapegoats.

imperfections inseparable from earthly life is because they believe that earthly life is the whole of life. If there is no other life but this, if this world exhausts the possibilities open to man, it is not surprising that some men should prove restless under adversity. Stoical resignation and equanimity are virtues which go ill with the spirit of secularism. A thirst to create an earthly Jerusalem is the direct emanation of an imagination incapable of transcending the here and now of finite reality. On this view, the nature of the Kingdom of God is the mystery that lies at the heart of the matter. The crucial distinction between men is theological. The utopians are consumed by the finality of all that is and has been. No redemption or compensation is possible beyond that which may be attained by our own strivings; and thus the incentive to strive stubbornly, recalcitrantly, even unto martyrdom can be powerful indeed. In the words of the original Pelagian heretic, 'Everything good and everything evil, in respect of which we are either worthy of praise or of blame, is *done by us*, not *born with us*. We are not born in our full development, but with a capacity for good and evil.'[1]

If, on the other hand, we are entirely in God's hands, and this life is but the shadow of a supreme and different reality, then the spirit is much readier to bow before the world's injustices and immoralities. Such a one will be more disposed to bow before a supreme will that is felt to be inscrutable as well as all-powerful. Retribution and reward, the restoration of the divine balance, the reconciliation of the wayward spirit of man, the possibility of bliss, these things are felt to belong to the realm of Eternity where they lie beyond the responsibilities of temporarily earthbound man.

Thus logic is stood on its head to prove that irreligious men are those who are eager to establish the right and the good, while truly religious men are those who realize that no good can come from stubbornly refusing to make an accommodation with the secular world. There is a remarkable constancy in the techniques of argument deployed by the apologists of the contradictions of the established order to confuse the multitude in their capacity to distinguish right from wrong. The following is an extract from *The Times* of a century ago:

[1] Pelagius, *Pro libero arbitrio, ap.* Augustine, *De peccato originali*, 14, 418; *Documents of the Christian Church*, edited by Henry Bettenson, World's Classics, 1943, p. 75

It is of no use for us to attempt to force upon our neighbours our several likings and dislikings. We must take things as they are. Everybody has his own little vision of religious or civil perfection. Under the evident impossibility of satisfying everybody, we agree to take our stand on equal laws and on a system as open and liberal as is possible. The result is that everybody has more liberty of action and of speaking here than anywhere else in the Old World.

These were the apologists of accommodation, the dealers in moral soporifics on behalf of the 'Establishment' whom Matthew Arnold assailed as apostles of atheism and quietism. The passage is worth quoting at length:

> ... I proceed to remark how not only do we get no suggestions of right reason, and no rebukes of our ordinary self, from our governors, but a kind of philosophical theory is widely spread among us to the effect that there is no such thing at all as a best self and a right reason having claim to paramount authority, or, at any rate, no such thing ascertainable and capable of being made use of; and that there is nothing but an infinite number of ideas and works of our ordinary selves, and suggestions of our natural taste for the bathos, pretty nearly equal in value, which are doomed either to an irreconcileable conflict, or else to a perpetual give and take; and that wisdom consists in choosing the give and take rather than the conflict, and in sticking to our choice with patience and good humour.

Once again we discern the familiar argument, caught and ironically pinioned by Arnold, that there is no unity of truth binding upon men, but only a plurality of echoing voices. Life ceases to be a challenge to evoke a response from our highest selves. It is whittled down to the level of a shabby mart where bargains are struck to obtain an accommodation between competing interests.

Arnold continues:

> And, on the other hand, we have another philosophical theory rife among us, to the effect that without the labour of perverting ourselves by custom or example to relish right reason, but by continuing all of us to follow freely our natural taste for the bathos, we shall, by the mercy of Providence, and by a kind of natural

tendency of things, come in due time to relish and follow right reason.[1]

The argument is the familiar one that reliance on our common frailty combined with a comfortable belief in Providence will better serve our welfare in this world than any strenuous and awkward striving after self-perfection.

The arguments of our contemporary apologists for the contradictions of our liberal, Christian, nuclear-armed fortress bear a striking resemblance to the 'philosophical theory' Arnold was at such pains to castigate. The following quotation is the concluding extract from a review by one of the most influential political theorists in Britain of the doyen of political thought on the other side of the Atlantic:

> But central to his entire discourse is Dr Niebuhr's justly celebrated view of man as a being doomed to imperfection, unable and unwilling to face this truth, and lured on by a fatal mirage of an earthly paradise conceived in terms incompatible with human capacities, engaged in destroying the real world in which alone at least some of his values could partially be realized. It is the eloquence and insight with which he urges his central thesis – that man's idealism and belief in the perfectibility of his species, so far from promoting either freedom or democracy, can be their worst enemy, and that it is man's realistic vision of his own imperfection that alone makes life tolerable on earth – that has made Dr Niebuhr one of the most interesting and influential thinkers of our day.[2]

The 'original sin' part of the argument is familiar enough. The theology apart, it reiterates the dictum that you can't change institutions until you have changed human nature, and combines with it a resigned assurance that human nature is eternally 'doomed'. On this diagnosis the world suffers on the one hand from a dearth of people endowed with a 'realistic vision' of man's imperfection, and on the other from a glut of self-sacrificing, altruistic wretches striving to improve the lot of their fellows. In fact, the remedy for the evil consequences that flow from violent intolerance is twofold: those who provoke it by their

[1] Matthew Arnold, *Culture and Anarchy*, 1869, pp. 128–30
[2] Isaiah Berlin, review of Reinhold Niebuhr's *Nations and Empires*, *The Guardian*, 25 November 1960

selfish behaviour should be rebuked; while those who seek to remedy injustice should confine themselves to non-violent resistance. But the 'realistic' are precluded from making these simple observations, since the privileged would be the first to be convicted by them. They accordingly prefer generalities which purport to demonstrate some mysterious metaphysical connection between good and evil – a paradox whereby the true welfare of men is put in jeopardy by their seeking to develop their own best selves; and their real interests best served by a faithful reliance upon their wonted compromises.

It is time to turn from what Arnold termed 'genial but pernicious anodynes' to conclude with a brief restatement of the positive response with which this book has attempted to concern itself. We may concede that there may be a relatively unchanging human nature. The important thing is that there is no fixed pattern or level of human behaviour. What can be attained by one individual, a microcosm of human nature, cannot in principle be excluded as beyond the reach of others. Human behaviour is made up of many elements, but the standard of aspiration which is accepted is crucially significant. And this is subject to influence by others. Nothing is more potent than the general level of expectation accepted by those we respect and in whose eyes we wish to stand well. The whole purpose of the 'detached realist's' description of how the world functions is to discourage us from adopting different standards, denounced as utopian and disastrous. In practice, people frequently appear equally hostile towards those who describe common practice truthfully and to those who are uncompromising in their moral aspiration. If the latter runs the risk of being labelled a 'prig', the former is assured of the title of 'cynic'. Truth of description undiluted by wishful thinking is a necessary safeguard against false optimism. But to allow our moral standards to be determined by the generally accepted level of behaviour is to put ourselves at the mercy of those of least repute. For they too affect the general standards of behaviour. An average is made up of the worst as well as the best. However difficult it may be to practise what we preach, there is no justification for preaching down to our standard of practice. For incessant struggle is a necessary part of the moral life. Phrases such as 'not allowing the best to be the enemy of the good' should put us on our guard, lest the purpose be to provide an excuse for doing that which is easiest. Circumstances may be stubborn, the dilemma fraught with anguish, the will driven beyond endurance. The really serious evil starts when we begin to persuade ourselves that what was done in extenuating circumstances was on that account the right thing to do. To engage in self-deception leads to a new and lower standard of value. Another common plea of the devil's advocate is to reproach the moral aspirant with his fallibility. If those who would seek to raise our standards can themselves be shown to be less than perfect, our own lack of effort is obscurely felt to have been vindicated. Archbishop Tillotson once saw fit to remind us that there is ambition in declining preferment as well as in seeking it. He may well have been right, but the remark would have come better from one less exalted.

As regards the facts of inequality which are allegedly inherent in human nature, no one wishes to deny the obvious truth that some people are more beautiful or more clever or strong than other people. Realists and pessimists often seem to suggest that their opponents are blind to these elemental facts, and thus distract attention from arguments which are as relevant as they are rarely met. They need to be stated briefly:

(1) Difference of stature, quality, ability, character may well require difference of provision or service or help or treatment to meet need; it does not require inequality of provision.

(2) Whatever the differences between people, it is morally important to all people that social provision and social relations should reflect an emphasis on all that they have in common simply as human beings instead of on their restrictive and crippling class differentiae.

(3) Inegalitarians evince a surprising reluctance to investigate the crucial question concerning existing unequal levels of development in people; namely, how far they reflect unequal circumstances and institutions which have produced retardation or inhibition of development or aptitude. The emphasis is rather on an alleged law of inherent or innate difference, despite the logical impossibility of empirically demonstrating such a law.

When a man like William Morris beheld the human consequences of the inequalities of condition of the industrial society he inhabited, the spectacle was intolerably painful to him. Driven by compassion and anger, he found himself impelled to leave the artist's comfortable retreat for the uncongenial atmosphere of street-corner hustings in his determination to do something to fight the evil. How, he asked, can we help the victims of oppression and at the same time rid ourselves of the guilt of participation in the injustice? And he answered his question in this way:

> By renouncing our class, and on all occasions when antagonism rises up between the classes casting in our lot with the victims: with those who are condemned at the best to lack of education, refinement, leisure, pleasure and renown; and at the worst to a life lower than that of the most brutal of savages in order that the system of competitive commerce may endure.[1]

It is possible to comment on this, as George Orwell would have done, by denying the sociological or psychological possibility of 'renouncing one's class'. But Orwell would not have questioned Morris's sense of the tragic reflected in such circumstance of human poverty and degradation.[2]

Anti-egalitarians are rarely willing to acknowledge the significant and evident fact that societies differ widely in their degrees of inequality. The discussion is frequently confined to abstract terms in which absolutist claims of equality are contrasted with an allegedly ubiquitous inequality. To take an obvious example, in many societies much less importance is attached to purely social distinction than in England. Therefore, if desired, it is clearly possible to move towards a more egalitarian social atmosphere in this country. Moreover, there are very wide divergences in sensitivity to social and intellectual class

---

[1] *Art and Socialism, Collected Works*, Vol. XXIII, 1915, p. 213

[2] Today even this is questioned by contemporary conservatives. The argument goes something like this. To describe aspects of reality as 'tragic' is a betrayal of the necessary virility of the conditions of life. Tragedy is a concept of art, and as such alien to the life of society and the world. To assert that the harsh lineaments of struggle and consequent suffering are tragic, is the offence of rationalism. Such an analysis can only have meaning if reality is contrasted with a measure of human perfectibility that is foreign to our nature. The human predicament, the human dilemma or crisis – the choice of language smacks of rationalism. They may have part in the vision of the artist, but are alien to life which is the subject matter of the social or political scientist. Kant's famous remark, 'Out of the crooked timber of humanity no straight thing was ever made' would be approved. But the form of expression would be deprecated as being shot through with rationalistic overtones, implying that it is a thing of sorrow that the crooked is not and cannot be made straight.

differentiae. For example, children below a certain age are oblivious to such matters, as not infrequently are people in love. It is therefore important to try to define the quality of a human relationship that is free from any such distortions. D. H. Lawrence's statement is not only an admirable summary of an ideal at which to aim, but is a reality at certain levels of experience for some people. Lawrence's point is the irrelevance of estimations and comparisons, of equality or inequality, where a genuine human relationship exists independently of the material world with its mania for owning things. 'When I stand with another man, who is himself, and when I am truly myself, then I am only aware of a Presence, and of the strange reality of Otherness. There is me, and there is *another being* . . . There is no comparing or estimating.' (*Democracy*, in *Phoenix*, 1936, p. 715)

The contrast between such a conception and existing status obsessions is painful enough. The permanent modification of human behaviour is not an easy matter. On the other hand, the slow move towards greater equality has been steadily maintained in the modern period, and there is much greater understanding of the nature of the problem. Human nature, as we know it, is undoubtedly weak and easily misled; but it is not inherently vicious. Much of the evil that occurs is attributable to the power of the few and the weakness of the majority. And the power of the few derives from the intellectual and moral confusion of the many. The evil in men can be overcome if enough people care enough, are sufficiently energetic and clear-sighted. How otherwise would the great social reforms of the past have been brought about? The vast majority will the good, but are loath to stand and struggle when currents set in motion by evilly disposed men begin to gather momentum. If the majority are weak, it must be remembered that they are still denied genuine educational means of intellectual and moral growth even in the richer countries. In every society a minority of powerful men are able to keep up a barrage of propaganda to the effect that the patriotic duty of men is to be prepared to kill their enemies. Again in virtually every society today there are men who strive to combat such falsehood, but everywhere they experience the utmost difficulty in reaching the public even where they are permitted to try. The authorities still wield great power and command deference. The most urgent task that confronts mankind is to break the authority of men and institutions whose position rests on violence or the threat of violence. It is monstrous to tell people that they must continue to prepare to slaughter each other, notwithstanding the deep repugnance to killing their fellow-men which exists in all normal human beings. To kill is very far from natural to man. As Dickens wrote, in discussing the pride which destroyed Mr Dombey: 'It might be worth while, sometimes, to inquire what Nature is, and how men work to change her, and whether, in the enforced distortions so produced, it is not natural to be unnatural.'

It is true that human beings have hitherto been liable to enter into relations of dominance and subjection with one another. Ambitious or aggressive egos expand their field of effectiveness, and weak or diffident egos comply or yield to them. Generally there is a limit beyond which no character is likely to be allowed to develop in the direction of aggression or submission. Individuals usually achieve equilibrium at a relatively fixed point along the spectrum of power. In purely personal relations it is not often necessary for power to extend as far as the use of force. This does sometimes occur, of course, generally where the weaker party is helpless as in the case of children, or in the case of adults when normal inhibitions are broken down by intoxicating passion or liquor. The one thing that emerged clearly from the individual case studies undertaken earlier in this book was the impossibility of any human relationship avoiding distortion to the extent that power enters into it. Even though the parties to the relationship may be quite unaware of the effect of their dominance or subjection upon themselves, the moral effect is nevertheless inescapable. A relationship is always vitiated in proportion to the degree of power present. Dominance is inseparable from pride or arrogance, while deference or compliance indicates weakness, if not servility, and is accompanied by resentment, conscious or unconscious.

Since power may be wielded without threatening or resorting to force, the question arises how to distinguish between power and influence. The distinction is important since while the contention is that all power is morally bad, influence obviously does not come within that category. By power is meant the production of desired consequences in the behaviour or belief of another, where the intent to exercise personal ascendancy is present in the one producing the effects. Motive is all important, although the motive may well be unconscious. Usually the victim of another's power will be aware of at least some sense of psychic constraint. But this is not necessarily the case. The victim may have long since come to accept his position and regard it as natural. The reader of the advertisement or the auditor of the mob orator may be entirely unaware of the extent to which his emotions are being manipulated. Nevertheless power is being wielded in each instance. The test therefore lies in the motivation, conscious or unconscious, of the agent of the desired effects. The fact that this evidence may not be accessible to us in any given case is irrelevant to the validity of the test. There may be border-line cases in which power and influence may prove exceedingly difficult to disentangle. Just as difficult cases are apt to make bad law, the fact that marginal cases occur should not permit us to blur the distinction between the two, which is generally obvious enough.

If men reject the logic of equality, they must necessarily live by the logic of inequality and power. Therefore the question must be posed: why is equality or living without recourse to power considered so utopian? Partly, no doubt, because human beings find it difficult to imagine any change of a kind that they have not hitherto experienced. But obviously the difficulty goes much deeper. Given the existing inequalities and resultant tensions and animosities, people find it impossible to imagine life on a secure basis without recourse to institutions providing violent sanctions. Therefore they readily acknowledge the rights of power, however much they try to soften the outlines of its face by the claim that power backed by majority consent is no longer power but democratic authority. Where there is agreement, there is no need of sanction. And it is the presence of the sanction that alone distinguishes the State from all other societies. Power has gone unchallenged for so long that decision-making has receded further and further from the lives of those directly affected. The result is the present terrifying quantum of power in the world, most graphically symbolized in 'Cuba week' of October 1962, when the fate of the world itself hung by a thread. Our most urgent problem is how to reduce this quantum of power sufficiently to provide a breathing space in which man may yet learn to grow to maturity and progress in moral development. This involves educating people to an understanding of the nature of power so that they can be persuaded to struggle against it.

The principal obstacle to an understanding of power is the intensity of the desire to possess it. In most people this stems not so much from a positive love of power, but from the fear that they will be insecure or impotent without it. People are readily persuadable that power is evil in the hands of their opponents: in their own hands it becomes 'just' or 'necessary' or 'democratic'. Communist and Capitalist, Conservative and Labour need no convincing that power is bad when wielded by the other. But there is always present a certain ambivalence arising from the fact that each is linked to the other by the common love of power. It is a curious love-hate relationship. While each denounces power as wielded by the other, each is ready to join forces with the other when the logic of power itself or the framework within which it is conducted is felt to be threatened. Within the parliamentary system, each respects the conventions, rules and ritual whereby each is allowed to rule in turn. Each will defend the system against its critics. Even in the international sphere, where the conflict goes deeper and is inflamed by emotions of nationalism, rival potentates generally engage in mutual State visits, inspecting each other's troops and guards of honour at the same time as engaging in mutual military espionage. Moreover, when direct-action unilateralists make a sudden incursion into the closed circuit of the upper reaches of power, the responses of the power world are significant. A unilateralist movement in Britain, West Germany or Greece is rightly seen by the Western Alliance as a potential threat to their power. Their hostility is accordingly unequivocal. But a threat to the West represents a potential strengthening of the East, so that it might appear reasonable to expect equally unequivocal expressions of support from the East. This is the case when the weakening of the enemy is by espionage. But British direct-action unilateralists arouse the suspicions, not the support of the Kremlin. Because unilateralism might by the force of its example prove contagious. And this would threaten the power of the East's ruling group no less than that of the West. While the rulers of the East have a vested interest in weakening the power of the West's ruling group, they have an even greater vested interest in securing the power of both

ruling groups against action that would threaten both equally.[1]
And this is the essential reason why negotiations for multilateral
disarmament between the Great Powers never succeed. They
are undertaken in order to appease a public opinion which
requires the fiction to be maintained that peace is being pursued.
The self-deception in this instance is so naked that the futility of
disarmament negotiations has even become a suitable topic for
episcopal wit at ecclesiastical assemblies. We are asked to
believe that those whose professional lives are ruled by the logic of
power, who owe their very positions to the success with which
they have understood and cultivated the arts of obtaining power,
are suddenly going to live by an antithetical logic and apply the
morality of trusting their most powerful rivals. Tolstoy has put
the truth of this as plainly as any man.

> To suggest to governments not to have recourse to violence but
> to decide their differences in accord with equity, is a proposal to
> abolish themselves as governments, and no government can agree
> to that. . . . it is the nature of a government not to submit to others
> but to exact submission from them, and a government is a govern-
> ment only in so far as it is able to exact submission and not itself
> to submit, and so it always strives to that end and will never
> voluntarily abandon its power.[2]

Why do men consent to be deceived in the one matter above
all that is vital to their welfare? A certain shrewdness in detecting
and pursuing one's own interest is, after all, widely held to be a
principal characteristic of man. Is it not odd that men remain
blind to the essential truth of the issue of war or disarmament
even when, as now, war would threaten the lives of all men? The
reason is that men are also highly sensitive to one other fact of their
common political, social and historical experience. Armed
men are powerful. To resist them might prove very dangerous,
particularly if I were to act alone. And there is always the
danger that others might be even more intimidated and that
I may find myself alone. Knowledge of the real reasons that lie

---

[1] After the unilateralist breakthrough at the Labour Party Annual Conference
at Scarborough in 1960, Mr Philip Noel Baker, M.P. rebuked the unilateralists with
the remark that he had just returned from the U.S.S.R. where he had learned that
'even' Mr Khrushchev did not support the British unilateralists.

[2] Tolstoy, *The Kingdom of God is Within You*, pp. 175–6. Even Tolstoy did not foresee that the day would come when a Government would dare to carry deceit and
hypocrisy to the length of setting up a Minister of Disarmament.

concealed behind the disarmament fraud is felt to be expensive knowledge.

Wagner: But then the world, man's heart and mind, are things
             Of which 'twere well that each man had some knowledge.
Faust: Why yes! – they call it *knowledge*. Who may dare
             To name things by their real names? The few
             Who did know something, and were weak enough
             To expose their hearts unguarded – to expose
             Their views and feelings to the eyes of men,
             They have been nailed to crosses – thrown to flames.

To pursue the path of virtue and emulate the good is not only not the surest way to rise in the world. It is incompatible with so doing, for goodness and power are antithetical. Goodness does not consist only of powerlessness, but where love is, power is absent. And since power is either keenly sought or keenly feared, the truth of love is also expensive knowledge. Bertrand Russell, speaking in the context of the murder of Jaurès and the acquittal of his assassin, wrote:

> 'Love thy neighbour as thyself' is a positive precept. But in all Christian communities the man who obeys this precept is persecuted, suffering at least poverty, usually imprisonment, and sometimes death. The world is full of injustice, and those who profit by injustice are in a position to administer rewards and punishments. The rewards go to those who invent ingenious justifications for inequality, the punishments to those who try to remedy it. I do not know of any country where a man who has a genuine love for his neighbour can long avoid obloquy.[1]

It has been the central contention of this book that Machiavelli was right when he insisted that the practice of power politics cannot by any logic be reconciled with the precepts of morality. He was wrong in inferring that the profession of prince could be legitimized by the amoral or immoral logic of *raison d'état*. But he was more honest than those who engage in the kind of self-deception that maintains that the State rests on will, not force. Tolstoy saw quite clearly, with Machiavelli, that the State necessarily rests on the logic of power and force. He also saw

---

[1] *Sceptical Essays*, 1928, pp. 118–19

quite clearly, again with Machiavelli, that this logic leads quite inevitably to the recurring explosion of the power tensions in war. But Tolstoy, unlike Machiavelli, drew the right inference from this; that man is bound by the law of his being to seek the truth and live in accordance with it; and that the truth is expressed in the law of love which is the antithesis of the law of violence. All history testifies to the fact that the law of love is by no means impotent to move men's hearts and minds. Had it been otherwise, mankind would have perished long ago; since power, as the world understands it, necessarily resides and must always reside with those whose moral sensibilities are sufficiently blunted to allow them to use such weapons. It is true that the law of love may prove expensive in the sacrifice it demands from the individual. But even if the conscience can be silenced in order to evade the sacrifice, the rewards of success and of power are incompatible with a man's best self and in any case fleeting. The strictly egocentric secular purpose has a bleak enough core in all conscience. 'Success? In few years thou wilt be dead and dark – all cold, eyeless, deaf; no blaze of bonfires, ding-dong of bells or leading-articles visible or audible to thee again at all for ever: What kind of success is that?'[1]

The truth may find a man wanting in performance, since fear is no mean adversary. The truth may appear to lead to the isolation of the individual when the many may prefer to walk with such 'truth' as can accommodate itself to 'silver slippers'. But what the truth will never do is to lead a man into the tortuous contradictions in which even good men find themselves involved, as they strive to keep within the bounds of what the world regards as sober common sense. The following extract from Edward Garnett's appreciative and perceptive short life of Tolstoy furnishes a good example:

> The Western critic in objecting with Mr A. Maude that ' "Non-Resistance" is one-sided and not really true to the facts of life' is of course pointing out the central fallacy that underlies Tolstoy's contention that 'humanity must be moved by moral forces and not by its animal requirements.' But in so doing the critic is cutting away the spiritual roots of Tolstoy's moral grandeur. Had Tolstoy compromised and adopted the 'Common-sense

[1] Carlyle, *Past and Present,* Proem

Christianity' of his European critics his gigantic, national figure would have shrunk into small dimensions.[1]

It is indeed wonderful how men deceive themselves. Garnett was a more than usually honest man, but the date was 1914. The central contention of Tolstoy's life and teaching was 'of course' fallacious, as we all well understand by the gift of common sense. Yet apparently it was precisely because of his scrupulous adherence to this central fallacy that Tolstoy bestrode the world like a moral colossus dwarfing the millions of common-sense men. What an odd universe it must be in which falsehood leads directly to 'moral grandeur', and truth to the 'small dimensions' of men who proceeded to slay one another by the million for reasons which have yet to be discovered. The wisdom of returning good for evil is very difficult to learn, but it is not impossible. The legacies of previous crimes, follies and weaknesses have perhaps loaded the dice against our generation. Our response must be in proportion to the magnitude of the challenge, for in the nuclear age we cannot afford to fail.

[1] Edward Garnett, *Tolstoy*, 1914, p. 88n.

Bibliography

I have asterisked critical works (as distinct from primary sources) to which I am especially indebted.
Unless otherwise stated, the place of publication is London.

CONTEMPORARY THOUGHT

J. O. Urmson, *Philosophical Analysis, its development between the two world wars*, Oxford 1956.

T. D. Weldon, *The Vocabulary of Politics*, Penguin 1953

A. J. Ayer and Others, *The Revolution in Philosophy*: with an introduction by Gilbert Ryle, 1956

Michael Oakeshott, *Rationalism in Politics* and Other Essays, 1962

Isaiah Berlin, *The Hedgehog and the Fox*: an essay on Tolstoy's view of history, 1953

George Steiner, *Tolstoy or Dostoevsky*: an essay in contrast, 1960

Basil Willey, *Nineteenth Century Studies: Coleridge to Matthew Arnold*, 1949

John Maynard Keynes, *Two Memoirs*, 1949

Norman Cohn, *The Pursuit of the Millennium*, 1957

POWER AND SOCIETY

*Guglielmo Ferrero, *The Principles of Power: the great political crises of history* (translated from the Italian by T. R. Jaeckel), New York 1942

Bertrand de Jouvenel, *Power: the natural history of its growth* (translated from the French by J. F. Huntington), 1952

Bertrand Russell, *Power: a new social analysis*, 1938

Crane Brinton, *The Anatomy of Revolution*, Toronto 1957

*Friedrich Meinecke, *Machiavellianism, the doctrine of* raison d'état *and its place in modern history* (translated from the German by Douglas Scott), 1957. Originally published as *Die Idee der Staatsräson*, Munich 1924

John Morley, *Machiavelli*, Romanes Lecture of 1897

Herbert Butterfield, *The Statecraft of Machiavelli*, 1940

Federico Chabod, *Machiavelli and the Renaissance* (translated from the Italian by David Moore), 1958

J. G. Fichte, *Machiavelli*, *Sämmtliche Werke*, Vol. XI, Bonn 1835

Hans J. Morgenthau, *American Foreign Policy: a critical examination*, 1952

Robert Jungk, *Brighter than a Thousand Suns*, Penguin 1960

POWER AND THE INDIVIDUAL

Sigmund Freud, *The Standard Edition of the Complete Psychological Works* (edited and translated from the German by James Strachey), 1953
Sigmund Freud, *Collected Papers*, 5 Vols., 1924–50
Ernest Jones, *Sigmund Freud: Life and Work*, 3 Vols., 1953–1957
*Philip Rieff, *Freud: The Mind of the Moralist*, 1959
Erich Fromm, *Sigmund Freud's Mission: an analysis of his personality and influence*, 1959
H. Stuart Hughes, *Consciousness and Society, The Reorientation of European Social Thought, 1890–1930*, 1959
R. E. Money-Kyrle, *Psychoanalysis and Politics*, 1951
John Stuart Mill, *Autobiography*, 1873, (World's Classics, Oxford 1924)
John Stuart Mill, *The Subjection of Women*, 1869, (World's Classics, Oxford 1912). Pagination in text is of 1869 ed.
M. St John Packe, *The Life of John Stuart Mill*, 1954
F. A. Hayek, *John Stuart Mill and Harriet Taylor: their correspondence and subsequent marriage*, 1951
The Letters of Robert Browning and Elizabeth Barrett, 1845–6, 2 Vols. 1913 Ed.
Samuel Butler, *The Way of all Flesh*, 1903, (Everyman Ed. 1933)

EQUALITY

*Leo Tolstoy, *The Kingdom of God is Within You*, 1893, (World's Classics, translated by Aylmer Maude, Oxford 1936)
Leo Tolstoy, *What Then Must We Do?*, 1886, (World's Classics, translated by Aylmer Maude, Oxford 1935)
Matthew Arnold, *Culture and Anarchy: an essay in political and social criticism*, 1869
William Morris, *How We Live and How We Might Live*, 1885
William Morris, *Communism*, 1893 } The Collected Works of William Morris Vol. XXIII. 1915
A. D. Lindsay, *The Essentials of Democracy*, Oxford 1929
R. H. Tawney, *Equality*, 1931
C. N. Cochrane, *Christianity and Classical Culture*, (Galaxy Ed. New York 1957)
William James, *The Varieties of Religious Experience*, Gifford lectures 1901–2. 1912 Ed.
*V. J. McGill, *Emotions and Reason*, (Blackwell Scientific Publications, Oxford 1954)
R. Osborn, *Humanism and Moral Theory*, 1959

Index